LAW
SCHOOL
CONFIDENTIAL

LAW SCHOOL

CONFIDENTIAL

The Complete Law School
Survival Guide:
By Students, for Students

Robert H. Miller

ST. MARTIN'S GRIFFIN
NEW YORK

www.stmartins.com

Design by Kathryn Parise

ISBN 0-312-24309-X

First Edition: July 2000

10 9 8 7 6 5 4 3 2 1

For Mom and Dad,
who made it possible for me to live the life
of a country lawyer. And for Carolyn,
who kept the faith that someday,
we'd walk in the sun.

CONTENTS

PART 2:
THE FIRST YEAR, THEY SCARE YOU TO DEATH

77

PART 3:

THE SECOND YEAR THEY WORK YOU TO DEATH

215

PART 4:
. . . AND THE THIRD YEAR, THEY BORE YOU TO DEATH . . .

313

AUTHOR'S NOTE

THIS BOOK WOULD never have come together without the help of many people who deserve a proper word of thanks. First, a hearty boomalacka to my literary agent and fellow Camp Belknap alum, Jake Elwell, for remembering me across the years, giving me my start, and providing the consummate professional guidance that every writer hopes for.

To my editor, Melissa Jacobs, for having the courage to reach out to a new writer, providing the enthusiasm to keep him writing, and making the suggestions/additions/deletions to ensure that he looks good doing it.

To Dean Gary Clinton, the heart and soul of the Penn Law "atmosphere of cooperation," for all the things he does to make Penn a different and better place than most law schools, and for honoring me with the contribution of his foreword to this book.

To Dean Janice Austin, for going where no dean of admissions has gone before in agreeing to take us all on a voyage into the previously unknown world of law school admissions policy, and, more important, allowing me to print all of it.

And finally, to my outstanding mentoring team: Carolyn, Keith, Joel, Steve, Alison, Allan, Pat, Bess, and Elizabeth for finding both the time in your busy schedules and the emotional fortitude to go back and relive the law school experience again in order to offer your counsel to others. It is a real thrill for me to be associated with all of you for posterity in the pages of this book.

Hopkinton, New Hampshire
May 2000

FOREWORD

SEVERAL YEARS AGO, at a law school orientation party, one of the new students came up to me and without introduction, threw his arms wide open, taking in the full sweep of Penn Law's summer-green courtyard and proclaimed to me, "I *own* this place!"

I laughed. In fifteen years of law school administration, no one—no dean, no trustee, no faculty member, no administrator, and certainly no student had ever said that before. Quickly thinking it over, however, I realized that he was absolutely right.

Since then, that message has become the core theme of advice I give to people contemplating a legal education, students starting out their first year, or those already deep into law school. *Own* the place, own the process, own your own time, and own the direction of your future.

Viewed from the outside, law schools are intimidating places. Viewed from the inside, legal education is often a confusing and sometimes a seemingly pointless process. Neither is necessarily true—and neither is deliberately true. Both views alienate the lay person from the attorney, and the law student from the educational process. After seeing this education up close for more than twenty years now, however, I can assure you that neither of these factors is deliberately crafted.

These views come about in part because legal education is neither sentimental nor romantic. Law school is a hard-edged training ground, meant to take the worldview of each law student (those things I describe as what we each inherently hold to be "good and true and right and just and beautiful") and shake this worldview to its foundation. The goal is to allow the gut "feelings" we each carry with us to be challenged right to their intellectual, rather than their emotional, roots. When this process is over, the process may have altered the student's values, bringing these values to a "higher" (some might say a more cynical) plane, or the student's values may precipitate out into exactly the same system held before. In either case, however, the student should now know the *reasoning* behind that value system. The core goal of legal education is to teach the student to ask the critical questions, "Why?" and "How?" of any situation. The student must learn to accept nothing at face value, but to learn the relationship of facts, learn to know why *this* is not *that*, and how any number of seemingly disparate situations, facts, ideas, or problems are related.

This brings me back to the notion of ownership, because as your world is turned around, your ideas are challenged, and you come to feel that not only do you not know, but you do not know *how* to know, it is natural to feel that the process is alienating and cruel, and that you are not nearly as smart as you thought you were. Ownership, however, means coming to understand and accept the fact that you are now part of a larger process, and at the same time, that you are becoming a product of that process. This recognition allows you to use the process to better advantage. The goal is to walk through the door each day feeling that you understand, if not each night's reading for each class, at least that you are fully involved in the process of your education.

The other significant aspect of taking ownership of your education lies in the contact you make with your classmates, professors, and administrators *outside* the classroom.

Most law schools attract a remarkably well-rounded group of individuals. Life and work experiences, political and social points of view, interests, career goals, hobbies, and educational values will cover a broad spectrum. Use that to your advantage. Stretch yourself, and allow your ideas and viewpoints to be challenged.

The student I quoted at the outset was, in some ways, the last person I would have expected to instantly know how to maximize his experience at law school. This student, in his mid-thirties, was a former street gang member from South Central L.A. who had finished college late and had held a series of jobs. Yet, his sense of joy in the opportunity, and his sense of ownership of that opportunity, never faded. He threw himself into it during his three years, eventually becoming president of a large student group, president of the student government, and vice president of his class.

When this student graduated, one of our professors—a man who had recently won both the law school's and the university's awards for distinguished teaching—said to me, "I always liked having Michael in my classes, because he could be depended to wade on in when everybody else was looking down pretending to search their texts. He wasn't always right, but he was always willing, and he always advanced the class. He took the chance of being wrong. And that's what I call a fine student."

Rob Miller was another such student. He came to Penn and jumped right in on every level. His eyes and ears were open, not just to the cases, but to the multilayered processes of attending a law school. He too "owned" his experience, and made it work for him. The result is this fine book that will teach you how to do the same.

—*Gary Clinton*
Dean of Student Affairs
The University of Pennsylvania Law School

PART ONE

So You Wanna Be a Lawyer . . .

HOW TO USE THIS BOOK

Is there anyone so wise as to learn
by the experience of others?
—VOLTAIRE

CONGRATULATIONS! By picking up and opening this book, you have just taken the first significant step toward building a productive, successful, and perhaps an even pleasant law school experience. Though you may not know it yet, law school can be an incredibly intimidating, foreign, and isolating place. Sure—at many law schools, you'll be assigned a 2L or 3L to serve as your "mentor," and if he or she isn't too busy, you might glean a few nuggets of wisdom from that relationship. Your school may offer a dean of student affairs, a team of orientation counselors, or a lecture to help you "transition" from undergraduate life or the working world into the new experience of law school. At the end of the day, though, it's still going to come down to you. In those desperate hours (and trust us, there will be many), after your mentors and counselors have given you all they can, it's going to come down to you alone, beneath the glow of your halogen reading lamp, hiding behind closed doors wondering, panicking, and crying out for answers.

And that's where I, and the rest of your *Law School Confidential* mentors come in.

We can relate, because we've just been there. We've given the "wrong" answer to a Socratic professor and sounded stupid in front of an amphitheater full of fellow students. Collectively, we've been caught unprepared, fallen way behind in our reading loads, botched exams, and received some horrible grades. We've papered our walls with rejection letters from employers and judges, thought about dropping out, considered alternate career choices, and anguished about choosing between coasts, cities, firms, and practice areas. We've feuded with members of our study groups and broken up with girlfriends and boyfriends who couldn't understand why we didn't have time to call or visit. We've worked on law reviews and journals, and we've been rejected by law reviews and journals. We've had articles published and articles rejected. We've thrived and stumbled in moot court competitions and legal clinics. We've pulled the all-nighters, blanked out during exams, cried behind our own closed doors, and felt the isolation first-hand.

Despite all of that, we also graduated, passed bar examinations in six different jurisdictions, got the jobs we wanted, and have just moved on into the world of legal practice.

We're not professors twenty-five years removed from the law school experience, clueless about the demands and requirements of law firm life, and waxing nostalgic about how wonderful the law school experience is. We were students, just like you, and three short years ago, we were where you are. We know that law school often isn't wonderful, and that it can be a cold, cruel experience for the unprepared.

We're here to give you the confidential "scoop" about law school—all the stuff the books written by professors will never tell you about. If you want the truth about law school—what it's going to take to get in, get what you want out of it, and get out with your self-esteem and personality intact, this is the book you want. We expose all the traps, dispel all the myths, cut through the rhetoric, and raise the veil which for so long has shrouded the law school experience in mystery and dread.

Possessing this book and applying its teachings will give you a distinct advantage over your classmates in almost every aspect of the law school experience. Most of all however, it will give you some peace of mind and help you to avoid making the same mistakes we made during the many weeks and months of hard work and isolation that lie ahead.

In a moment, I'll be introducing you to your mentoring team— the group of recently graduated students from law schools around the country who will guide you through the next three years with their wisdom, advice, and experiences. First, though, a bit of advice about how to get the most out of this book. Whether you are a college student thinking about law school, a working person contemplating a career change, a student already in law school, or the parent, friend, or significant other of someone in law school just trying to understand what your loved one is going through, this book has something to offer you. Determine which of the following sections is most applicable to you, and read accordingly.

I am a college student thinking about applying to law school, or I'm thinking about changing careers and applying to law school

Great! If your law school experience has not yet begun, you've just stumbled upon a wealth of information and resources that will make your entire experience easier, less stressful, and, we hope, more successful. We suggest that you read this book from cover to cover before you begin the application process to confirm for yourself that you really *do* want to go to law school, and to get a good overview of the entire experience to help inform your interviews and application essays. Once you've read the material, familiarized yourself with law school terminology, and have a basic grasp of how the law school experience will proceed, you should then go back and read each of the individual chapters again as they become applicable to your experience.

I've already been admitted to law school, and I'm nervous . . .

Yeah, well join the crowd! Almost everyone entering law school is nervous about it because of the mystique associated with the experience. You, however, have come to the right place at the right time. Unlike your classmates, who will fumble nervously through the first few weeks if not the entire first semester not knowing exactly how to proceed, you will be escorted around the pitfalls and provided with a step-by-step, proven plan drawn from the experiences of the mentoring team you're about to meet.

Take the time between now and the first day of classes to read this book cover to cover. Don't worry if you don't understand everything right away. Just familiarize yourself with its content and with some of the basic ideas and concepts it presents. Then, when law school begins, keep *Law School Confidential* within arm's reach and let it be your escort through each week of each semester, guiding you safely through the jungle that so many of your classmates will get lost in. Use it to measure your progress and to keep track of where you are.

This is a book of wisdom. Put it to work for you.

But I'm already in law school . . . I wish I found this sooner

Yeah, us too. The difference between us, though, is that at least you can still benefit from this book. We had to learn most of this stuff the hard way! The fact is, it's never too late to start.

If you are already in the throes of law school, we recommend reading the entire book anyway—as there may be some earlier hints and suggestions that you can still capitalize on and apply. Then simply go to the table of contents, find where you are in your law school career, and begin in earnest. Read forward to the end of the book to get a feel for what's to come, and then concentrate on specific chapters as they become applicable to you.

I'm the parent, friend, sibling, or significant other of someone going to law school

Want to give your friend or loved one the best gift you could ever give her at the time she needs it most? You have it in your hands. Before you wrap it up, though, you may want to skim it over yourself. In it, you'll soon discover why your law student isn't returning your phone calls, letters, or e-mails, doesn't have time to come home to visit, and is frequently tired and cranky when you call. If you're close to a law student, the experience will touch you, too—and the better understanding you have of law school's incessant demands on time and energy, the easier it will be to accept the virtual loss of your loved one for the next three years. Your job is to be as understanding and forgiving as possible, and to place as few demands as you can on your law student. Reading *Law School Confidential* will help you to understand why by giving you some familiarity with the experience.

That said, it's now time to meet the mentors who will guide you through the next three years. As you progress through this book, you'll be able to follow their progress, recognize and learn from their mistakes, and watch their careers develop before your eyes. You can and should model some of their actions, choices, strategies, and experiences.

At the end of our law school careers, each of us walked away from law school shaking our head and muttering to ourselves, "I wish I knew then what I know now." You are in the unique position to have that wish granted.

It's time to get busy!

The *Law School Confidential* Mentors

JOEL WATTENBARGER
Red Bank, New Jersey

B.A. Yale University
J. D. Harvard Law School

Harvard Law Review

1L summer: summer associate, Kirk-
patrick & Lockhart, D.C.
2L summer: summer associate,
Ropes & Gray, Boston, MA

After graduation: associate,
Ropes & Gray, Boston, MA

The biggest factor in my decision to go to law school was the three years I spent as a paralegal in Washington, D.C., after graduating from college. I found that I really enjoyed the atmosphere in that firm—I had never experienced such a concentration of bright, motivated, and responsive people. I also enjoyed the work I was doing, helping companies understand and respond to complex legal and business problems. I was also attracted, unsurprisingly, by the money that can be made by lawyers. A word of warning, though: Because I had to take out significant loans, it will take close to a decade for my "investment" in law school to start "paying off."

Knowing what I know now, I would probably do it again. However, I would consider business school more seriously than I did four years ago—anyone who is considering a career in corporate law should consider life as a client, rather than as a lawyer!

Know what you're getting yourself into. I almost applied to law school as a senior in college, primarily because I didn't really have any idea what I wanted to do, and law school seemed like a respectable way to put off the decision for a few years. In retrospect, applying at that time would have been a huge mistake. I wasn't emotionally prepared for three more years of any school (much less law school) at that point in my life; and I wouldn't have had any clear idea of where I might be headed at the end of the three years, but I would have been deep in debt nevertheless. If you don't know why you're going to law school, don't go.

CAROLYN A. KOEGLER
Bronxville, New York

B.A. Tufts University
J.D. University of Pennsylvania Law
   School

H. Clayton Louderback legal writing instructor

1L summer: summer associate,
   Dow, Lohnes & Albertson, D.C.
2L summer: summer associate,
   Bingham Dana, Boston, MA

After graduation: associate, Sulloway & Hollis, Concord, NH

I went to law school because (1) I was told by a number of people that law school really teaches you how to "think" in a way that even the best undergraduate education really does not; (2) because I felt that no matter what career I ultimately chose, even if I decided not to practice law, that people would take a woman with a law degree more seriously than they would take a woman without one; (3) because I thought that a law degree would open up more opportunities for me; and (4) because I majored in history in college and I wasn't sure what else to do with that degree!

I don't regret my decision to go to law school at all, but I think this is because my father was generous enough to pay for it. As a result, I don't have to worry about paying off student loans, and I was able to take the kind of position I really wanted. I got a terrific education and a degree which has opened up opportunities to me that I never would have had without it. I do also feel that people take me more seriously when they find out that I have a law degree.

Having said all of this, I would not necessarily have made the decision to go to law school had I been required to pay for it myself. I have a number of friends who are very unhappy practicing law, but cannot leave their jobs because they have to pay off enormous student loans. After struggling through a tough three years in law school, they are now stuck in jobs they despise for the better part of the next decade. I enjoy my present job, working in a smaller law firm, in a smaller community, where I am getting a lot of hands-on experience, and where the work I do actually impacts clients I know and talk to. Knowing that if I ever stop enjoying it, I could just decide to do something else without worrying about having to make loan payments makes a big difference, though.

KEITH KOEGLER
Bronxville, New York

B.A. Amherst College
J.D. Vanderbilt University Law
    School

*Vanderbilt Journal of Transnational
    Law*

1L summer: internship with crimi-
    nal law judge
2L summer: split summer doing
    part-time work for two Nashville, TN, law firms

After graduation: in-house counsel for start-up technology company
                  associate at Ritchey, Fisher, Whitman & Klein P.A.,
                  Palo Alto, CA

Like many people, I backed into law school. At Amherst, I received the classic liberal arts education which meant that I didn't really start thinking about a career until my senior year, when I began scrambling to find a way to support myself after graduation. I chose to paralegal for a large national law firm for a year, because I couldn't think of anything better to do. The experience was miserable and after a year, I applied to law school because what else was I going to do with my B.A. in history?

I now work at a small firm in Palo Alto doing corporate securities work for start-up technology companies and I couldn't be happier. My hours are reasonable, the work is interesting, and the people are fantastic. But I think I'm unusual—most of my friends are at large national law firms and are miserable.

ELIZABETH DECONTI
Albany, New York

B.A. Yale University
J.D. University of Miami Law School

University of Miami Yearbook of
    International Law Vice
    President, Moot Court Board

1L summer: studied evidence and
    European community law—
    University College, London
2L summer: summer associate, Pyszka, Kessler, Douberly & Massey,
    Miami, FL

After graduation: associate, Holland & Knight LLP, Tampa, FL

When I entered my senior year of college, I was torn between going to graduate school and going to law school. My prospective field of study in graduate school was very narrow, and there was not much room to grow. Teaching positions were at a premium, and the "greats" under whom I had studied did not look to be ready to vacate their posts for a long time. I was determined that whatever I did should be worthwhile both to me and to society, and I began to get the idea that I would not have the opportunity to leave much of a mark on the world as an academic.

I decided that more opportunities would be available to a lawyer. The field was wide open, jobs were plentiful (that year), and the law seemed to be a door opener to a variety of other careers including business and politics. Even within the law, I saw many opportunities, including working for a law firm, public interest group, or even in the judiciary. It did not occur to me at the time, however, that the world is overflowing with lawyers, that jobs are not easy to come by, and that most of all, it takes something special to distinguish oneself from the crowd.

Would I do it all again? I honestly don't know. There are times when I miss spending my day studying the perspective of a Renaissance painting . . . Now, though, my days are filled with different kinds of excitement—finding a client a way out of a difficult business trap, arguing

11

hearings, and developing well-reasoned legal arguments in briefs to courts. I suppose if I had not had the "legal experience," I would not know what I was missing. Surely I would have been a very happy academic. As a lawyer, though, I can keep my love of art history and Shakespeare as a hobby and I can have the law as a career. It would have been difficult to do the reverse.

PATRICK CLOSSON
Exeter, New Hampshire

B.A. The University of New
    Hampshire
J.D. Boston College Law School

*Boston College International and
    Comparative Law Journal*

1L summer: New Hampshire
    Attorney General's Office
2L summer: summer associate,
    McLane, Graf, Raulerson & Middleton, Manchester, NH

After graduation: associate, McLane, Graf, Raulerson & Middleton,
    Manchester, NH

I majored in history in college and decided in my senior year that I was not interested in pursuing a career as a historian. Having made the decision not to be a historian, the remainder of my senior year I struggled trying to figure out what I wanted to do with the rest of my life. In the midst of this uncertainty, I adopted law school as a contingency plan. I figured if I got into law school, I could put off answering "The Question" for a few more years. On the day I graduated from college, I had a stack of rejection letters and had been waitlisted twice. I then started looking for a job and ended up as a customer service representative for an HMO, answering questions from angry New Yorkers who were angry with the service they were getting. After about two weeks on that job, I had learned all I could about angry New Yorkers and HMOs, and I realized that whatever career I chose, it would have to be something that challenged me every day. Shortly after that, I received an acceptance letter from Boston College, and I knew law school was my next step.

A career as a lawyer includes many of the things I was looking for in a career—including the ability to solve problems, help people, and be challenged intellectually. Knowing what I know now, I would do it again. A solid foundation in the law is useful in any pursuit, and the skills learned in law school are transferable to most careers.

ALISON GABEL
Brooklyn, New York

B.A. SUNY Binghamton
J.D. University of Pennsylvania Law
    School

Journal of International Economic Law

1L summer: Public Interest
    Healthcare Outreach Project—
    Senior Citizen Judicare
2L summer: summer associate,
    Simpson Thacher & Bartlett, NYC

After graduation: associate, Simpson Thacher & Bartlett, NYC

I decided to go to law school because I thought the law would be a good way to satisfy a bunch of different interests I had (public service, public speaking, and being challenged intellectually on a daily basis) all in one. I also decided to go to law school because it's what I thought smart people did if they didn't go to med school. Getting into a good law school seemed to be a good way to prove to those around me that I was smart. I didn't have the foggiest idea what I was going to do with my law degree.

Through my participation in this book, I hope to give some advice about getting through the many hard, negative parts of law school. It's really important to focus just as much on enjoyment as achievement, since much of law school is so competitive, and you can't win everything. I want to help people understand how to achieve, get better grades, and be successful on the job search, but most importantly, I want to help explain how to keep your perspective in order to come out of the law school experience a happier, better person for it.

I now practice trusts and estates at a big law firm in Manhattan. I like both my job and my firm. From first to third year, I learned a great deal about balance—I worked hard in school, but I made time for part-time jobs and tried to keep active socially. I still try to do that today. I have to say that if I could go back, I wouldn't change much. I learned a great deal, both academically and personally, and I found law school to be an enjoyable, rewarding, and valuable experience.

ALLAN KASSENOFF
West Orange, New Jersey

B.S. Columbia University
J.D. University of Pennsylvania Law
    School

Journal of International Economic Law

1L summer: New Jersey Attorney
    General's Office
2L summer: summer associate,
    Kaye, Scholer, Fierman, Hays &
    Handler, NYC

After graduation: associate, Kaye, Scholer, Fierman, Hays & Handler,
    NYC

I decided to go to law school because the work involved seemed both interesting and stimulating to me, and because it pays well.

I really enjoyed law school. Once you get the hang of it, it is a really rewarding experience. I am now practicing litigation at Kaye, Scholer in New York City. From day one of law school, I was always planning to work at a large New York City firm, and it has worked out really well. I love what I do 90 percent of the time.

BESS FRANZOSA
Durham, New Hampshire

B.A. University of New Hampshire
M.S. Boston University College of
    Communication
J.D. Boston College Law School

Boston College Law Review

Law clerk to chief judge Paul
    Barbadoro, United States
    District Court, NH

1L summer: legal department, City of Waltham, MA
2L summer: summer associate, Goodwin, Procter & Hoar, Boston, MA

After graduation: associate, Goodwin, Procter & Hoar, Boston, MA

I went to law school because I wanted to be a prosecutor. I had worked for four years as a reporter and editor, and I had covered and/or followed coverage of many heinous crimes. I found myself frustrated—because I was a journalist, I was forced to be a constant bystander. I wanted to *do* something rather than simply watch and criticize or comment.

If I could go back, however, I would not do it again. The cost of law school, financially and personally, has outweighed the benefits for me. The loans I had to take out to pay for law school will preclude me from becoming a prosecutor for a long time, so my original motivation for going to law school now seems foolish, or at least really naïve. By the time I have paid off the debt, I don't know that I will even want to continue to practice law. I think it is particularly poignant that at a graduation party for one of my classmates from law school, one of the guests asked all of us about our plans. There were five graduating law students there, and all five of us said, on the day after graduation, that we weren't sure we wanted to be lawyers.

I wanted to be a prosecutor, but joined the labor and employment group at a large firm because I have to pay back $1100 per month in loans. I enjoy labor and employment law, so it may turn out to be a good change which I'll stick with. I do wish I had inquired more about law school and the legal profession before I went into it, though.

STEVEN WEITZMAN

B.A. University of Maryland at
   College Park
J.D. University of Pennsylvania Law
   School

1L summer: summer associate,
   Thomas Foley, Wilmington, DE
2L summer: summer associate,
   Seward & Kissel LLP, NYC
   University of Pennsylvania
   Journal of Labor Law

After graduation: associate, Seward & Kissel LLP, NYC

I didn't decide to go to law school—it was just something I was always going to do. When I was a little kid, my cousin came to visit my family. He was a lawyer in New York, and he had a nice car and told interesting stories and seemed to have a glamorous life. From that, while I was just a little boy, I decided that I would be a lawyer too. It seemed to fit me personally, since I was always argumentative, logical, and quick thinking. Nothing better ever came along to replace that aspiration, so here I am.

Knowing what I know now, I would definitely still go to law school. It was a great experience for me, and it has led me to a great career.

CHAPTER 1

Thinking About Law School?
Think Again . . .

Know thyself.
—SOCRATES

THE MOST IMPORTANT PIECE of advice that can possibly be given to you, the prospective law student, is really very simple. Surprisingly, perhaps, it has nothing to do with how to study or how to write a good exam. It is not about how to glean wisdom from the dusty pages of the supreme court opinions that shaped our country, or how to make the law review, or how to impress an employer in a job interview. Those things are important, but they're all secondary.

The most important advice that you can get as a prospective law student isn't even about law school. It's about you—and it can be summed up succinctly but completely with a single word.

Commit.

Huh?

Commit. That's it. "To carry into action deliberately." Commit.

Show up for your first day of law school with only a vague notion of why you're there—without a clear set of reasons for putting yourself through the punishment you're about to endure—and you'll be setting yourself up for a miserable and unfulfilling three years. Show up committed, with a well thought-out set of goals supported by reasons for attaining them, and the experience can be exhilarating.

The choice is yours. You picked up this book looking for

answers, or maybe a "quick fix" that will put you ahead of your competitors in the rough and tumble world of law school. You have it in one word: commit. That's it. Don't "decide" to go to law school. Don't "try" law school. Commit to law school. That is the pure axiom of law school success. Commit, or forget it—for in law school, to quote an ancient Jedi master, "there is no try."

Still with me?

Now . . . about the cocky guy next to you who just put this book back on the shelf with a "Hrumph" after reading these first few paragraphs—don't worry about him. That's the overconfident guy who will spend the first many weeks of law school casually reading cases, partying in the bars, and teasing you about studying too much. Learn to love that guy because he's someone you're going to flog on your first-semester finals. Trust me on that, because I used to know that guy.

He was me.

Step number one on the road to your commitment to law school is to ask yourself one critical question.

Why do you want to go to law school?

No really. Think about it. What's driving you? Why do you want to go to law school? Force yourself to come up with an answer.

Okay, now be honest. Does your answer, or something like it, appear on this list?

- because my mom/dad/sibling/relative/friend is a lawyer
- because I took the LSAT and got a really good score
- because I'm not good at science and wouldn't be able to get into med school
- because lawyers make good salaries and have financial and/or job security
- because most of the people at my school are applying to law/med school
- because I watch *Law & Order/Homicide/L.A. Law* and think they're interesting
- because I read Grisham/Turow/Baldacci novels and find them fascinating

- because I don't know what else to do and law is a respectable profession
- because my parents/relatives/teachers/friends think I'm a "born lawyer"

If it does, all is not lost. It just means that you need to rethink your motivations, because these just aren't going to cut it for you. Let's dispel some illusions.

My relative the lawyer made me do it

First of all, what is it about your parent/sibling/friend the lawyer that makes you want to follow him into his profession? Is it the money? The prestige? Do you even know whether this person is happy practicing law? Have you asked him lately? More importantly, have you ever followed this person through a typical day—or even better, a typical week? Ever ask this person what he likes least about the law, or about how much time he spends in court compared to how much time he spends with his nose buried in the books? Ever ask how long it took him to make partner, or how many hours a week he had to work on the road to becoming partner? These are revealing questions that may help you explore a career in law more realistically. Ask them before you romanticize your relative, the lawyer.

I can't ignore this amazing LSAT score, can I?

Why not? The LSAT is allegedly an aptitude test that predicts how well you'll do in law school, but the effectiveness of this correlation is controversial and much-debated. A good LSAT score is a tremendous asset when applying to law schools. In fact, there's a whole chapter in this book devoted to teaching you how to get the best possible LSAT score. What is certain, however, is that the test bears almost no resemblance to what you'll be doing in law school, and even less to the actual practice of law. Both law school and law practice require well-developed research and writing skills, and to a lesser extent, oral advocacy proficiency, none of which is tested on the LSAT. There are no legal concepts tested on the LSAT, which in many ways, is basically a souped-up, trickier SAT. Yet some would use a good LSAT score to justify law as a career choice. A good LSAT score may bring you to the dance, but it's no guarantee that you'll be happy to be there.

I don't have a mind for science, so . . .

Otherwise known as the old, "I can't be a doctor because I couldn't hack Orgo, so I might as well be a lawyer" rationale. Where's the logic in that argument? We're not playing the game of *Life* here—this is the real thing. Contrary to the beliefs of many, there are other career choices besides law, medicine, and investment banking. Maybe you should explore some of these. Take a year off to travel, learn a language, teach, write, or work for a non-profit or volunteer organization. Start your own business. Think a little and figure out what it is that you like to do. Just don't fall into this ridiculous three-track mind trap and go straight for the law school applications because all your friends are doing it. To quote your mom, "If all your friends jumped off the Brooklyn Bridge . . ."

It's the economy, stupid

This one is one of the biggest misconceptions of them all. If you're going into law because you think it's your road to riches, stop, and go directly to business school or ignore the advice in the last section and become an I-banker. That's where the real money is these days. While it's true that associates in big city law firms make six-figure salaries right out of law school, in a good year, I-bankers at comparably large investment firms make that much in *bonuses*. Similarly, a successful business idea can bring you a partner-level salary two or three years after start-up, not to mention stock options and a flexible work schedule.

Remember this—the average lawyer's salary in the United States is still about $40,000 per year. Sure, partners at big city firms may pull down a million a year . . . but it may have taken them fifteen to twenty years of eighty hour weeks, two failed marriages and a heart attack to get there. Meanwhile, the prosecutors you've romanticized may make as little as $25,000 a year while working the same hours. So don't kid yourself. A career in law does provide some job security and a good assurance that you and your family won't starve on the streets, but if money is your primary motivator, there are much easier ways to make your millions.

This ain't Hollywood, son

That brings us to the unspoken reason why many people go to law school—the secret longing to be Tom Cruise in *The Firm*, Gregory Peck in *To Kill a Mockingbird*, Sam Waterston in *Law & Order*, or Johnnie Cochran in the O. J. Simpson case—uttering phrases like, "if the glove doesn't fit . . ." to a worldwide audience of millions, and bringing the opposition to their knees with a brilliant legal checkmate. Unfortunately, this too is a romanticized picture of the law. Most lawyers never make guest appearances on *Larry King* or get to parade secret, star witnesses into court to the gasps of the gallery. To 95 percent of practicing lawyers, law is not a glamorous profession. If your aspirations about law school center on supercharged days before a jury, a worldwide audience, and invitations to appear on national television after your latest victory, it's time to refill your prescription.

Most lawyers, even the really good ones, typically toil in the state and lower federal courts, often on mundane legal issues. Most lawyers will never argue before the United States Supreme Court, and an appearance before a circuit court of appeals or a chance to break new legal ground may only occur once or twice in a career. That's not to say that your days as a lawyer won't be interesting or intellectually challenging. Many of them will be. But they won't be like what you see in the movies.

Finally, remember that even what you see on *Law & Order* is the culmination of hundreds of hours of hard work in the library reading cases, developing theories, drafting court briefs and memoranda, and taking depositions from unwilling witnesses in law firm conference rooms—things the producers will never show you on television. For every hour of court time you log, you may spend fifty hours reading, researching, and writing. If you become a civil or criminal litigator or a prosecutor, you'll have your days in court before a judge and jury—but if you go to work for a big-city firm, it may take you five to ten years before you see a courtroom, and even longer before you'll try your own cases. In the meantime, you'll be a researcher—analyzing issues, finding applicable cases, and writing memoranda to the more senior associates and partners in the firm. You'll typically be asked to work sixty to eighty hour weeks, late nights, and at least some weekends.

Your fate is typically better in a smaller firm, or working for a state or federal prosecutor. Doing so can bring these opportunities much more rapidly—often within the first year or two, but these positions typically pay much less.

On the corporate side, it is much the same story. If you want to become a dealmaker in a large city, you'll need to get in line. For the first few years, you'll be paid handsomely to draft boilerplate agreements and spend late nights at the printer arguing over the placement of commas in merger agreements and initial public offerings. Remember that at a big firm, there are up to sixty starry-eyed associates in your "class," all of whom want the same plum assignments that you do. Someone has to do the scut work, though, and for the first few years, that will be you. While smaller firms again offer more rapid opportunity, the deals are also smaller. Further, someone still has to copyread these agreements—and that someone is still going to be you. Oh—and if you're thinking of going the in-house route, remember that most corporations won't even consider hiring someone right out of law school. You'll need some years of firm experience first, so you're back to square one again.

Of course, there are exceptions to all of these scenarios. Partners in big firms will occasionally take promising young associates under their wings, channel them interesting and important work, or provide them with uncommon opportunities to sit "third chair" in a trial, or to help "put the deal together." Be clear, though: These are the exceptions, not the rule. The road to partnership is paved with the broken bodies of disillusioned associates who became bored and disenchanted with the work they were given and left voluntarily, or who, after seven years spent toiling in the mines, were told that they were not on the partner track and should look elsewhere for employment. In a typical large firm, of an entering class of forty associates, one or two will survive to make partner eight or ten years later.

Hey you! Yeah, you—the one with the distressed look on your face about to reach for the "How to Survive Medical School" book. Relax. It's not all bad. It's just that there are so many people out there with misconceptions about law practice that we needed to clear the delusions away up front in order to approach this experience with more realistic expectations. Now that we've done this, it's time for more introspection. Let's explore whether you have an accurate picture of what your law school experience will entail. As you read the questions that follow, carefully consider the answers that come from within. Pay particular attention to the "Yeah, buts . . ." that come up. Trust me—it's better to deal with this crisis now than to experience it a month into your first semester . . .

A Realistic Evaluation of Your Fitness for Law School

Go somewhere where you can be undisturbed for the next thirty minutes or so and force yourself to answer the following questions honestly. What follows below is a realistic picture of what the day-to-day grind of law school is all about. In fact, in many ways, it's also an accurate picture of what the day-to-day life of a young lawyer is like, too. So forget the glamorous pictures of law practice you've seen on television and in the movies and be honest with yourself. While very few people will find themselves completely in love with the thought of spending their next three years holed up in a library, if what you see below is too far out of sync with what drives you, your misery may last much longer than the three years you'll be in school.

- How comfortable are you with the idea of spending the majority of each day in silence, reading difficult material?
- Do you, or could you have the stamina to read dry, complicated material for four to six hours a day, every day?

- Are you self-reliant, or do you depend on others for constant encouragement, evaluation, and/or affirmation?
- Can you seize the main points of an assignment and move on, or do you typically get hopelessly bogged down in detail?
- Are you disciplined enough to get up and attend classes every day?
- Are you comfortable speaking out in class and speaking and arguing in front of others?
- Have you been able to "will" yourself through difficult periods in your life?
- When you don't understand something—are you capable of teaching yourself?
- Do you enjoy doing research, searching through books in a library or online databases for pieces to a puzzle or "the answer" to a problem?
- Do you like to write critically and analytically?
- Is your personality more proactive than reactive?
- When you've given your very best effort, will you be able to sleep at night knowing that you've done the best you could, or are you more likely to beat yourself up wondering if there was more you could have done?
- Are you ready to make the law your life for the next three years, by subverting most of your hobbies, other interests, and your social life to serious academic dedication?

It's probably obvious from the way these questions were worded, but you're looking for mostly "yes" responses—or at least the probability that you'll be able to work up to "yes" responses on each of these questions. If you've had too many "oh-ohs" during this evaluation, you should take that as a warning. For example, if you don't like to read, you're making a big mistake applying to law school. In order to help you examine your readiness for law school, let's develop these areas more completely.

The reading load

The typical law student will read in excess of three thousand pages of case law, hornbooks, and outlines during a fifteen-week semester. In that semester of 105 days, that means roughly thirty pages of reading every day if you read seven days a week without ever taking a day off. At an average rate of ten pages per hour, that means three hours of reading per day, every day, with no weekends, holidays, or excuses. Naturally, that's an unrealistic expectation—but realize, of course, that when you start taking days off, the missed reading starts backlogging and piling up on other days. In my own experience, in the first year of law school, I generally read for about four hours a day, six days a week. That of course, is in addition to class time, and time spent outlining what you've read. But we're not talking about the time commitment yet, just the reading. Recognize what you're signing up for. If you can't fathom yourself reading law for about four hours a day, six days a week, you might want to start reevaluating your career choice.

The discipline

In law school, there is really no substitute for discipline. The problem is, most of us have never had to exhibit the kind of discipline that law school requires, and many prospective law students underestimate just how much discipline that is. I've already suggested to you that, whatever your practices were in college, skipping classes because they're too early in the morning, too boring, or because you're too tired or too hungover must become a thing of the past when you get to law school. Missed classes mean missed notes, and even if you get the notes from someone else, chances are you won't understand them. Since classes often build on the material introduced in prior classes, if you miss a critical class, you might fall off the wagon. Trust me when I say there is no greater discomfort than realizing that because you missed an important lecture, you are the only person in your section that still doesn't understand a concept.

There is simply no substitute for putting in the time. You must go to class every day, struggle through the difficult material, take notes on the professor's hypothetical scenarios (called "hypos"), and pay special attention to what parts of the material the professor stresses in class. The benefits will soon be obvious, as it is often these very things that show up on the exam.

In your upper years, after you have a few semesters of law school under your belt, these rules will change somewhat, and we'll get into these modifications in later chapters—but for you, the prospective 1L, you're looking at the need to string together two to three semesters of near-perfect attendance. Are you disciplined enough to force yourself through those tough days when pulling the covers over your head sounds a lot better than a 9 A.M. lecture on collateral estoppel?

Of course, just being there isn't enough. You need to be there with the reading done and outlined, taking supplemental notes, and ready to respond when that fateful day arrives when you are called upon to be the Socratic crash-test dummy for the class. Given that we've established that you really can't afford to miss classes, "I didn't do the reading, so I'll just blow off the class" doesn't work in law school. Knowing the importance of discipline and everyday preparedness, the professors can be really unforgiving if they catch you unprepared.

During my first year at Penn Law, the unthinkable happened in only one class, during the second-to-last week of the semester. The unfortunate individual, a friend of mine, had already started studying for exams, and had not read the case being discussed that hour. The class, Civil Procedure, was being taught by the acting dean of the law school—a younger but equally intimidating incarnation of Professor Kingsfield from *The Paper Chase*. The exchange went something like this:

"Mr. Brown (not his real name)—what happened in *Hanna v. Plummer*?"

A long silence, as heads began to turn and stare at Mr. Brown.

"Mr. Brown?"

Mr. Brown furiously scrambled to locate the proper page in his commercial outline . . . Members of the class, starting to realize what was about to happen, began to whisper to each other and giggle nervously.

"Is something wrong, Mr. Brown?"

More silence, then . . .

"Uhh . . . I'm going to have to pass."

"Not likely, Mr. Brown!"

More silence as the professor and student stared each other down.

"Mr. Brown, are you trying to tell me that you are unprepared to discuss this case?"

The professor continued to stare at Mr. Brown, waiting for a response . . .

Poor Mr. Brown didn't manage to find anything sensible to say about *Hanna v. Plummer,* and was badly humiliated before the entire section of almost eighty students. He was the first and last student caught unprepared by the professor that semester. He was also called on for two consecutive days after that day—and I'm happy to report, he gave good answers both times. Needless to say, however, you really don't want this to happen to you.

A couple of more practical thoughts to close this section on the requirements of discipline. The average yearly tuition in a private law school is now approaching $25,000. Assuming eight subjects per year, or four per semester, that breaks down to $3125 per subject, and assuming three classes per week in each subject during a fifteen-week semester, about $70 per class. For every class you miss, you're throwing away $70 that you'll never see again.

If that doesn't work for you, this—the ultimate example of why you need discipline in law school—probably will. As we've discussed previously, to accomplish your reading load for the semester, you need to read about thirty pages a day, every day. If you blow off Friday's reading for whatever reason, that means you'll need to read forty-five pages on Saturday and Sunday to be ready for Monday. If you really goof off and don't read on Saturday, you've left yourself ninety pages to read on Sunday—which is already more than can be realistically handled in a day. This is why there are really no weekends off in law school, and this example clearly illustrates just how easy it is to get hopelessly behind in your reading load.

You must be disciplined!

The atmosphere

As I've mentioned before, the study of law is a lonely proposition. Yeah—there are study groups—but you don't get to a study group until you've read the material for the week. Are you the kind of person who can sit alone in a library carrel and read for a few hours after class every day and then go home and outline the day's reading alone under the midnight oil? Isolation is a reality of law school that many people have difficulty dealing with. My group of friends made it a point to get together on Sunday nights for a few hours to play poker, but aside from that, it wasn't uncommon for me to go the entire week without seeing them outside of class. You need to be ready for that. While some schools may tout softball leagues, intramural sports, and other activities, for your first two years of law school, those things will be much more the exception than the rule. For most people, the cappuccino after class, the hour at the gym, or the thirty minute "library break" dinner you grab with a friend will be the extent of your social life. That takes some getting used to. Is it something you can handle?

Other people have substantial difficulty getting used to the competitiveness and contentiousness of everyday life in law school. If you dislike competitiveness, there are things you can do—like applying to schools known for providing more cooperative atmospheres—but this won't completely eliminate your problem. Most schools still operate, at least during the first year, via the Socratic method. In other words, you'll go to class, and a professor will ask a question related to the reading you prepared for that lecture and then call on someone to respond—perhaps even requiring them to stand while providing their response. The interrogation rarely ends with one question, often stretching on for fifteen minutes or more, while you're up there, intellect exposed to the entire class, sweating out answers. In many cases, when you're stumped, other students will eagerly volunteer the correct answers (though in Chapter 9, we'll suggest that you not do this), which can leave you feeling humiliated and incompetent.

Finally, at some of the most competitive law schools, the competition can turn ugly. People hide books needed for common assignments or horde the best outlines passed down by upperclassmen to give themselves an advantage in exams. Sometimes, people even intentionally play mind games with you to try and throw you off. Some schools are notorious for harboring atmospheres like this, and I encourage you to avoid these places at all costs. But the truth is, at any school where students are graded on an absolute curve, there is bound to be some nastiness as exams draw near. If you are easily rattled or respond badly to the stress of academic competition, you may want to reconsider how well your personality fits with the realities of the law school experience.

The writing

It's been said before, but it bears repeating. Words are the lawyer's tools, and writing is the lawyer's craft. If you don't like to write, and if you're not fully committed to becoming a master legal wordsmith, you're in for a miserable three years, and an even worse career. At a minimum, all lawyers draft letters to each other and to their clients. Corporate lawyers spend a lot of their time drafting or amending contracts and other agreements. Litigators, however, can spend weeks on end crafting motions and memoranda of law to various courts.

Given the importance of writing in legal practice, you'll have a first-year class that will teach you the finer points of legal research (where to find cases, statutes, legislative history, and the like in books and online), and writing (everything from how lawyers write, to proper legal citation form). You'll do a lot of writing in this class, encompassing everything from an opinion letter to a client to a full-blown appellate brief to the United States Supreme Court. Your instructor will dismantle your current writing style and, hopefully, turn you into an economic, laser-sharp legal tactician. The conversion will likely be rough on you, because legal writing emphasizes precision. Every word must be chosen carefully to convey the desired meaning—nothing more, and nothing less. There is no room for flowery prose. Many students find this style arduous and frustrating. Further, the fact that the legal writing class is graded pass-fail at most law schools communicates a terrible message—encouraging students to relegate legal writing to "if I have time" status. Don't make a critical mistake by taking this class lightly, because after graduation, your legal research and writing skills will define your aptitude as a lawyer more than anything else. How much real estate law you remember, however, may never matter to you again.

You'll utilize your legal writing skills at almost every turn in law school—in writing essay exams, in the law review writing competition, in moot court competitions, in writing a law journal "Note" or "Comment," and in any externship you may pursue. Every employer will require a writing sample as a prerequisite for a callback interview, and no judge will grant you a clerkship without first evaluating your ability to write.

I trust that you get the message here. If you don't like to write precisely, and don't think you can warm up to it, you might want to consider a different line of work.

The commitment

At least for the first two years, law school is an all-encompassing task. Nights, weekends, and holidays will all be sacrificed to the cause. You'll be eating, sleeping, and dreaming law. Most of your conversations will center on law, to the point where you may discover that you have difficulty talking about much else. There will be stretches during the first two years when you won't have enough time to return phone calls. Letters will go unanswered, and bills will go unpaid. You'll be forced to abandon most, if not all of your most cherished hobbies. There simply won't be enough time left in the day for most things. Not if you're going to stay on schedule.

Sure—you can cut corners, and turn in a lackluster performance now and then. It's your future. But every grade you get, and particularly the ones you get during your first year, counts.

A lot.

Every stumble closes a door. In a great legal market when the economy is booming, you might survive a stumble or two. If the market tightens, however, or if you're after one of the really plum jobs, you can't afford putting forth anything less than your best effort every day. In the rough and tumble world of law school, sometimes even your best effort won't be good enough.

The law is a jealous mistress. Be forewarned.

Plan Your Application Process in Advance

Well, you're still with us, which is a good sign. Although Chapter 3 will take you step-by-step through the law school application process, there are some significant scheduling issues which we need to address now, while you're still thinking about law school. Most schools now use a "rolling" admissions process, meaning that they admit, waitlist, or reject students as their applications arrive instead of commencing the evaluation process on a stated date. Some schools using rolling admissions will make offers to attractive candidates (or reject unqualified candidates) within a week to ten days of your application being complete. What this means for you, of course, is that you must have your applications filed, complete, and ready for evaluation as early in the process as possible to give yourself the maximum opportunity for success.

Needless to say, if one of your top-choice schools admits you early in the process, your application stress will be greatly reduced, and you'll be in a much better position to haggle over money and/or to secure loans at favorable rates. On the flip side, if you wait until the last minute, most of the slots at your top choice schools may already be filled, leaving you to compete for whatever slots and whatever financial aid money has not already been committed to other candidates.

Recommendations

Most law school applications require two or three recommendations. Unless you're coming to the law from another career, two of these recommendations should be required to be from college professors, and the third from the source of your choice. Obtaining recommendations takes time, particularly if the professors have to write them for many people, or if you need many versions personalized to each different school. Accordingly, a good benchmark is to disseminate your recommendation forms sixty days in advance of the date you hope to complete your applications. We'll address how to select and solicit your recommenders and provide several hints about how to keep the process running smoothly in Chapter 3.

For now, just remember to plan sixty days ahead for the receipt of your recommendations.

Essays

Most law school applications require two to five essays. Many or all may have word limits or space restrictions. You heard it when you applied to college and you'll hear it again here—essays can make or break your application. Near-perfect grades and LSAT scores are commonplace in admissions offices at the best law schools—so in making the tough calls between numerically identical candidates, nothing is more impressive to an admissions committee than a piece of tight, concise, well-crafted prose. Good writing, however, takes time and considerable effort. Don't expect to have the luxury of essay overlap that you enjoyed in college, where you could simply adapt the same essay to every school you applied to. For law school, you may have to craft at least one different essay for every application you file.

Request your law school applications in July so you'll receive them as soon as they are published, typically in mid-August. Make a list of the different essay topics, determine how much overlap there is, and get started as early as possible.

Your criminal history

Huh?

That's right. Your criminal history. You are applying to *law* school, after all—and most schools will be asking you to document any arrests you've been subject to, and any court appearances you've made for anything other than routine traffic tickets—and they may even want to know about those if you've had too many of them. If there are any skeletons in your closet, assemble the documentation now so your applications won't get held up.

If you've ever been arrested or been a defendant in a court proceeding, admissions committees will want to know the name of the court, its address and phone number, the date and docket number of your case, the disposition, and any fines or other punishment you received. For those of you considering a cover-up at this stage—don't. You might get away with it, but most law schools won't automatically disqualify individuals with checkered pasts anyway. Three years down the road, however, an extensive character and fitness investigation background check awaits you before you can sit for the bar exam. They'll find anything you've tried to cover up—and they won't be as forgiving as the admissions office might be.

With this in mind, if you have a criminal history, contact your state bar association and inquire about the likely effect your past might have on your ability to pass the character and fitness investigation. Better to find out now than to spend the tuition and three years of your life only to find out that no state considers you fit to practice law.

The LSAT

Finally, you must determine when you will face the LSAT—the great law school gatekeeper. The LSAT is offered four times a year, in February, June, October, and December. Scores can take up to six weeks to be processed and sent to the schools, and your application will not be considered complete—and will not even be looked at—until your scores are in. Accordingly, most applicants in a given year will take the LSAT in June or October in order to complete their applications by November. Taking the exam in June is the wisest choice, because it leaves room for error in case you are sick, have a family emergency, or experience one of the few circumstances which warrant canceling your scores. We'll address the LSAT more fully in the next chapter.

The big picture

Stepping back, then, you should have penciled in (1) a June or October LSAT date, (2) compiled a final list of schools and written application request letters to be sent out no later than August 1, and (3) made your recommendation requests no later than September 15. Your applications should begin arriving at the beginning of September, and you should immediately dissect them.

Make a list of all the essay requirements, figure out how much overlap you have and how many separate essays you'll need, and get busy writing.

Remember, your deadline is to have everything in the mail by November 1.

CHAPTER 2

Your Five Most Critical Hours:
How to Beat the LSAT

Labor conquers all things.
—HOMER

ACCORDING TO the powers-that-be, the Law School Admissions Test, or "LSAT," is the "great equalizer." Theoretically designed to measure aptitude and fitness for law school, its goal is to take the entire pool of law school applicants and put them through an examination which "levels the playing field" by providing a vehicle to evaluate everyone on a single objective scale. Such a measurement is needed, the argument goes, because the inherently subjective nature of essays and recommendations and relative degrees of grade inflation make it otherwise difficult to separate applicants based on merit.

As a result, we have the LSAT, the great gatekeeper to the doors of law school—and with it, a healthy dose of both good news and bad news.

First the bad news.

The LSAT is required for admission to any of the 196 law schools that are members of the Law School Admissions Council (LSAC). Not surprisingly, all of the top law schools, and the overwhelming majority of second and third-tier schools are members of the LSAC and, thus, require the LSAT.

Most law schools take LSAT scores extremely seriously. Although exact admissions "equations" are among law schools' most closely guarded secrets (see the interview in the next chapter for much more on this), most law schools use some kind of formula which combines a student's undergraduate grade-point average and strength of undergraduate institution with that student's LSAT score to compute a raw score for that student called an "admissions index." This index is then used to rank the applicants. At many schools, an applicant whose admissions index falls well outside the school average may not ever get a second look. And the news gets worse. Although exact figures are not known, at the majority of schools, LSAT scores account for at least half, and in many cases more than half of the weight of the admissions index. In other words, bombing the LSAT, in many cases, will be fatal to your admissions hopes.

> When I decided to try to get into law school, I realized that my score on the LSAT was going to decide where I went to law school, and prepared with that in mind.
>
> —Pat

So what, you ask, is the good news?

The LSAT is nothing more than a big game, and it is a game that you can get good at. The structure of the exam is virtually identical from year to year, and it is a test that rarely surprises anyone with its content. There are a finite number of "tricks" that the exam employs—simply rehashing the same tricks over and over again in subtly different ways. Although the LSAT is very challenging and poses severe timing issues for many students, it is a challenge that can be overcome if you are willing to put in the time. The LSAT's formidable reputation as the "great gatekeeper" and the "breaker of dreams" has been earned primarily from the experiences of the unprepared and the uninformed. This is not a test that you'd be advised to take cold, but it is a test you can master.

So what is this "LSAT" anyway?

The LSAT is a 101-question exam comprised of 175 minutes of multiple choice questions (including one unidentified experimental section used to test future exam questions) and a thirty-minute essay question. The exam is divided into five thirty-five minute timed sections each testing one of three different "categories" of questions. In no particular order, these "categories" include reading comprehension, logical reasoning, and logic games. The LSAT will always be comprised of two logical reasoning sections, one reading comprehension section, and one logic games section. The wild card is the experimental section, which can be another section of any of the above types. During any given exam session, more than one experimental section will be tested—so one student's exam may contain an experimental section of logic games, while another student's exam may have an experimental reading comprehension section. There is really no way to tell which section of an exam is the experimental section, so you have to treat each of the five sections the same way.

Your "raw score" on the exam is simply the number of questions you answered correctly. There is no subtraction made for incorrect answers, so you should be sure to fill in an answer choice for every question even if you have to guess blindly on the questions you didn't get to consider. Your raw score will be converted to a "scaled score" between 120–180 based on a formula which will normalize the LSAT you took with LSATs given in the past five years to account for differences in difficulty between exams. Your scaled score will then be assigned a percentile ranking which will compare your score to the scores of all other students who took the identical exam.

The reading comprehension section

Don't be lulled into complacency—this is not the same reading comprehension section you aced on the SAT. This is major-league reading comprehension. The dense passages of up to 450 words each will be chosen from one of four general fields: law, humanities, social sciences, or natural sciences. Each passage will be followed by five to eight questions. You are allotted thirty-five minutes to complete the entire section, usually comprised of four passages and twenty-seven total questions. Not surprisingly, although reading comprehension is usually perceived to be the least threatening of the LSAT categories, it often poses the most serious time constraints. Accordingly, building speed will probably be the focus of your practice in this section.

Logical reasoning

With two multiple-choice sections of twenty-four to twenty-six questions each (forty-eight to fifty-two total questions), logical reasoning questions constitute half of the LSAT. Generally, these questions pose a short argument, and then one or two questions requiring you to analyze or evaluate that argument or draw logical inferences from it. These questions generally follow one of several basic patterns that you should memorize and learn to recognize as part of your preparation.

Logic games

The logic games section is almost always the most dreaded of the LSAT sections, in large part because it is the least familiar. Invariably, there are four different scenarios, or "games," each followed by four to seven questions based on it. A typical game poses a hypothetical example, such as one in which there are eight seats around a table, and eight dinner guests. There will then be several statements about who will and won't sit next to whom, who must be seated together, etc., and you will then be asked to respond to several questions about possible seating arrangements.

Although these games can be fascinating and even fun to work out casually on a rainy day, they can bring students to tears under the strict time constraints of the LSAT. Accordingly, on this section more than any other, studying the different "types" of games and their hidden tricks and the strategies for dealing with them can pay huge dividends on exam day. As Allan notes, "the only way to master the games section is to take multiple practice exam sections."

It is usually the logic games section of the LSAT that causes students to panic and waste precious time fretting—leading to exam disasters. Knowing this ahead of time, and preparing accordingly, will give you a big advantage over your competitors.

The minutiae and related suggestions

As noted, the LSAT is offered four times a year, in June, October, December, and February. You should take the exam no later than the October term in the fall of your application year to ensure that admissions offices have your completed application as early as possible during the admissions season.

In 1999–2000, the registration fee for the exam was eighty-eight dollars (which can be waived upon proof of financial hardship and the filing of the proper forms) and must be received by a deadline one month prior to the administration date. With an additional late fee of fifty-three dollars, you can register up to two weeks before the exam.

You'll have a wide choice of test administration centers offering the exam—and you should not overlook the strategic advantages of making a wise selection. At the time I registered, I was living in New Haven, but despite the familiar exam center and setting, I had no desire to take the exam in a room filled with several hundred frenetic Yale students and a bunch of way-too-serious graduate student proctors. Instead, I opted to travel home to New Hampshire for the weekend, and to take the LSAT at the exam center at the tiny liberal arts college in my hometown—where I felt that I would have a psychological advantage, and might benefit from more relaxed proctors. Instead of taking the exam in a room of 250 students, I took it in a room of ten students. My friends in New Haven tell me that their graduate student proctors were confiscating food and beverages at the door. My proctor allowed us to have whatever we wanted, and actually baked cookies for us to eat at the break. Although food is technically "prohibited" in the LSAT, I'd at least try to bring in a couple of rolls of Life Savers or some raisins for a little sugar boost when you need it, an energy bar to eat at the break, and a bottle of water. If they get confiscated, they get confiscated. You might, however, get lucky, and get to consume them.

Maybe you don't care about any of these little "advantages," and that's fine. I, however, find stress to be contagious—and I wanted to assure myself of every possible edge I could get. The LSAT was hard enough by itself, and I found that my choice of test centers made a big difference to me.

Wherever you decide to take the exam, you should visit the exam center at least a day before the exam to get a sense for where it is located, what the room is like, and how warm or cold it is, so you can dress properly. No matter where you take the exam, I'd also bring a pair of earplugs and plan to use them. If the guy next to you has a cold and sniffles incessantly, it will disturb your concentration and throw you off your game. I've known people who would have gladly paid a hundred dollars for a pair of earplugs to counter a clanking radiator, a jackhammer out in the street, or construction noises in the exam building. The day you take the LSAT will be one of the most critical days of your academic life. Plan for every contingency.

> One helpful thing I did was set an alarm for the week before the exam and wake up every day and do practice questions so I could get used to thinking like that early in the morning.
>
> —Alison

So what about the test prep courses?

Stanley Kaplan and The Princeton Review both offer excellent LSAT preparation courses that you can take either on tape or live and in person. I've had many friends who have taken one or the other and been extremely satisfied with them. The courses are relatively expensive, generally around five hundred dollars, but by most accounts, are well worth the investment.

"I took the LSAT twice. The first time, I prepared minimally on my own and ended up scoring in the 90th percentile. This wouldn't have gotten me into the schools I wanted to go to, so I took the Princeton Review prep course, took the test again, and scored in the 95th percentile. I would definitely recommend taking one of these courses," Keith noted.

I did not take one of these courses. I ordered as many actual sample tests (with answers) as I could, and bought a couple of the readily available study guides (The Princeton Review and Arco) at the local bookstore. I studied hard for about six weeks (several hours a day), memorizing all the tricks, building speed, and doing thousands of sample questions until I was routinely hitting my target score on released exams taken under actual exam conditions.

You probably know someone who took the LSAT cold without doing any advance studying at all and pulled a 175. I know someone like that too—but it wasn't me—and you shouldn't expect it to be you either. It took me six weeks of pretty intense training to get in range of the score I needed. Whether you do a course with one of the reputable test preparation centers, or prepare on your own, plan for about the same time frame, and take test preparation seriously.

I bombed it—I know it—Should I cancel my score?

Many, many students walk out of the LSAT administration thinking that they did significantly worse than they actually did. Unless you were physically ill during the exam or you *know* that you drastically underperformed your goal on more than one section (say, by wild guessing on many more questions than you intended in more than one section), you should consider allowing your test to stand and see where you are after your score comes out. Do not simply cancel your score because you are nervous about your performance. Everyone is.

> Don't cancel your score just because you feel badly when the exam is over. I came out of the exam feeling terrible about it, and thought very seriously about canceling my score. I don't know if it was that I did badly on the experimental section and lucked out, or whether it was a tough exam for everybody, but I ended up scoring in the ninety-third percentile, which was enough to get me into the school I wanted.
>
> —A mentor

You'll have five days after the administration of an exam to decide whether or not to cancel your score. The Law School Data Assembly Service, or "LSDAS," reports aborted exam attempts to the law schools you selected to receive score reports—and law schools are suspicious of canceled exam attempts. Further, you cannot take the LSAT more than three times during any two-year period—and canceled exams count.

If you take the LSAT more than once, LSDAS will report each separate score and then average the two scores together. Most schools will look at the average as the more accurate indicator.

CHAPTER 3

Applying to Law School:
Bait the Hooks Carefully and
Cast the Nets Wide

'Tis fate that flings the dice,
And as she flings
Of kings makes peasants,
And of peasants, kings.
—JOHN DRYDEN

MOST OF US who applied to college filed applications with a relatively small number of schools. Your guidance counselor probably advised you to pick two or three schools in each of three tiers. The highest tier contained your "reach" schools, where your chances of admission were unlikely or uncertain, but most desired. The middle tier contained the schools which were a good numerical match for you based on their mean GPA and SAT numbers, where your chances of admission were a good possibility. Finally, the third tier contained your "safety" schools, one or two places, typically including your state university system, where your chances of admission were virtually assured. For others among us, a single application to one's state university may, for financial or other reasons, have been the only alternative.

The law school admissions process, however, is entirely different. The admissions criteria are different, the required documentation is different, there isn't always a state school available to you, and admission is virtually never certain. Accordingly, as Joel notes, "for applicants with borderline numbers, I recommend applying to as many as fifteen, or even more schools. There is less variance between law school applications than between college applications, so it's not that hard to crank out a bunch of apps without diluting the overall quality of each one."

Steve agrees. "Apply to four or five schools that you think you can get into and that you would not mind going to, and then apply to as many other schools as you can in the range above those schools. While it may seem like a waste of money and a waste of time to send out so many applications, you never know where you're going to get in, and so the time and money spent applying must be viewed more like a long-term investment. If the result is that you get into a school that is higher on the list than you expected you would get accepted to, the time and money will be well worth it."

Another mentor expressed his frustration at the seemingly random way the process is conducted, and the even more random array of results he got in the application process. "It made no sense at all. I got into the number three school in the country, and rejected by one of my safety schools. I just have no idea what the admissions people are looking for."

With this is mind, *Law School Confidential* is proud to present the advice and insights of Dean of Admissions Janice Austin of the University of Pennsylvania Law School. Dean Austin was an admissions officer at Columbia Law School for eight years and the director of admissions at the University of California at Hastings Law School for five years before becoming the dean of admissions at Penn at the beginning of the 1994–95 academic year. She brings eighteen years of law school admissions experience to your side at this critical time, and she speaks with an unsurpassed degree of candor and alacrity. At the end of the chapter, we'll return to provide you with a couple of additional strategies and suggestions based on their own experiences.

Dean Austin, first of all, I'd like to thank you for taking the time out of your busy schedule to speak directly to the future generations of law students who will read this book. As you know, the focus of this book is to provide those future generations of law students with the inside secrets to success in law school, and I have to say, speaking at least from my own experiences, there is nothing more baffling or unpredictable than the law school admissions process—so I'm really thrilled that you agreed to participate in this project.

You're very welcome. I'm happy to provide whatever advice I can.

Let's start at the beginning. Who is generally on an admissions committee at a law school?

Well, first of all, not all schools have them. Those that don't generally have a dean of admissions and his or her staff working autonomously. Those schools that do have committees generally involve faculty members, current students, and the professional staff in the admissions office. Faculty members are typically appointed to an admissions committee by the dean or associate dean of the law school. Because of the volume of work involved over a short term, there usually are not a lot of faculty members chomping at the bit to be appointed. You need workhorses.

How do students get on the committee and what is their usual role?

Students usually come on to the committee through the student government. Students on some committees read files, others just help to decide general admissions policies. Usually, the volume of files a particular school receives dictates how the committees work. Faculty members can't read every file at high volume schools.

How does an admissions committee at a particular law school formulate its admissions policy?

It depends on the type of school we're talking about. The most selective schools have the opportunity to construct an admissions process in a way that's going to give them an extraordinary class. Probably two-thirds of the law schools out there don't have that luxury—many schools have to admit almost all their applicants in order to field a class—so they are less selective and less engaged in discussion about the admissions criteria that they use.

So what does it take to get into one of the top law schools in the country?

There is clearly a distinction between the most selective schools and the less selective schools in how they conduct their admissions processes. The first assumption that people tend to make about the most selective schools is that we only want people with high LSATs and high GPAs, but I always tell people the most selective schools are not going to fill their class with everyone who has a 4.0 and a 175 LSAT score—they could, but that's not their goal. Obviously there are some ranges dependent on the selectivity of the school and the overall quality of the program, but it's much less numbers driven than people think.

I've got to try and pin you down on this, because this is what students out there thinking about applying to law school are most interested in hearing about. Aren't there typically some minimum numbers that you have to surpass in order to have your application taken seriously at a top law school?

Yeah, sure. I always say to students, you have to have a B or better and an LSAT around 160 to get into the ball game at the most selective schools. I'm a baseball fan, so I'll use a baseball analogy—at this stage, all you want to do is get into the game. You can get in with a bleacher seat, and you can get in with a box seat, it doesn't really matter. Once you get into the ballpark, you're going to see the game. The secret is understanding the process and getting over that first hurdle.

How do schools decide what these cutoff points are? Isn't it kind of arbitrary to decide that a student with a 160 LSAT gets over the hurdle, but a student with a 159 doesn't? I mean, that could come down to one question on the exam. It could come down to a guess!

Well, it never comes down to a raw number like that. Schools generally use a validity study to suggest what weight to attribute to LSAT and GPA to predict a certain law school first year average. Law services is the keeper of the validity study for the law school admissions council. Every year, member law schools have to send each student's first year grades to law services. Law services then enters these grades into a formula that determines by what weight students' undergraduate GPA and LSAT scores predict their first year grades, and sends the validity study back showing the formula. When you get the results for the prior class, you tweak the formula between LSAT and GPA to get a coefficient factor as close as possible to 1—which would be the proper weight to give to students'

GPAs and LSAT scores to perfectly predict their first-year grades. Some schools then tweak their formula to some degree, but at Penn, our formula hasn't changed in the last decade.

Is this combination of GPA and LSAT score what is commonly referred to as an "admissions index"? Can you be any more specific about how these two factors are weighted in calculating the index?

The validity studies show that the best predictor of performance in law school is a combination of LSAT and GPA. Taken alone, GPA is better—because the LSAT is a sprint and the GPA is a marathon—four years of successful work tends to stand up better than a one-day wonder who has gotten an outstanding score on the LSAT but has an underachieving GPA. The index varies among the different schools. For us, the formula incorporates your LSAT percentile, your mean LSAT (the average LSAT score of the students from your undergraduate school who have taken the LSAT in the last five years), and your "rank in class," which is computed by taking the percentile rank of your GPA compared to the GPAs of the other LSAT test takers from your undergraduate institution during the past five years.

So the quality of your undergraduate college or university is considered?

Oh yeah. Penn's faculty, and the faculties of many top schools, give weight to the undergraduate school that you went to—that's why the mean LSAT and class rank are used instead of straight-up GPAs and LSAT scores. The person in the middle of their class at Williams will inevitably have a higher index than the person at the top of their class at Chico State because of the weighted values. That's why it's important to read files and not just rely on the index—otherwise, the person with the 4.0 from Chico State who may be spectacular could get overlooked, while the person who was mediocre at Williams but had the advantage of the Williams name and the higher index could win out.

Does the admissions office use this admissions "index" to develop some kind of "rank order" of applicants?

Indices are used to rank order files when they come in. We got

3800 applications this year and we need a way to put them in some kind of alpha order—schools want to be able to admit their most admissible students as quickly as possible—so you need to be able to read from the top down in terms of making the initial offers quickly, and then you need to read from the bottom up to let those people know what's going on. The files at the top and the bottom present the easiest read—it's the files in the middle that cause you the most difficulty. We use the index to determine what order the files are read in. We read every file at Penn—but the rank order helps me to prioritize my time. It takes me 8-10 minutes to read a file. Since we want to get offers out as quickly as possible in order to be able to do admitted students days over the spring to help lure students to the school, and to get financial aid and scholarship merits awards out—you have to read from the top down.

Okay, so once a file has passed the initial hurdle and makes its way into your hands, what is it you're looking for?

I don't read books anymore because I read 3500 short stories every year—I see this as my reading. When I talk to applicants, I tell them that once their file is in my hands, their life is my short story, and gets the next ten minutes of my undivided attention. Every file gets read by me at least once—and I say at least once because people whose files end up in the waitlist pile get read by me again and again. What I usually attempt to do is step into people's lives. You know, we ask the questions we ask for very specific reasons. Even the most benign optional questions that most people think are throwaways or just for demographic analysis are actually really important—things like where you were born, where you grew up, where you went to high school, where your parents are and whether or not they are alive, what do they do, whether you were a first generation college graduate—these things really help to give me a sense of the person behind the application. So that's where I start. Once I have that picture, then I look to see where you went to school, whether you transferred in or out, whether you spent time abroad. I look to see what kind of extracurricular activities you participated in while you were in college to determine whether you were a leader, or were at least active on campus, or whether you were strictly a library person who had no interest in becoming involved.

What happens once you've looked at these background questions?

Well, once I have a general impression of who you are, I usually look next to see whether you've followed instructions, and how neat you were in your preparation. This is your presentation of yourself, so I am hoping to find that it is thorough and complete. I'm still at the "gathering an impression" stage. Did you scribble the application in pencil, or were you manic and fit it perfectly into a printer, which is next to impossible? When I was at Columbia, we also had a handwriting expert take a look at signatures to provide further insights.

What happens once you have this "impression" of an applicant?

Then I usually take a look at your transcript to see what kind of grades you had. I'm not just looking at the letters, though. I'm looking for the story behind the letters. For example, say I'm looking at someone who went to a public high school in California. If the applicant started off as an engineering student at MIT and then transferred to Cal State Long Beach to become a philosophy major after his first year—I know that the first year grades at MIT are all pass-fail, so I assume that this person struggled, and was probably miserable being an engineer. Then I look further. After the student's transfer, his philosophy grades at Cal State Long Beach are really good, that's where he's from, he's back home in the more comfortable environment of his community now, did some things on campus, had decent summer jobs there—well, to me this looks like a pretty good candidate—someone who struggled initially, but found himself.

Then what happens?

Well, once I have some sense of the story your grades are telling me, I usually look at the letters of recommendation for some confirmation of this. Recommendations are kind of tough, though, because if you've played your cards right, no one is going to say something bad about you—and if they do, then you were really dumb for asking that person to write on your behalf. On the other hand, every now and then I get a recommendation that compels me to write a thank-you note to the recommender—either because the person is such an extraordinary writer, or because the recommendation is so insightful, or so helpful.

48

Is it true that there is a certain "secret language" that you're looking for in recommendations—certain words that recommenders use to convey more to you than they seem to be conveying?

Yeah, I get letters that on their face seem fine, but to me, are clearly lukewarm and say to me "take this person at your own risk." It is very rare to have someone just come out and say that in a letter, but I read eight to ten thousand letters of recommendation a year, so the buzzwords, the clues, the telltale language, when it's there, jumps right out at you.

Can you give some examples of this?

Things like "interesting student—shy in class," or "so-and-so is always involved in the conversation, but occasionally irritates classmates," or "so-and-so's writing style is underdeveloped." A dead giveaway is the recommendation which intentionally misses the mark by making complementary observations like—"this person is very attractive" or "a nice person" without providing any specific examples.

How much weight do you give to "celebrity recommenders" like senators, congressmen, famous lawyers, etc.?

Recommendations from senators, representatives, governors, movie stars, Fortune 500 CEOs don't mean a whole lot if it's clear to me that they're just there for the name—some of them are easier to get than you think, because we vote for these people. The people that you really need to get are the people who grade and evaluate your work, the people who see you in class every day and respond to your questions, the people who you see in office hours, the people who you know have written letters for other people applying to law school. The way higher education is shaping up in this country, with large classes, fewer tenured faculty, more graduate students teaching classes—many students tell me that they just don't know the big-name professors that well. That's okay. It's okay to get a recommendation from a T. A. who knows your work well instead of the sterling professor of international law whom you've never spoken to. It's easy to hide behind your letters of recommendation—but you can't hide from me. If you only get letters from your senator and the named partner at your father's law firm who last met you when you were two, then I begin to question where the substance is. I start wondering why no one knows you well enough to write substantively on your behalf—and then I begin looking at that in conjunction with any other suggestions present in your file to support that impression.

So when does the personal statement come in? Is it really important?

That comes next. By this point, I have a pretty good sense of who you are. I've looked over your grades to see if they tell me a story, and I've looked over your recommendations to see if they confirm or contradict that impression. Now, I'll skim the first two paragraphs of your personal statement—and that usually tells me a lot—mainly what kind of writer you are. I had some files at home with me over the weekend and I couldn't believe how poorly these people who are seniors in college, were writing. When I see that, my immediate thought is usually 'Am I going to release this person who is such a lousy writer into society with a Penn Law degree? I don't think so.'

So you're looking more at the writing style of the personal statement than the content of the personal statement?

Only initially. I can usually tell what kind of writer you are by skimming the first two paragraphs. I think about the content later.

What's next?

Now I take a more thorough look at your transcript. I'll check and see what school you went to, the courses you selected, and the grades you got in them, and compare this performance with your LSAT score to see if the LSAT is about what I would have predicted. Again, I'm looking for the story. Do you have a 3.8 from Berkeley with good course selection, but a lousy LSAT score—which tells me that you either had a bad day, or are you a poor standardized test taker? If I see that, I'll look to see if you were kind enough to provide your SAT score on one of my optional questions. Did you get a 900 combined on your SAT but go to Princeton undergrad and get a 3.7—to suggest to me that you just can't do these standardized tests but that you'd be fine as a student in class? Did your SAT underpredict your performance in college—such that I might expect your LSAT to underpredict your performance in law school?

Would you advise a student who bombs the LSAT to take it again?

When students call me to ask me whether they should take the test again, I always ask them to really take a gut check and evaluate whether they gave it their best shot the first time. Did you walk out of that test feeling really good, or did you walk out crawling on your belly? If you felt like you crawled out on your belly then you probably need to take the test again. But if you feel like you studied hard, you did all the preparation, you got a good night's sleep the night before, you weren't sick in the test room, and you stayed pretty much on your goals and did everything you could—but you still didn't score, there's probably no need to take the test again. Statistically, people usually don't raise their scores very much the second time around.

Does taking the test more than once weigh against you in the admissions process?

If you do take the test again, tell me why you decided to—I always wonder about it, especially if your score increased dramatically the second time. An increase of five raw points can translate into fifteen percentile points, but how am I supposed to evaluate that without a context? When I come across a person who has taken the test more than once and raised their score significantly but doesn't tell you why—then I wonder, well, did the person just have a bad day the first time, were they sick, was there a family crisis? There are times when it is appropriate to take the LSAT twice and there are times when it is inappropriate.

How are two disparate scores evaluated?

So much of what happens in our offices is driven by outside forces—and by outside forces, I mean rankings in various publications and other things—most schools will take the higher of the LSAT scores when making admissions decisions—so that's usually of some comfort to candidates. If you took the test once and got a 163, and then took it again and got a 164, that's not going to make a difference to me. On the other hand, if you took the test once and got a 163, then took it again and got a 169—well, six points could be about fifteen percentile points, that could be a big deal—especially if it's in keeping with the other predictors in your file like your GPA. But give me a context to understand the difference.

So now the ten minutes are up. You've finished reading a file for the first time. What happens to it? Do you assign it a score, make an immediate decision, assign it to a pile?

I play chess here in my office—if you look around the room there are files in a lot of different spots for a lot of different reasons—that's how I move files around. I can't speak for how every school does it, but I'd say that for most schools, the director of admissions or the dean of admissions gets all files—and as the files become complete, they live in giant file cabinets. I go to the cabinets and pull a certain number of files to read every day—and after I've read the file, I'll make some kind of preliminary decision—it's usually pretty easy at the top and really easy at the bottom, although there are always people at the top with perfect grades and scores that just make you pause and say, well, there's just something weird about this person—there are too many holes or they look like a great student but they haven't done anything to contribute. Having great grades and scores does not mean that you're going to be an automatic admit. Likewise at the bottom, there are always some people that look like bootstrappers—and there's something in their files that makes me look beyond the numbers. Those people typically live on my windowsill for awhile until I see how the class is developing.

What are the different outcomes that a file can get at this point?

We have a lot of decisions that are available to us—I can admit somebody, I can reject somebody, I can put somebody on a waitlist, I can put somebody in a "hold" category which I equate to a plane circling an airport waiting for a runway to clear so it can land on one of the other decisions, or I can ask people for additional information—like their fall semester grades—if I'm looking for confirmation of a trend. I can ask people to come in for an interview—which I don't advertise, and don't do all that often, but which I will do if I have questions about a person, or if I know that Penn is their first choice and there's something that I need to know about the person before I can make a decision about them. I may give them a call, or I might ask them to write their personal statement again, or to get me more letters of recommendation, or get an updated copy of their transcript to see if an upward or downward trend is holding up. So files move around. I try very hard not to send out any rejection letters, except to early-decision candidates, during the holiday season. So things might just back up in here around then. Depending on the time of year, files may be in all different states of decision.

What's the story with early decision?

There are twenty-seven schools that have early notification processes now—which means that you apply by a certain date, and check off a box on the application to indicate that you'd like to be considered for early decision. If you apply for early decision, you'll have an outcome in December. At Penn, about four hundred people apply early decision—and the one thing I know about early decision is that it produces a relatively high yield.

At what stage do the faculty members on the committee get to read the files?

Faculty read the files of those people at the top and the bottom that are giving me trouble. So I'll give them the person at the top who is a great numbers person but a weird character or a noncontributor, or the person at the bottom who looks to have pulled himself up by his bootstraps but has a really low GPA, like below a 3.0 or even a 2.5. I also typically give them the career changers, older people with advanced degrees coming to law school in the middle of their lives, and the "cookie cutters"—the people in the middle who would all be great students here. Since we can't admit one thousand of them, I leave it to the faculty to pick and choose these students since they will be the ones teaching them.

Is there ever any contentiousness among the members of the committee in choosing which students to admit?

Like all committees, the dean, when choosing the composition of the admissions committee tries to get some balance, but regardless of how the committee is composed, it always shocks me how similarly our votes come out—the conservative faculty members and the liberal faculty members usually come to the same conclusions about which students should be admitted—which makes me feel good. I think that's one of the reasons why admissions is such a successful administrative process here at Penn. I'd say that better than ninety-eight percent of the time, the faculty and I come to the same conclusion on a file.

How does it ultimately get decided? Is there a vote?

I make a bunch of decisions on my own, but a vote is taken on every file that I distribute to the faculty members. For those files, each faculty member on the committee gets one vote, and I get a vote. We have three faculty members on the committee, and of the files I give them, each of those three faculty members will read the file once. Different schools work differently though—at schools like Stanford and Yale, which get a lower volume of applications, every faculty member reads files. Conversely, at a school like NYU, which might receive six-thousand applications, they have more administrators or outside readers reading files.

What is the most common mistake people make on their applications?

Not caring. Your application is the only presentation of yourself you will make to a school. There's only one school in the country that routinely and systematically interviews its entire applicant pool—so for the most part, it's a paper process. Whatever ends up in that envelope is what we see about you. Presentation and neatness count. Were you careful in your personal statement? I appreciate that some personal statements overlap and that you will use the same personal statements for more than one school—but needless to say, it is probably deadly to your application if in the essay you send to Penn your last sentence says that you really hope to get into Georgetown.

Are those kinds of mistakes common?

Oh yeah. I see that stuff all the time. Be careful. Typos and grammatical errors in the personal statement are also widespread, and deadly. The way I look at it, someone who submits a personal statement with grammatical errors or typos in it is just giving me advance notice about what kind of student and what kind of member of the community they're going to be when they get here—so those are usually deadly errors to an applicant. Get someone to read and edit your personal statement and give you some feedback on it.

What is the biggest gaffe a student can make on an application?

Trying to grab my attention by being too creative. I love being creative—but this is a tricky line, because you're applying to professional school here. When I was the admissions director at U.C. Hastings, this woman sent a shoe in the mail, and said something like—now that I have my foot in the door, I hope you'll offer me admission. The problem is she also sent the shoe to a friend of mine who was the director of admissions at U.C. Santa Clara. There are only one hundred seventy-eight accredited law schools—so there are only one hundred seventy-eight of us who do this job around the country and we talk all the time, so if you do something stupid to one of us, more than likely, we're going to talk about it. The thing is, we were talking about this to a third friend who was the director of admissions at U.C. Davis, and we were going to have him send both shoes back to her and say something like, you should have stepped into Davis, but we didn't do that for fear of doing permanent damage to the woman's psyche.

Any other examples?

Yeah, this year, I got an application attached to a life preserver with a note that said something like, this is to help my application stay afloat in the sea of competition. People send books, cassettes, CDs, videotapes, sketches, paintings, and artwork. This year, an applicant sent us a bunch of soaps that she made. Anything that fits into a file, I can deal with. I never watch the videotapes, I farm those out to my staff. People are now starting to tell us to check out their websites—but I farm these out to my staff too and they pre-screen these for me, and if there's something really cool, then I'll check it out.

How important are legacy, ethnic, socioeconomic, gender, and race in the law school admissions process?

We don't have any quotas for anything. These are the things that make admissions both exciting and disturbing. I would hope that as academic institutions, we would be free to set the policies that we want to enable us to enroll the classes that we would like to get—but these days, a lot of this is controlled by outside forces, and there are more legal ramifications associated with what we do than ever before. At Penn, as an institution, legacy has always been important—but it doesn't have the impact that people may think it does. There are many more legacies that get denied here every year than there are legacies who enroll. More often than not—people are understanding of this, and acknowledge how much more rigorous the law school application climate is here these days. In terms of ethnicity, socioeconomic factors, other interesting factors like disadvantaged backgrounds, first generation college, immigrant status—we don't have a formal affirmative action policy, which I think is great, because it gives us the flexibility to conduct our process as we see fit without a mandate on either end dictating what kind of complexion of class we should enroll.

What happens to people on the waitlist? How long should they hang in there?

That's a tough question. I feel really bad and my heart really goes out to the people who end up Phi Beta Kappa at a third-tier undergraduate school, and have a decent LSAT score but the reality is, that's usually not strong enough to get in here, as amazing as that sounds. But I don't like to just send these people away with a simple rejection letter, so I might just waitlist that person in recognition of their accomplishments. I won't be able to enroll every person with a 4.0 who applies to Penn Law school from one of those places, but I can probably waitlist them. I think that to get waitlisted at one of the top law schools in the country really says something. It says that someone read their file carefully, recognized the significance of their accomplishments, and did not simply look at the name of their school and their numbers and then pitch their application into the reject pile. As they go to law school somewhere else and then move on into their careers, I think they'll still remember that—they may not feel as good as they would have if they had gotten in, but hopefully it will give them some confidence and be something they can hang onto as they go forward. This is something I saw at Columbia and have also seen used at some of the other very selective schools. When you're faced with thousands of applicants applying for less than three hundred seats, you're going to have to deny admission to some spectacular people, and I would rather give some form of recognition to these people than just send them some cold, informal rejection letter that leaves them wondering whether anyone even looked at their file.

So what would you say to a person sitting on the waitlist still hoping against hope to get in?

If I'm going to go to the waitlist during the summer, it means I have some seats to fill. I can't afford to be shooting blanks at that point, so I have to go to people who I know will enroll. So the person that has written me every week since April gets noticed. On the other hand, if I pull a file that I think looks really good, but I haven't gotten any correspondence from the person since she was waitlisted four months ago, and I go out to my staff and find out that she hasn't ever called or written to supplement her application—I can't take a chance on that person with the limited amount of time I have left at that point.

So the squeaky wheel gets the grease?

Well, to a certain extent. You don't want to be obnoxious or to become a nuisance, but at the same time, you want to remind us that you're out there. There was a person I remember when I was the admissions director at U.C. Hastings that was sitting on the waitlist during the summer and traveling in Europe, and she sent us postcards every three days from the various places in Europe that she was traveling—just simple reminders that she was still waiting and hoping to hear from us. Well you know what? She got in, because when I had a spot open up and needed someone who I knew would come at the drop of a hat, guess who I thought of?

Imagine that you're sitting with your nephew or niece and have two minutes to give him or her a last bit of advice about applying to law school. What would you say?

Pick your schools carefully—it's okay to apply to fifteen, but of the three schools you get into, focus, figure out where you're going to be happiest, and really make the commitment. Do a self-evaluation about how realistic you are as an applicant at a particular school, and then, if you feel like you have a shot, do what you need to do to get noticed. You don't want to be loud and draw too much attention to yourself, but you want to make sure that you are recognized in this process. Good luck!

There are a few other strategies that you may want to employ in planning your approach to law school applications. As with everything else in this book, these strategies are culled from personal experience, and will help you avoid some of the critical mistakes we made.

ADDITIONAL STRATEGY 1: Try to decide where you want to practice before you apply

I know, I know, you don't have any idea what you want to do with your life, so how are you supposed to know where you want to live? Well, guess what? If you read the first two chapters of this book, you should already have an appreciation for the importance that foresight and planning play in determining the success of your law school career.

Hey, if you get into Yale or Harvard, that's great. You can keep this book around for some humorous bedtime reading and cease to worry about any of this stuff, because you'll pretty much have it made. But the rest of us might want to heed this advice: Figure out where you want to settle down before you apply to law school.

Why?

It's simple. If you don't get into one of the top fifteen or so law schools in the country, it's going to be pretty hard to get a job outside the region where your law school is located. If you already know where you want to live, however, you can file applications with the top law schools, and then hedge your bets by applying to the better regional law schools near the city where you hope to practice. This strategy has several advantages. First, you can virtually neutralize the placement problems associated with attending a regional law school, because you'll want to practice in the region to which your regional law school primarily places its students. Second, in applying to that law school, your desire to stay and practice in the region can make a compelling case for your admission. Third, if you are admitted, you'll greatly reduce your stress during recruiting season knowing that before you even started, you've maximized your chances of getting a job in the city or region of your choice. We'll talk much more about the role regional preferences should play in your application process in the next chapter.

ADDITIONAL STRATEGY 2: File your applications as early as possible

Dean Austin made a pretty clear point in her interview earlier in this chapter—the early applicant pool produces a high yield of accepted offers and matriculating students. As a student, that should tell you two things: (1) as an early applicant to a law school, you are signaling a preference to attend that law school, and with competitive numbers, may increase your odds of admission; and (2) if you send out your applications late in the application season, many of the seats in the class may already be filled. There is really no need to mince words here—you must file your applications as early in the application season as possible to maximize your chances of success. This process is competitive enough without putting yourself in a hole out of the gates. Aim to have everything in the mail by November 1.

ADDITIONAL STRATEGY 3: Proofread everything

Yeah, I know I'm being redundant, but Dean Austin couldn't have been clearer about this. Typos and sloppiness can kill your chances of admission. If it isn't absolutely perfect, don't send it out.

ADDITIONAL STRATEGY 4: Visit your top schools and then reference your visit

Remember, you need to stand out. Visit your top choice schools and figure out why it is that you really want to matriculate there. Is there something about the school's general philosophy that draws you to it? Do you hope to study a certain subject in depth with the tenured faculty member who is the acknowledged expert in the field? Do you want to participate in a dual degree program that is better at that school than elsewhere? When you visit the campus, drop into the admissions office and introduce yourself to the director of admissions. Don't brown nose, but don't be afraid to make that person aware of your attraction to the school, and the reasons for that attraction. If you do get to speak to the admissions director, send a note a few days later thanking him or her for the time spent talking to you. Later, try and reference your campus visit and reinforce your reasons for applying somewhere in your application.

About four weeks after you send out your applications, drop a quick letter in the mail to each school highlighting any recent achievements or accomplishments, enclose any subsequent grades you have received, reiterate your interest in attending the school, and express a willingness to discuss your candidacy further at any time. Include a phone number and e-mail address just in case.

These are all ways to keep your name fresh in the minds of the admissions offices at your top choice law schools, which, as Dean Austin suggested, can be helpful to your chances of success in a largely faceless process.

Finally, be sure to respond immediately to any requests by admissions offices for more information and don't even consider turning down an interview if you are lucky enough to be offered one.

ADDITIONAL STRATEGY 5: Attend any informational sessions given by the admissions office in your area

If you're still in college and attend a major university, you may be graced with an "informational visit" from one or more law school deans of admissions. Do not pass up these opportunities. Go to the events, introduce yourself, mention that you have applied, and express any true feelings about the school, and your reasons for wanting to matriculate. During the course of her interview with me, Dean Austin referred to several conversations that she remembered from this year's round of information sessions.

In a game where success can turn on being remembered, you must capitalize on whatever opportunities you are given—and opportunities like these in your own backyard are about as easy as it gets to do so.

CHAPTER 4

Choose Your School Wisely

*The first step which one makes in the world,
is the one on which depends the rest of our days . . .*
—VOLTAIRE

FOR MOST OF US, the choice of where to go to college depended first and foremost on the availability of sufficient funds. If the funds weren't there, the state university provided an adequate solution, and in a great many cases, provided a better-than-adequate educational experience. If funds were available, we made our decisions about which school to attend based on school size, interest in potential major programs of study, availability of sports teams and recruiting, and proximity (or lack thereof!) to home. Choosing a law school, however, is an entirely different enterprise and properly involves a much different thought process than choosing an undergraduate institution. The good news is that the number of relevant factors that must enter the calculation for choosing a law school is much smaller. The bad news, of course, is that since there are far fewer factors to consider, each takes on far greater significance. I run through each of these factors, in order of their importance, below.

The school's regional and national reputation

I'm sure you're familiar with the *U.S. News and World Report* "ranking" system for graduate schools. Published in March of every year, "The Best Graduate Schools" issue lays out where each of the 178 accredited law schools falls on the all-important continuum from "first to worst." These rankings are often quite controversial, and because the law schools know how much emphasis prospective students place on them, law schools frequently try to "massage" their numbers in a way that raises their relative ranking. In other words, relative rankings are accurate according to the criteria used by *U.S. News*—but the criteria used to determine these rankings may not be the ones you should use.

So how should you use this information?

Well, first of all, there is usually not much disagreement about which schools are the top ten or twelve law schools in the country. If you look back over the past few years, the same names are always there: Yale, Harvard, Stanford, Chicago, Columbia, N.Y.U., Berkeley (Boalt Hall), The University of Pennsylvania, The University of Virginia, Duke, The University of Michigan, Cornell, Northwestern, and Georgetown. Forget (for now) where any of these schools ranks within the top tier—as they frequently tie or move up or down a slot or two from year to year. The bottom line is, if you get into one of these top tier law schools and perform respectably, you'll be positioned to do just about anything you want to do. You should know, however, that even among these very top schools, only Yale and Harvard are not subject to some regional bias with respect to placement. Students at those two schools are sought after with identical vigor by firms and judges all over the country. After Yale and Harvard, however, regional preference begins to play a role in impressions about a school. For instance, lawyers and judges on the west coast refer to Stanford as the "Harvard of the West," and often prefer its graduates to those from any other top school. Similarly, Duke is often called the "Harvard of the South," and its students are the gold rush for firms in the large cities of the South, while students from the University of Chicago, the "Harvard of the Heartland," are the top draw in the Midwest.

In other words, the majority of students from Duke tend to stay in the south or mid-Atlantic region, where lawyers and firms lust after them. Students from Penn tend to roam the I-95 corridor from New York City to Washington, D.C., where their placement numbers are strongest, and many students from the University of Chicago tend to stay in the Midwest.

What does all of this mean to you?

Pay the greatest attention to a school's placement record

The number you should be most concerned about is the school's "placement record"—that is, what percentage of its graduates have gone on to gainful employment, and more importantly, *where?* You can find the overall number in the *U.S. News* survey, although some schools have been known to lump any gainful employment, whether law-related or not, into these numbers. You may have to make some calls to get the more critical numbers.

And what are they?

Every law school placement office keeps records of what percentage of its graduates have gone *to each region of the country*—the number that is most critical in your decision about what law school to attend. You may be very proud of your acceptance to the East Boise State Law Center, but if their placement record reveals that 98 percent of its lawyers stay in Idaho and the other 2 percent go to Montana, and you know you want to practice at a large Boston firm—you're setting yourself up for a titanic struggle.

Does this mean you could *never* go to a Boston firm from East Boise State? No, of course not, but you could win the lottery tomorrow, too, and then all of this would be irrelevant. The point is, if you know you eventually want to work in Boston, you'll have a much better chance to achieve that goal if you go to a good regional school in or around Boston than you will coming out of a good regional school on the west coast. Like it or not, this reality plays itself out in every region of the country, every year, to the disappointment of countless law students. As the quote at the top of this chapter suggests, your choice about which law school to attend will likely carry with it immediate consequences about where you'll end up practicing and living for your first few years out of law school. Don't make that choice uninformed.

The harsh reality

What I'm about to say is probably the most controversial thing you'll find in this book. Few professors or law school placement officers will ever admit this to you (for obvious reasons), and no other "how-to-do-law-school" book will tell you this either—but based on the experiences of the *Law School Confidential* mentors and a number of other law students we've known—it's one of the most important pieces of advice you could possibly have as you think about applying to law school.

Brace yourself.

If your goal is to work for a firm, and you don't get into one of the top fifteen to twenty law schools, and you are not interested in practicing in the city, state, or region where that non-top-twenty law school is located, you're better off re-applying and trying again.

That's right. Refuse the offers you get from regional law schools, and try again next year. Try to raise your LSAT score, work for a year or two as a paralegal or a legal intern with a public service organization to gain some law-related experience, and then reapply. The numbers simply do not support you if you're planning to make the leap from a small regional law school to a New York mega-firm. If you don't believe me, check the numbers yourself. Call any big city firm and ask it for a list of the law schools where last years' associates came from.

"In applying to law schools, you should really be thinking about where you want to be living down the road. Obviously, you won't be forced to live in the same city or area of the country that your law school is in forever, but there is no denying the regional control that every law school has. It is easier for a Harvard graduate to get a job in Boston than in San Francisco, and the opposite is true of Stanford graduates, and this state of affairs is magnified tenfold for graduates of less prestigious schools. Don't think of going to Kent if you can't see yourself settling down in the Midwest, or to American if you have no interest in living and working in D.C.," Joel observes.

I know at least six people who got good grades at regional law schools, passed bar exams in various states, and still had an extremely difficult time finding jobs. In getting rejection after rejection, each of them was given the same reason.

"No one at our firm has any first-hand experience with anyone who has graduated from your law school."

Remember, lawyers are risk-averse—and with very few exceptions, they're going to choose the known commodity. They're not going to be willing to "give you a chance," unless you have a really compelling story to tell.

Why put yourself through this?

The take home message here is this—if you're going to accept an offer from a "regional" law school—make sure you're committed to practicing for at least a couple of years in that region. Forget the exceptions. There just aren't enough of them to make the chance worth taking.

Philosophy

The last of the "Big Three" concerns that you should consider is the prevailing "philosophy" at a school and how this philosophy meshes with your own. Is the school widely known to be an unfriendly, overtly cutthroat, and competitive place where people hide books and refuse to work cooperatively? (There are a few very well-known examples of such places which threats of libel prevent me from disclosing here—but just ask around—they're easy enough to discover.) But let's put some concrete examples behind this label of a "cutthroat" school. Legendary stories aside, here are some questions to ask to make the determination of whether a school is cutthroat or not:

- Are grades posted on the hallway walls by name or readily ascertainable numbers for everyone to see, or are they distributed confidentially?
- Does the school compute and publish grade point averages and class ranks each term, thereby encouraging students to openly compete with each other for numbers?
- Are positions on law review determined strictly by grade, or can some people write on every year?
- Does the career placement office (1) assign employment interview slots by class rank, or (2) allow the employers to select which students to interview according to class rank,

or (3) do the students get to choose which employers to interview with?

- How often do books needed for common assignments go missing? (You'll need to call the head librarian to get the answer to this one.)
- Do students share outlines and willingly help each other out?
- Do students socialize after class in intramural sports leagues and other extra-curricular activities?
- Are there regular law student "Happy Hours" and other events?
- Is there an active social committee at the law school?
- Is there a "student union," or other area where students go to "hang out" with each other between classes or after class?

If you decide to attend a law school with a reputation for being "cutthroat," realize what you're getting yourself into *before* you enroll. Aside from the more difficult social interactions you may experience with your classmates and the increased stress associated with open competition for grades, your performance on single-day exams may prevent you from involvement with a host of other experiences that open doors to your future. For example, getting on your school's law review is the gateway to getting a judicial clerkship. If your school seats people on law review only by grade-point average, one bad exam could compromise both your chance to make the law review, and your chance to get a clerkship!

On the other hand, a school where the law review considers a combination of grade point average and performance on an independent writing and editing exam, or simply lets some people "write on" based on their high performance on this writing and editing exam, creates a much more student-friendly environment. Ditto for job screening interviews. If your school lets the employers pick you, they may screen you based only on your grade-point average, which increases the stress level associated with grades, and decreases students' willingness to cooperate with each other. If the school uses a random lottery or lets you choose which employers to interview with—that situation is diffused.

The biggest factor in my ultimate decision was the atmosphere of the schools. I took tours of the schools, and I spent a lot of time talking to students. I asked about the atmosphere, the stress levels, and the general sense of the relationships that the students had with one another. Talking to the students that were already going to the schools I was considering was a big help in deciding which place was right for me. While administrators and books can tell you a lot about a school, nothing beats the firsthand information you can get by talking to the students who are already there and asking them the right questions.

—Steve

Make certain that you know your school's philosophical stance on these issues before you decide to enroll. In some cases, it may help you make decisions between schools. How you weight this factor with the other factors you need to consider (reputation and placement success) is entirely a personal choice. Each choice carries consequences, and it's up to you to decide what is most important.

But what about . . .

Whether your law school is in the middle of an urban war-zone, or located in a pastoral country landscape? What the climate is like? Whether the law school is near the rest of the university or not? How close it is to the beach, the mountains, and good skiing? How attractive the people are there? Whether you'll be able to bring your dog with you or not?

Yeah, I know you're thinking about these things. I certainly did. Just don't let them cloud your judgment. Worry about the "Big Three" factors discussed above. After all, you're going to professional school—and as I've illustrated above, the choices you make are going to have a dramatic effect on your life and career. You're not going on vacation, and this is not college anymore, Toto. Let these other issues intervene to influence your choice *only* when the schools you are choosing between are otherwise indistinguishable based on the more important "Big Three" factors.

The academic strength and reputation of the schools I was considering was priority number one. You go to law school to get a good job, and if you attend a top-ten law school, you'll get one.
—Allan

Oh—a final word. Be incredibly wary about choosing a law school based on its proximity to a girlfriend or boyfriend. As I've mentioned earlier, law school is a very disruptive experience and a supreme test of the strength of relationships. If yours doesn't survive and leaves you marooned somewhere you don't want to be, you're going to be very, very unhappy.

CHAPTER 5

An Investment in Your Future:
Funding Your Legal Education

If you would know the value of money,
go and try to borrow some.
—BENJAMIN FRANKLIN

OKAY—so you've thought carefully about applying to law school, chosen your schools wisely, filed perfect, carefully crafted applications, and beaten the LSAT. For all your trouble and accomplishment up to this point, you'd think that you'd be in line for some sort of reward by now, right?

Yeah, well think again.

Once the jubilation of actually having beaten the odds and gotten into the school of your dreams wears off, you'll need to welcome yourself back to reality. The cost of your law school education, including tuition, room-and-board, books, study aides, supplies, transportation, and personal expenses is about to set you back as much as $125,000 depending on your choice of school.

I went to law school because I wanted to be a prosecutor but starting salaries for assistant district attorneys in Massachusetts were about twenty-seven thousand dollars when I got out of law school. I'm going to be paying about eleven hundred dollars a month for the next ten years in student loan payments, and after taxes, that salary would barely cover my student loans. I didn't go to law school to get rich, but I didn't expect to get poor. I think it's disgusting that in order to get the degree to

get the job I wanted, I had to take on a debt load that pre-
cluded me from accepting that job.

—Bess

There is a great deal of financial aid available, in the form of
scholarships, loans, grants, fellowships, and work-study programs.
Most of your classmates will be depending on some sort of financial
assistance to help get them through the door, and you'd be foolish
not to explore whether the kitty might hold some assistance for
you. In any case, however, unless you're independently wealthy or
were blessed with incredibly generous parents, you're going to
need to get the money from somewhere, and you're going to have
to pay it back. Here's what you need to know.

Sources of funding

There are many different sources of financial aid for law students. The larger private law schools—those with sizable endow-
ments—offer generous financial aid packages to top students.
Other law schools may offer low-interest institutional loans. There
are many other private scholarships, fellowships, and grants to
apply for—many of which are targeted toward specific groups of
applicants, including minorities, women, residents of particular
states, children of veterans, or students who are committed to practicing in the public sector after graduation—and are available from
foundations, corporations, benevolent associations, local bar associations, social clubs, religious or business organizations, and veterans organizations. There are several different federal loan
programs available, and, of course, private institutional loans from
banks and other financial institutions are always available to students with good credit histories. Finally, the federal work-study program may be an option in your second or third years to help bridge
the gaps in your aid package.

How do you decide which route is the best for you? Without a
doubt, the financial aid offices of the law schools that admit you
will be the best resource for information about how to fund your
legal education. Inquire about the most common ways that students at that particular law school fund their legal education. Ask

for any information and paperwork the financial aid office can provide you. At the very least, a discussion with your prospective school's financial aid officer should get the ball rolling for you.

General suggestions

If you know that you will need financial aid to fund your legal education, do not wait until you have been offered admission to begin applying for financial aid. In December of the year in which you are applying to law school, get a copy of the Free Application for Federal Student Aid (FAFSA) from your university's financial aid office, from one of your prospective law school's financial aid office, or online at http://ww.faffsa.ed.gov. This form was developed by the U.S. Department of Education as a general need-analysis tool for use by all law schools you designate to receive it. Contact the financial aid office of each school to which you are applying no later than December 31 to verify each individual institution's financial aid filing requirements. Many schools require additional documentation (like copies of your tax return or additional institution-specific paperwork) in addition to the FAFSA.

As soon as possible after January 1 of the year in which you are applying, complete your federal income tax return. Keep a copy, as many schools will request a supplementary copy before determining your need package. Using the information from your tax return, complete the FAFSA form by providing all the information it requests, and send it in. Completed FAFSA forms cannot be filed prior to the first of the year, but should be filed as soon as possible after January 1 to afford you the best chance of getting an optimal aid package.

The law schools you designate to receive the FAFSA will each make independent determinations on your eligibility for institution-based and federal financial aid. Because costs and expenses vary from school to school, the aid packages offered by different law schools may differ widely. As an applicant to graduate school, you will automatically be considered "independent" from your parents for the purposes of securing federal financial assistance. Individual law schools, however, may require you to provide information about your parents' income in determining your eligibility for institution-based scholarships and loans, and such requirements will vary from school to school. Contact each institution's financial aid office to confirm your compliance with school-specific requirements.

Some terms they'll throw around in your aid package

Your "financial need" is the total cost of your law school education, including tuition, room-and-board, books and supplies, and living expenses, (collectively known as your "student budget") minus what you are able to personally contribute toward satisfying this amount. Your "unmet financial need" is your "financial need" minus any scholarships, fellowships, or grants you have received. Note that your "student budget" will vary from school to school depending on the school-specific costs and cost-of-living differences from city to city, but it will never consider any personal consumer debt you may be carrying.

After completing its analysis, each law school's financial aid office will send you a financial aid package explaining your eligibility. Most students receive offers including several different types of aid in combination—often consisting of a partial scholarship, an institutional loan offer, and eligibility for federal loan programs. Once you receive each school's financial aid eligibility letter, begin the federal loan application process immediately.

Federal loan programs

Federal loan programs are funded by the United States government. The amount of funding available each year is dependent on the national budget and the priorities of the political party currently in power. Most federal loans are need-based. These loans constitute the most common source of financial aid after institution-based scholarship awards.

The Subsidized Federal Stafford Student Loan (SSL)

The Federal Stafford Loan provides up to $8500 a year to students who can demonstrate the required degree of financial need, have registered for the selective service (if applicable), and are not in default on any previous student loans. There is an aggregate loan ceiling of $65,500 which includes undergraduate loans made under this program, and undergraduate and graduate loans made under the Unsubsidized Federal Stafford Student Loan Program (discussed below). Interest, which is variable, is paid by the federal government as long as you remain in school at least half time. You must begin repaying the loan six months after you graduate, drop out, withdraw, or attend school less than half time, and you then have ten years to repay the loan in full. Subsidized Federal Stafford Loan applications can be obtained from any financial institution that participates in the program, or from any law school financial aid office.

The Unsubsidized Federal Stafford Student Loan

Under current federal guidelines, a student may borrow up to $18,500 in combined subsidized and unsubsidized loans. Any amount of aid the student receives in a Subsidized Federal Stafford Student Loan, thus, is deducted from $18,500 to determine a student's maximum eligibility level for the Unsubsidized Federal Stafford Student Loan. This loan is *not* need-based, and, thus, is available to any student who has registered with the selective service (if applicable), and is not in default on any prior student loan. There is an aggregate loan ceiling of $65,500 which includes undergraduate loans made under this program, and undergraduate and graduate loans made under the Subsidized Federal Stafford Student Loan Program (discussed above). Interest, which is variable, accrues immediately. You must begin repaying the loan six months after you graduate, drop out, withdraw, or attend school less than half time, and you then have ten years to repay the loan in full. Unsubsidized Federal Stafford Loan applications can be obtained from any financial institution that participates in the program, or from any law school financial aid office.

Federal Perkins Loan

The Federal Perkins Loan is administered by individual participating law schools and offers an aggregate ceiling of $18,000 (including undergraduate loans). Eligibility is need-based and determined by the individual law school based on information provided in the FAFSA application. Federal Perkins Loans are available to students who have registered for the selective service (if applicable), and are not currently in default on any other student loan. The interest rate is fixed at five percent. You must begin to repay the loan nine months after graduation, and have ten years to repay the loan in full.

The Federal Supplemental Loan for Students (SLS)

The SLS provides up to $10,000 per year (up to an aggregate of $73,000 including undergraduate loans) to any interested student. The student must, however, have first applied for a Federal Stafford Student Loan. Interest, which is variable, begins accruing immediately. You have ten years to repay the loan in full.

Private institutional loans

Private loans from banks and other financial institutions are approved on the basis of an evaluation of the student's credit report and credit history. Students with poor credit will generally be denied these loans. There are any number of private loan options available to credit-worthy borrowers. Shop around at several different financial institutions to find the most favorable rates, terms, and conditions.

Federal work-study

Given the rigorous demands of law school, particularly during the first year, financial assistance from the Federal Work-Study program is best left as a last option during the second and third years of law school. Under this program, law students work on campus performing a wide range of school-specific services for which they are compensated. Information is generally available in any law school financial aid office.

Your day of reckoning

Unless you attend a well-endowed private law school, most of your financial aid will probably come from federal loans, and accordingly, you will likely graduate with a large debt burden that may take you up to ten years to pay off.

"I have over $100,000 of debt. Think about that. It's like a mortgage. It's a huge obligation. Even though salaries are great right now in the legal world, it still takes a great deal of time to pay off debt like that. If you're going to go to law school on student loans, make sure that you really want to do it and make sure that you understand what being a lawyer is really like, because you're obligating yourself to it for a long, long time. It's going to take me ten to fifteen years to pay off my loans," Steve warned. Others agree. "Ten years. Maybe seven or eight if I stay at a big firm and am really vigilant about paying them off," Alison added. The list of your mentors goes on.

Ten years at eleven hundred dollars a month.

—Bess

Ten years at nine hundred dollars a month.

—Joel

My wife and I are allocating the majority of our incomes to paying off my student loans, and will be for the next four or five years. Although we're making a good income, we have little to show for it.

—Pat

We're hammering home this point, and putting a real price tag on it, to force you to really think one more time about your commitment to the choice to go to law school, and to reevaluate the practicality of your plans after law school. As Bess noted earlier, her debt burden is keeping her from doing the kind of work that drew her to law school in the first place. Steve experienced a similar reality.

"While it is sad to say, my loans kept me from doing the kind of law that I wanted to do. I always envisioned myself as a prosecutor, fighting the bad guys and doing something that had meaning to it. The reality, though, is that there isn't any money to be made as a prosecutor, and the bank won't accept the meaningfulness of your work in lieu of the payment on the loans you owe them, so I entered the corporate world and am practicing asset securitization. Truth be told, I enjoy the work I'm doing, but if I didn't have my loans to deal with, I would be doing criminal work."

If you're still insistent, save as much money as you can before and during law school, and attempt to minimize your credit card and other consumer debt in anticipation of this reality. As a federal loan recipient, you will be required to attend an exit interview prior to graduation. During this interview, your financial aid officer will review your loans with you, and help you develop repayment schedules and options to suit your needs. Keep accurate records of this meeting.

Finally, some schools offer loan forgiveness, or Loan Repayment Assistance Programs (LRAPs) to graduates who accept public interest positions. These programs are school-specific and vary widely. Call your law school's financial aid office or public service department for further information.

PART TWO

The First Year,
They Scare You to Death

CHAPTER 6

The Ten Things You Must Do
Before Classes Begin

A man who suffers before it is necessary
suffers more than is necessary.
—SENECA

RECALLING MY OWN EXPERIENCES, the weeks leading up to the first day of law school were filled with good intentions and fraught with anxiety. Knowing little about the intricacies of the law, I bought books about the American legal system and the United States Supreme Court and its justices and pledged to read them over the summer.

It never happened.

I dusted off the Constitutional Law casebook left behind from an undergraduate class and pledged to read a case a day, every day in order to get one full subject ahead of the field.

You guessed it. On the first day, I made it about halfway through *Marbury v. Madison* (which, as you will soon discover, is the first case in just about every Con Law casebook ever published), and that was the end of that. I never read another page the whole summer. Never even finished *Marbury*. So much for good intentions!

Fortunately, it is entirely unnecessary to read cases before you go to law school. If your interest supports it, you can pick up a book about the supreme court at the local bookstore and read it for pleasure, surf the many law-related sites on the Internet, or simply follow the latest happenings at the supreme court on the pages of the *New York Times*; but you certainly don't *need* to do any of these things. I spent the summer before law school hanging out with fifty-five twelve-year-old kids at a boys overnight camp teaching them how to swim and water ski, coaching the camp swim team, and leading kids on hikes in New Hampshire's White Mountains. Camp closed for the season on a Saturday morning, and by the time the sun sank low in the Sunday sky, I was pulling into Philadelphia to begin my law school career. Talk about culture shock!

The day I arrived at law school, I couldn't have named more than three of the nine current Supreme Court justices if my life depended on it (although as I was soon to find out, there were people in my class who could have recited each justice's complete biography from memory). In the end, however, all of this was inconsequential. The summer before law school is the last experience of true freedom you'll have for at least the next three years. Make the most of it, and don't impose a bunch of silly obligations upon yourself in the name of "preparation."

Having said that, there are ten things you *should* do before classes begin to make your life easier and to complete time-consuming preparations before time gets scarce. The following list is broken down into things you should do before you arrive at school, and things you should do after you arrive but before classes begin. Go through the list carefully and plan accordingly so that you'll have enough time to complete each item on the list before your first day of class. Don't procrastinate! Once classes begin, any of these things will take valuable time away from your studies.

BEFORE YOU ARRIVE ON CAMPUS

1. Read this book from cover to cover

I said it in the introduction, but it bears repeating here. You have in your hands a complete book of wisdom to guide you through your three years of law school. It is a complete map of the landscape with all known pitfalls and obstacles identified—but like any other map, in order for it to be useful, you need to familiarize yourself with it ahead of time so you'll know where you're going before you actually get there. Reading this book once through before you get to law school will assure you that you'll know enough of the lingo and vocabulary so you won't feel stupid at orientation events, and it will put you in the pole position at the start of the race. Plus, if you're anything like me, you'll be thirsting for all the information you can possibly gather about the experience that awaits you. It's all here, so drink up. Just leave the worksheets for the day when you're going through the chapter for real.

> The biggest mistake I made was not taking time off between college and law school. Once you start law school, you begin down the path to becoming an attorney, and once this process has begun there is no looking back. The first year is very stressful, and after that, you become focused on getting a job.
>
> —Pat

2. Arrange for housing

No later than early to mid-summer, you'll need to start making arrangements for law school housing, and right away, you'll have to make a critical choice. Do you want to live in on-campus housing (if there is any) where you'll likely be surrounded by classmates with whom you can study and commiserate, or would you prefer to strike out on your own? At many schools, you may have a third choice—opting to live in the off-campus apartment building or townhouse complex preferred by students from your law school. Usually, a quick call to your law school registrar's office can reveal this location to you, since the Registrar has every student's school address. Make this call so you'll have a complete set of information with which to make your decision.

> The biggest mistake I made in getting ready for law school was arriving in Philadelphia the day before orientation. I should have moved in a few days earlier, set things up, and spent some time getting to know the city and the campus. Instead, I spent three weeks traveling in Costa Rica, moved out of New York City in a rush, and stumbled into Philadelphia at the last minute. That was a bad idea, because I never caught up with all the things I wanted to do to get ready.
>
> —Carolyn

Living on campus certainly has its advantages, including ease of acquisition and proximity to classes and the law library. Renting graduate housing space will spare you the need to search for an appropriate apartment, and perhaps more importantly, will spare you the potential headache of dealing with a landlord. Many graduate dorms will come furnished, or at the very least, will provide major appliances, and should anything need repair, you can count on your university's custodial services to be available to attend to your problems promptly. Many law schools also offer convenient nine-month leases, which will save you the hassle and risk of having to sublet your apartment during the summer. You should also not underestimate the convenience of rolling out of bed at 8:55 A.M. in time to make your dreaded 9 A.M. class, or having the ability to go back and forth from home to class and the library with ease. At many schools, up to half of the first-year class will opt to live on campus.

Students in the law dorm tend to bond readily. Friendships form easily out of the mutual misery of the long hours spent studying in close quarters. Mixers, happy hours, poker nights, and other social events also typically originate in the dorms. Study groups will form out of these friendships, and consequently, it will be easier to find course outlines and to learn about good hornbooks and study aides if you live in the dorm. Living on-campus during your first year of law school is not a bad idea if you think you'll be able to stand being around your classmates all the time . . . but that's a *big* if.

The closeness of the living quarters can also breed competition, anxiety, and stress. You may get up to use the bathroom in the middle of the night, look out the window, and discover that many of your classmates are still up reading. How will that affect you? In the dorm, there is *always* talk about how late people stay up, how many pages ahead in the syllabus certain people are, who is brilliant, and who seems to be struggling. There's always one jerk who will try to whip the class into a frenzy by passing along false information, or try to rattle individual members of the class, and unfortunately, he always seems to live in the dorm too. Finally, you'll need to consider whether you'll be able to disconnect yourself from the stress overload that will electrify the dorm come exam time. Everyone will talk about exams. People will stop by to ask questions that may unnerve you. People may experience nervous breakdowns.

The biggest mistake I made in getting ready for law school was living in the dorm. The absolute worst, worst, worst! To feel like a person, I needed a real apartment, and the dorm was also a rip off financially.

—Alison

As for dealing with an unknown, off-campus landlord, to pervert a Latin legal standard—*caveat rentor*. Living away from the law school will certainly afford you some space, and the peace of mind to be able to remove yourself from the fray each night. Distance can certainly lend perspective. If your chosen law school is in a rural area, you may be able to rent a house, bring your dog, and build a low-stress law school life that few others will experience. If you're in the city, apartments are likely to be larger and cheaper than your on-campus housing. In either case, however, there are other important factors to consider.

First, living off campus means that you'll have to find a suitable place. Do you have the time or the inclination to spend several days setting this up? If you do, remember that you'll be traveling to and from class every day—often late at night. How close is the nearest public transportation? How safe is it, and how often and how late does it run? Are you willing to put up with this inconvenience in order to get some space? Second, if your pipes leak, the radiator bangs and whistles all night, or the hot water heater breaks down, it might be a while before it gets fixed. How willing are you to put up with the crapshoot of an unknown landlord? Finally, pay attention to the noise level around the apartment, and if at all possible, visit any potential living space at night to determine whether it is quiet enough to study there. Is the apartment located above a bar where crazy drunks getting into fights will keep you up all night? Do the neighbors in the apartment next door practice piano every evening or host opera recitals in their living room? Are the neighbors hard of hearing such that their TV will be on so loud you can't concentrate? Will there be early morning truck traffic, or loud deliveries to wake you every morning at dawn? Don't laugh—each of these scenarios is drawn from a mentor's sad-but-true real life experience living off campus. If you opt to live off campus, research your choices carefully, because once you sign the lease, the place is yours for at least a year.

Actually, I made another big mistake. If I had spent more time I would have chosen a more modern apartment. The building

I chose was very old, and it took a lot of calls and a lot of work just to regulate the temperature and to get things fixed when they broke.

—Carolyn

On balance, I think living in the dorm was a good choice for me during my first year of law school. It was where the majority of my classmates at Penn lived which made it easy to develop friendships and feel like part of a group. Although law school is not college and should not be expected to resemble it, living in the dorm first year did invoke some memories of college—which was comforting to me.

"I think choosing to live in the dorms was the best thing I did in preparing for law school," Allan agreed. "It was a great way to meet people and make friends. It was also advantageous to always have fellow classmates around to discuss classes and share outlines with."

Whatever you decide, spend as much as you can afford to assure yourself of a comfortably large and quiet living space. Finally, and perhaps most importantly, be *very* wary of taking on a roommate in law school, even if that roommate is an old friend living and working in the city you're traveling to, or studying in another graduate program. The *last* thing you need in law school is a clash of schedules, conflicting work or sleep habits, or someone with annoying quirks or an antisocial personality. It seems that most of the law school horror stories you hear about arise out of these situations. *Take this advice to heart.* There will be many times in law school when you'll just want to hide behind closed doors and be alone. If you *must* take on a roommate, find a medical student. They're never home anyway.

Once you've decided where you're going to live, there are two more critical things to do. First, call the appropriate sources in advance so the phones will be working, the power will be on, and the cable and Internet hooked up upon your arrival. There's nothing worse than having to wait three weeks for phone service. Finally, if you're moving into an apartment, check with the management company to see if you have to schedule a move-in time. Many city buildings require you to use freight elevators that are key-operated and scheduled well in advance. Forewarned is forearmed.

3. Use the summer to get in shape

No, I'm not kidding. The long hours of reading and thinking that you'll be doing in law school takes stamina, and a daily work-out can refresh you, clear your mind, keep you awake and alert, and make your days more productive. Of course, you don't want to have to deal with the soreness and adjustment associated with a new workout program once law school begins, and you'll want to capitalize on the many benefits of being in shape from the first day anyway—so start now! Begin a physical workout program in June or July to increase your fitness and stamina so that it will be a regular part of your routine, and easy to continue, once law school begins. Many of us made time in our daily schedules to run, blade, bike, shoot hoops, play tennis, or participate in an aerobics program, and those of us who did swear that it made a difference.

4. Read now, sign up later

Beginning in late May or early June, you'll start getting inundated with mailings, pamphlets, and brochures. There will be note-taking services and "buy now and save" offers. There will be the pickup and deliver weekly laundry service, and the weekly dorm room linen service. There will be offers for meal plans and "exclusive" graduate student-only "dining clubs." The campus computer center will urge you to buy a computer. There will even be bar review organizations trying to get you to sign up for their classes three years in advance! Everyone will be hocking something. So how do you wade through this blizzard of materials and separate the necessary from the wasteful? How do you know what you need?

It's really quite simple. As each of these "act now!" offers comes in, log them in on a list, throw the brochures and order forms into a big manila envelope, and wait. I'll let you in on a little secret. Almost all of these "but you must act now!" offers miraculously reappear for "one week only" during the first week or two of classes. When you get to campus, talk to your upperclass mentor or other 2Ls and 3Ls about the various items on your list. Scope out the typical patterns of behavior at the law school and *then* buy. Other than a computer (see below) which may be offered at an unbeatable price, there is nothing that these organizations are selling that you can't wait until you arrive on campus to purchase. The last thing you want to do is sink two thousand dollars into the "prestigious graduate-only dining room" only to discover that it is a long, inconvenient walk from the law school, and that you have just condemned yourself to three meals a day with two dorks from the physics lab and a horde of arrogant and elitist business school students networking their heads off.

Remember the simple lesson of this section—read now, buy later. It will save you much money and aggravation.

5. Buy a computer and become computer-literate

Although you won't see them in old *Paper Chase* reruns, computers, and particularly laptops, have become a way of life in law school. Because many people can type faster than they write, taking a laptop to lectures and typing your notes in outline form can be a big time saver. The great thing about taking notes this way (and we'll get more in depth about this in Chapter 8), is that at the end of each class, you'll have a rough outline of the material you covered, which you can then go back and easily supplement with material from your hornbooks and commercial outlines. Then, with a simple click of a button, you can have a fresh, clean, updated copy of an outline-in-progress.

"Yeah," you say, "but I'm old-school. Got through college using loose-leaf paper and spiral-bound notebooks, and I can do the same for law school."

Sure you can . . . but remember, getting the edge in law school is about making little distinctions—doing things just a little bit better than your classmates do them. So why waste time writing things over and over again, cramming supplemental material into the margins only to find your notes illegible and disorganized?

You'll also want to have a computer to access LEXIS and Westlaw, the online legal databases that you'll need to conduct research. Without a computer, you'll find yourself relegated to the dreaded, understaffed and always-breaking-down computer clusters in the library—on their schedule, and at the mercy of their equipment. Many schools also charge for your research printouts, often as much as ten cents a page. You can do the math, but I'll save you the trouble. Getting a decent laptop computer with a modem and printer is worth going into debt, taking the second pre-law school summer job, or even selling your car. I'll stop just short of telling you that it's essential to have one, but you'll certainly be at a disadvantage without one . . . and for you "old schoolers" out there—you can't surf the Net from a spiral-bound notebook.

So now that I've convinced you about the merits of getting a computer, what computer should you get? As I mentioned earlier, a laptop is preferable because it's portable. As for choosing between a MAC and IBM-compatibles, it's best to contact your law school to find out what platform they support. Once you've done that, in ninety-nine out of one hundred cases, you'll find out that law schools use exclusively IBM-compatibles. Thus, if you have an IBM-compatible, you're set. But where does that leave you if you're a MAC user?

I was a devoted Apple user for my entire pre-law school life and dragged my MAC desktop and laptop off to law school with me. I quickly discovered, however, that the entire law school environment was IBM-based. Networks were configured for IBMs, the latest versions of legal research software were released first in IBM-platforms, most disk-based outlines were IBM-based, and most of my classmates had IBMs—which made being in a study group and trading class notes more difficult. The law review and other journals were also all running on IBMs. Suffice it to say that for purposes of convenience, study group coordination, and your own sanity, if your law school is IBM-based (which it almost certainly will be), and you haven't yet purchased a computer, you're better off buying an IBM-compatible. Can you live with the MAC you already have? Sure. I did it for all three years, and I made it through just fine . . . but I have an IBM-compatible now. Needed it for my clerkship because the United States federal court system is IBM-based, and so is the firm I'm going to next year.

As for what "toys" to get along with the computer, get one with as much RAM as you can afford—as some of the research software is vast and cumbersome to run on slower computers. A fast modem and a durable, reliable laser-quality printer are also essentials. The fast modem is for convenient, rapid, and reliable downloading from on-line research networks, and to speed up your Web surfing on often overcrowded University networks. You'll need the laser-quality printer because many professors now expect nothing less.

Campus computer sellers generally offer competitive prices, but usually only on certain brand names, and their "bundles" rarely feature the most updated technology. I hopped on the Net, went directly to my manufacturer's web page, had a system custom built for my needs, and had it in my hands in ten days. If you don't already have a computer, you can also call the manufacturers directly, or use any of the reputable computer mail order companies to order a system. Any of these methods are safe and reliable, and tend to get you the most computer for the least amount of money.

6. Check in with the registrar

Trust me—you'll be thanking me out loud for this piece of advice. Among the piles of paperwork you'll receive during the summer before law school will be a form from the registrar's office. It's standard issue at just about every educational institution nowadays, and chances are, you'll remember running around with your parents trying to track everything down for the one you filled out for college. On it, you'll have to provide a complete, updated list of your vaccinations, medications, and any health conditions your school should know about. Many schools will also ask for a copy of your social security card and/or birth certificate for your file. During the course of your law school career, you'll need many other "important papers" as well, so here's a timesaver that will spare you serious frustration.

Get yourself a folder—and if possible, pick one that is brightly colored so you'll never misplace it. In it, place one copy each of your birth certificate; your social security card; your medical history (including a complete and updated history of all inoculations); and your driver's license or state-issued ID card. Then get three certified copies of your undergraduate transcript (you'll need to request this in writing from the registrar at your undergraduate institution and pay a small fee for it); one uncertified photocopy of your undergraduate transcript (which, obviously, you can make by photocopying one of the certified copies); one certified and one uncertified copy of a transcript for each graduate degree you carry, if any; and one photocopy of each of your undergraduate and graduate diplomas, and add these to the file. Finally, toss in your original, current passport.

Some of these items, like your medical history and two forms of identification, will be required before you are allowed to register for classes. Others, like certified copies of your undergraduate transcript may or may not be required to matriculate, but will certainly be required by employers and/or judges during employment recruiting, or judicial clerkship season. You'll probably need to provide copies of your undergraduate diploma to your law school registrar in order to graduate. As for the passport, more than one person I know had a partner come into his office during a summer associateship and say, "I need you to fly to London with me to help with these depositions I'm taking. We'll be leaving on Wednesday."

Don't be the schmo who has to refuse the trip because you don't have a current passport. Get one, or renew the one you have, put it in the folder, and forget about it. It might also come in handy for your spring break in Tahiti (after you've made real money during a summer associateship, of course), or conversely, when you make your first really big blunder during said summer associateship and need to rapidly flee the country.

AFTER YOU ARRIVE ON CAMPUS

7. Set up "headquarters"

By this stage, you've probably picked up on my "law school is war" analogy, and at risk of belaboring that symbolism further, I raise this vitally important point. Every general needs a headquarters, and so will you. If you've been paying attention thus far, it should also go without saying that once law school begins, you need to hit your stride as quickly as possible.

"The biggest mistake I made was thinking that law school was just an extension of college," Steve notes. "Don't kid yourself. It's not. College was a lot about fun, and most of the people spent more time having fun than working hard. Law school was not like that. It was much more intense much more quickly than I thought it would be. There were a lot of older people there, and a lot of serious people, too. What I failed to realize was that the people in law school all had a pretty easy time in college, and that they viewed law school as a stepping stone to top job placement. I wasn't expecting that people would come in from day one taking everything so seriously, and that was the hardest adjustment I had to make."

Once classes begin, there may not be time to take a weekend off to shop for furniture, build more shelf space, or unpack and get yourself organized. Think about the recommendations that follow before you get to campus, so that once you're there, you can efficiently and effectively set up a well-provisioned and properly outfitted headquarters for yourself.

Depending on where you fall on the anxiety scale and whether you're moving into an empty apartment or a furnished dorm room, accomplishing this mission might take you an afternoon or a week. Start by remembering the fundamental premise of this book: You're looking for little edges on the competition . . . and being organized and ready to go on the first day of classes is one of the biggest of those little "edges."

So what do you need? Start with the most critical item. You *must* have a good bed.

Huh?

That's right. A bed. I know, I know . . . you were expecting a desk, a good reading chair, or some secret hornbooks, right? All of those things are coming. Let me explain, however, why a bed deserves the top spot on the list.

When the battle begins, you may be working eighteen hour days with regularity. The only way you can pull that off for any length of time and stay sharp is to sleep really well when you finally do get to sleep. On many, many days in law school, the only thing separating the hundreds of pages of reading and outlining that you'll be doing seven days a week is the time you spend sleeping—refreshing your brain. So forsake the rickety iron frame and foam mattress likely to await you in your dorm room, and buy yourself something comfortable. Many law students choose large futons that can convert into couches, or actually spring for real beds. After so many years in dorm rooms sleeping in dorm beds or mattresses on the floor, you might have forgotten what it's like. Getting a good bed is one of the biggest favors you can do for yourself, as a restful night's sleep is truly one of law school's most precious commodities.

The next absolute "must" is a good fan, or two if you hate moving them around. Remember that it will still be summer when law school begins, and no matter where in the country you are, it's hot in August. Seeing that tossing back too many cold ones might disrupt your concentration, you'll need to find another way to beat the heat—and your fan will likely be the best way to do it. Then, when summer fades, the dormitory heating system roars to life, and you discover that your dorm room thermostat doesn't actually do anything, you'll have two choices: (1) open the windows (which, at least in Philadelphia usually produced noisy distractions like street fights, gunshots, and blaring sirens, not to mention pollution), or, (2) *voilà*—turn on your fan. Having fans is a key to both comfortable studying and restful sleep. Trust me on that.

Now we get to the desk.

When shopping for a desk, avoid anything fancy that doesn't provide you with a sprawling top to spread things out on. Little antique desks just won't cut it here. You don't need lots of little drawers, compartments, and cubbies. You're not trying to please Martha Stewart, or your mother. Many nights, you're going to want to have three or four books and your laptop computer open on your desk at the same time. Plan accordingly. For your purposes, a door on cinderblocks or a large table will provide a better workspace than the most elegant antique rolltop. Think *space*.

Next, you'll probably want to consider investing in some species of file cabinet. For about fifty dollars, I went down to the nearest office supply superstore and got a rolling two-drawer wood file cabinet which doubled as the stand for my laser printer. (Remember—think *space*—this got the printer off my desk and up off the floor.) I got a bunch of hanging folders to put inside the cabinet and created a file for each of my classes to store the syllabi and handouts. I started separate files for recruiting correspondence, writing samples, resumes, bank and credit card statements, paid bills, and a few other things. I also placed my yellow "important information" folder in the file cabinet for safekeeping. Again, staying organized is the key. This categorized "catch-all" system proved an easy way to keep paper organized—off my desk, but at my fingertips if needed.

Finally, you'll want to be sure you have adequate shelf space. Your law books and hornbooks will accumulate faster than you'll believe—and you'll need a good place to keep everything. Invest in a sturdy bookcase or build some solid shelves so that you can keep your books and hornbooks in good shape and close to your desk.

Other items that you'll probably want to have to outfit your "headquarters" include a TV and VCR, a microwave, your stereo system, a dorm-sized refrigerator, or whatever you need to outfit your kitchen if you have one. Don't plan on having time to cook elaborate meals. though. Simplicity and speed are of the essence here.

Oh—and make sure you have a reliable alarm clock. You'll definitely need that.

8. Learn the "lay of the land"

Once you've arrived on campus and set up your living and working space, take an afternoon to wander around the city or town that you'll be calling home for the next three years. Get a feel for where things are on campus. Do you know the names of the different law buildings and how the room numbers work? Can you find the campus bookstore? The gym? The undergraduate library? Next, get a subway map and a bus schedule and start to figure out how the routes work. Buy a couple of rolls of tokens. Determine how long it takes you to get from your apartment or dorm room to the law school. Do you know where you'll be able to get a taxi when you stumble out of the library at midnight and don't feel safe walking home? Figure it out.

Have you found the place where you'll get your morning coffee on the way to class? Mapped out a safe jogging or walking route that you'll use to let off steam? Found a clean and affordable gym near home or school that you can join to ensure that you'll work out regularly?

Do you know which bank you're going to be using? My advice here is to open a no-frills checking account with the bank nearest to your apartment. Make sure the bank has an ATM machine—and even better if it also has one near the law school. Over the course of three years, those service fees for using someone else's ATM will really start to add up. Don't spend time worrying about interest rates. You need to face the reality at this point that you'll be wasting a lot of money to save time and satisfy your id over the next three years. Having a free ATM machine nearby is the key issue.

Did you find a good grocery store that can supply you with the necessities of your diet? What about places where you can go to get a quick sandwich between classes, or a late night snack after a long night at the library? Have you located a cool neighborhood bar to meet friends for a drink on the weekends, or a bookstore to spend a stolen hour reading something other than law? What about the movie theater which will provide you with your most common form of entertainment during law school? Is there live music anywhere in the area to refresh your spirit? Have you found a sanctuary where you can go to be by yourself, get grounded, and regroup when the pressure mounts? Do you want to join a church or a synagogue?

There won't be a lot of time available to find these places once classes begin. You need to do it now.

9. Update your resume

You probably haven't even thought about your resume since you finished filing your law school applications. Nearly eight months have passed since then. You have changes to add! For one thing, you're in law school, so you'll need to add your new school information at the top of the "Education" section with the designation "J.D. expected, 20xx." Beyond that, at least your home address, phone number, and e-mail have changed, so take care of those. Did you graduate from college last May? With a degree in what? Any honors? Get it down. Did you work over the summer, or just terminate your long-term employment? Update!

If you've made it this far, it's probably safe to assume that you have a resume, and know what belongs on it. What you may not know is what a resume for a legal job should look like. Your career placement office will likely accept and review resumes starting sometime in October—a service you should take advantage of. But since you're doing this now, here's some preliminary advice about what your legal resume should look like. First and foremost, remember your audience. You're writing for the heavy-starch, dark-tie-on-white-shirt Brooks Brothers crowd, so think "conservative." That means heavy white bond paper—the best you can afford, and coughing up the extra money for real laser printing. Choose a clean, crisp, and simple font from the New York or Times families. Use a clear layout with separate sections for "Education," "Professional Experience," "Publications" (if any), and "Interests and Hobbies." Include lots of white space, and vary the typeface within the same font, using bold caps, underlining, and italics thoughtfully, but sparingly, to set off the different sections and draw the eye. You want your resume to look friendly and invite the reader to continue.

Present in inverse chronological order, with your most recent accomplishments first. In the "Education" section, be sure to list your college degree and the date it was conferred. Add a list of academic honors and a carefully chosen list of college activities. The general rule for inclusion is, if something illustrates your skills and relevant interests, or distinguishes you as a person, you'll probably want to include it. Sports, writing, drama, teaching, outdoor, and leadership activities are all relevant to consider. That you were your fraternity's beer-pong champion, on the other hand, is best left for a night in the bar with your fellow associates once you're safely employed. You'll also want to keep your discussion of high school to a minimum. The name and city of your high school is sufficient unless you did something to particularly distinguish yourself there, either academically, or in writing or legal-related activities. For example, if you were the valedictorian in a class of eight hundred, or the editor-in-chief of the national award-winning high school newspaper, those things would merit a line on a legal resume. But nobody will care that you were the president of the bridge club. Mention bridge in your "Interests and Hobbies" section so that anyone interested in bridge can engage you on that subject.

Start the "Professional Experience" with your most recent job. If you've been a perpetual student, the rule-of-thumb is to include summer employment for the past five years. If law will be your second career, legal employers will be generally interested in where you worked over the past decade. If you've only been out in the workforce for a year or two, use year designations (e.g. 1987–88) for full-time employment, and summer designations for summer-term employment (e.g. Summer 1998).

Include a "Publications" section only if you have any written publications you deem worthy of inclusion. Relax, relax—you won't be the only person who doesn't have any. . . .

Lastly, include an "Interests and Hobbies" section at the end of your resume to fill out the picture of who you are. Are you an avid hiker, golfer, or skier? Do you sail, run, or play an instrument? Do you write fiction on the side? Interestingly, the items in this section typically draw a lot of fire in employment interviews because you're liable to encounter interviewers who share your interests. Given that people are naturally drawn to people with like interests, the power of these connections should not be overlooked.

As for the controversial topics of sexual-orientation, race, politics, and religion, you're on your own, but unless you're adamant about joining a firm that closely reflects your religious and political beliefs, I'd avoid these hot button topics. Keep in mind that the white-shoe world of law is no different from the rest of the world as to the way these topics will play. While your work on behalf of your religion, political party, or sexual preference may be admirable, impressive, and a vital part of who you are, recognize that if you include these topics on a legal resume, you might end up alienating potential employers.

Finally, it goes without saying that your resume must be as tight as it can be. Practice verbal economy by challenging the necessity of every word. Use the most active, descriptive verbs possible, and be certain that there are no typos, misspellings, or stray marks. If, after you've strained to cut all the fat out of your resume, it still stretches onto a second page (or even more if you're coming to law from another career), that's fine. If you're certain everything on your resume is relevant to a legal employer or manifestly illustrative of you as an individual, then you can safely ignore everyone who tells you that your resume *has* to be one page long. Trust me, if you have enough relevant credentials to stretch to multiple pages, your employers will read them.

So why, you ask, is all this talk of resumes stuck in the middle of this chapter? Easy. In this chapter, you're learning about the things you need to do before law school begins. You need to update your resume now so that it will be sitting in a folder in your files ready to be sent out to employers come the beginning of 1L recruiting season in November. You see, the first-year employment rat race begins on November 1, which, by agreement of most accredited law schools, is the day that law school placement officers can begin working with 1Ls. The problem is, come November 1, you'll be swamped with work and heading into the most critical period of the semester. There won't be time for resumes then. In fact, most 1Ls will ignore the lure of recruiting until after their fall semester finals in mid-December, when most of the plum 1L positions at firms and public interest placements have already been claimed. But not you. Come November, you'll be ready.

10. Get your books, study aids, and other supplies
If your school is like most schools, your first-year class will be broken down into two or three "sections." Everyone in your section

will likely follow the same schedule, and have all of the same professors. At least three days before classes begin, and probably much sooner than that, your first-year professors will have posted your section assignments. They'll probably be posted on a class bulletin board somewhere in your law school. There will likely also be syllabi and course packets, handouts, or other materials. Get the packets and handouts, and then take your syllabi directly to the bookstore. Be sure to bring along a couple of large backpacks to haul your materials home.

When you get to the bookstore, buy a new copy of each of the *required* books. In law school more than most other programs, it's important to buy new because you'll be marking your books up like you never have before—and working around a previous user's extensive notations can be frustrating and distracting. Be sure to buy the right edition, and to get any paperback supplements offered with the book. Often, an author will put out a paper supplement between editions to keep up with the most recent case law in a particular area. These thin pamphlets are easy to overlook.

If the professor "recommends" a particular hornbook, you'd be advised to pick up a copy—chances are the professor will either lecture out of parts of it or at least refer to it. It may also prove extremely helpful to your understanding of the subject.

Wait on anything the professor lists as "optional." These books are frequently either written by your professor, or contain contributions by your professor. You'll probably never need anything "optional" for a critical part of the class—but your professor would be happy to collect the royalties if you want to oblige.

Next, go to the stationery section. After you've loaded up on your favorite types of pens, binders, and legal pads, find the highlighters and follow these directions carefully. Buy at least six each of green, yellow, red, blue, and orange. Yeah, I know that's thirty highlighters.

Trust me on this. You'll learn what these are for in Chapter 8.

Finally, head for the section of the bookstore where the legal study aids are kept. These are huge business for the bookstore, so they should be prominently displayed. Chances are, there are three or four choices for each of your subjects. So how are you supposed to decide which ones to use?

Consult the list below. Find the subjects that you are taking this term, and immediately buy the study aid(s) listed after the subject name. These are our consensus picks of the best study aids and commercial outlines available for each subject. If you can't find them all at the campus bookstore, don't worry. Flip to the end of this chapter and contact one of the companies listed there. They have all of our recommended outlines and will overnight mail anything you need. The most important thing is to get your commercial outlines immediately—since they will play a vital role in the way you study from day one.

Recommended commercial outlines

Civil Procedure:	Civil Procedure: Examples & Explanations (Glannon) Emmanuel's Civil Procedure Outline
Torts:	Gilbert's Torts Outline Torts: Examples & Explanations (Glannon)
Property:	Gilbert's Property Outline
Contracts:	Emmanuel's Contracts Outline
Constitutional Law:	Emmanuel's Constitutional Law Outline
Criminal Law:	Gilbert's Criminal Law Outline

Remember that you really won't have time to consult more than one or two commercial outlines in a particular subject, so don't buy everything the bookstore has. We recommend the products listed above.

Finally, as we were going to press, a new and exciting internet-based product was just hitting the market. Produced by a company called LearningLaw (www.learninglaw.com), the product, called "Aristotle," provides a series of online, hyperlinked overviews of the first year subjects which will give you a much-needed contextual framework for each subject from which you can then expand and supplement with case law from your lectures and material from your hornbooks and other commercial outlines.

After taking our bar review classes in preparation for the bar exam, many of us noted that having a framework of black-letter law for each subject at the beginning of law school would have been immensely helpful. This is what LearningLaw seeks to provide with Aristotle. Check them out.

Bonus: Go to orientation!

Finally, this note. Go to the orientation events. Law school can be an extremely lonely and isolating place. The experience is made much more tolerable if you can find a trusted friend or two among the masses—and grabbing a beer at orientation and mingling with your classmates is one of the best chances you'll have to do this in a relaxed atmosphere. Once classes begin and conversations turn almost exclusively to the daily grind, it is harder to get to know people.

The two or three days of orientation events will probably be the most fun you have in law school until you're a third year student. Go forth and enjoy the last days of unburdened time. It is frequently during these first few days over a beer at these orientation events that memorable conversations, important bonding events, and the formation of study groups occurs. But you have to be there to be included.

Contacts for commercial outlines

Lerner Law Book Co., Inc. (www.lawbooks USA.com)
www.Lawbooks.com
www.Barrister Books.com
www.amazon.com
www.barnes and noble.com

CHAPTER 7

So What Is a Tort Anyway?
A Brief Overview of the
First-Year Curriculum

It is enough if one tries merely to comprehend
a little of this mystery every day . . .
—ALBERT EINSTEIN

BY NOW, you should have gotten the idea that a great many people apply to law school without the vaguest notion why they're doing so. Not surprisingly, this lack of information also extends to the first-year program of study, and the entire law school curriculum.

"Not me," you say . . . "I know a lot about law school. I've read the first six chapters of this book."

Okay then, what's a tort?

"Huh? A tort? Uh . . ."

Most American law schools offer a standard first-year curriculum that includes courses in Contracts, Real Property, Civil Procedure, Torts, Criminal Law and/or Criminal Procedure, Constitutional Law, and a full-year course in legal writing. In some schools, one or more of these classes might be offered as a full-year course, pushing one of the others, often Criminal Law or Constitutional Law, to second-year status. Further, one or more of a limited list of "elective" courses, often including Administrative Law, Labor Law, Legal Theory, Economic Theory, or Legal History may be offered during the second semester to provide a bit of variety.

In this chapter, we harbor no illusions of providing an exhaustive analysis of the first-year subjects. That's why you go to law school. This chapter is included for the day during the summer before your first year of law school when your mind starts to wander toward the end of August, and you start asking yourself, "So what am I going to be studying next fall, anyway?" It is just an overview—to both sate your summertime curiosities and whet your appetite for the study of law.

THE SUBJECTS

Civil Procedure

Affectionately referred to as "Civ Pro" by students, or simply "Procedure," by the professors, Civil Procedure is typically one of the most intimidating and most feared of the first-year courses. Admittedly, understanding some of its more abstract concepts like subject matter jurisdiction and the infamous "*Erie* question" may be more difficult than memorizing the elements of common law robbery in Criminal Law, or negligence in Torts. This fear and intimidation, however, can be successfully dispelled by discovering and understanding the broader purpose of the course and studying the rules "in action" with a good hornbook—a strategy which will be discussed at great length in the next chapter. By following this approach, you will discover that an elegant, sensible structure underlies the rules of procedure—and that the system actually "makes sense."

A civil action is an action brought to enforce private rights and/or seek private remedies in which money damages or some other court order is sought. It may be easier to conceptualize civil actions through the use of a negative—a civil action is "any non-criminal case." Civil Procedure, then, at its most basic level, is the study of the rules, procedures, regulations, and process governing these non-criminal actions in state and federal courts.

Because the rules of civil procedure govern a broad spectrum of cases, from garden-variety contract disputes to high-profile First Amendment challenges, the first thing to realize when you're reading a case for Civil Procedure is that you're not really concerned about the underlying substantive law dispute. It's not the contract issue or the First Amendment claim you need to evaluate. Instead, in Civil Procedure, you need to be on the lookout only for the procedural questions *underlying* the case that the court was forced to decide.

Most national law schools teach Civil Procedure from a federal court perspective, and consequently teach the Federal Rules of Civil Procedure—a compendium of eighty-six rules which governs every aspect of bringing a civil action in the federal court system. Most professors require you to own a copy of the federal rules, but even if yours doesn't, you should buy a copy—as reading the applicable rule will greatly aid your understanding of the case law precipitated by that rule. In addition to providing a complete list of the rules, the "Rules Pamphlet" or "Rule Book," as your professor will likely refer to it, will contain instructive "Advisory Committee Notes" stating the intended function of each rule, and the purpose of any amendments thereto. Penned by the drafters of the federal rules, the "Advisory Committee Notes" often hold the key to ambiguous language in a rule, or even to an entire case!

If you go to a smaller state law school, your course in Civil Procedure may focus on the procedural rules of the state courts where your law school is located. Like their federal counterparts, state courts are also governed by rules of procedure. Unlike in the federal court system, however, where the same *Federal Rules of Civil Procedure* govern your case whether you're in federal court in Alaska or Florida, each state's court system has its own rules of procedure. Fortunately, most state courts' rules of civil procedure are closely modeled after the federal rules. Radical departures by state courts from the federal rules of procedure are uncommon.

So what, specifically, will you learn in Civil Procedure?

First, you will learn how to determine whether you can bring a case in state court, federal court, or both, and which courts within those systems are available to hear different cases. This question, which raises issues of "subject matter jurisdiction," "personal jurisdiction," "proper venue," and "removal," encompasses the first broad area of Civil Procedure—choosing the proper court to hear your claims and making sure that you don't run afoul of that court's jurisdictional rules.

From there, you will discover how lawsuits are shaped through the evidence-collecting procedures of interrogatories, discovery and depositions, joinder of additional culpable parties after the commencement of the lawsuit, and supplemental jurisdiction over additional claims involving those parties. You will learn how courts can hear counterclaims and cross-claims between these parties, and you may even delve into the complicated world of complex litigation and class actions.

Once you have your court properly chosen, all necessary parties in the lawsuit, and all claims on the table, you will need to decide which law governs the case. Federal statutory law? State statutory or common law? If so, which state's law? In considering these issues, you will encounter (1) the infamous "*Erie* question," which requires you to determine whether the issues raised in a federal court case implicate federal procedural law or state substantive law, and accordingly, which law to apply, and (2) the choice-of-law conflicts that arise when citizens of different states appear in a federal court, each alleging that the law of his own state should govern the lawsuit. In trying to make sense of all of this, you will likely address the policy underpinnings of the *Erie* decision, and the troubling problems of horizontal and vertical "forum shopping," where plaintiffs try to seek out the court which will apply the most favorable law to their claims.

You will then learn about how cases can be derailed and ended prematurely through the motion to dismiss, the motion for summary judgment, and the motion for judgment as a matter of law. Finally, you will learn how the concepts of "Res Judicata" (claim preclusion) and "Collateral Estoppel" (issue preclusion) can bar a plaintiff from relitigating events or particular issues that have already been resolved on the merits in a prior claim.

Civil Procedure is one of the most complicated, but most enjoyable of the first-year subjects, because it is your undeniable entrée into the world of law. In studying Civil Procedure, you learn the blueprint of the American legal system, and slowly discover how our entire system of civil justice fits together. Working through the rules to the point of mastery can be a long and extraordinarily frustrating process, but when the clouds finally do part, the elegant simplicity of the system of American civil procedure will be yours to keep.

Contracts

Anyone who has read *The Paper Chase* or has seen the movie probably lives in fear of Contracts. In reality, however, the course in

Contracts is one of the most practical and common-sense driven courses you will ever take in law school. At its essence, the study of contracts is the study of how the law protects an original understanding or agreement between two or more parties, as manifested in a contract, from the subsequent misfortunes, changes in circumstances, accidents, later-discovered misunderstandings, or intentional breaches by one or more of the parties to that contract.

During your course, you will learn the three primary components of contract formation: offer, acceptance, and consideration, and what is required of each component in order for a valid contract to be formed. You will learn about the defenses to contract formation including the absence of mutual assent, lack of valid consideration, illegality of the underlying contract, and incapacity to contract. You will also learn the defenses to contract enforcement, including when to apply the statute of frauds (which bars the enforcement of oral contracts concerning certain subject matter, and all oral contracts which cannot be completed within one year), and when the principles of impossibility, impracticability, frustration, and unconscionability can bar the enforcement of a contract.

From there, you will address the rules of contract interpretation, including how to resolve disputes over contract language and how to apply the "Parol Evidence Rule" (which holds that when the parties have reduced a contract to a writing which is intended to be the full and final expression of their agreement, any other prior or contemporaneous written or oral expressions cannot be interpreted to vary the terms of the written contract). You may also discuss the rights and responsibilities of third-party beneficiaries of the contract.

Finally, you will learn what happens when a contract is breached, and what different kinds of damages and other remedies are available to the non-breaching party.

The course in Contracts is typically taught using both case law and Article 2 of the Uniform Commercial Code (U.C.C.), a special set of codified rules which govern all contracts for the sale of goods.

Finally! So what *is* a tort, anyway?

A tort is an act or omission, perpetrated by one individual against another, for which a civil remedy is available. There are intentional torts like battery; economic or dignitary torts like defamation; and torts of negligence, strict liability, products liability, and nuisance. You'll doubtless cover them all, but regardless of how obscure your professor tries to get with the doctrine—no matter how much cost-benefit analysis and economic theory he tries to teach you—Torts is still probably the most straightforward, black-letter subject you'll have during your first year of law school. Don't lose the forest for the trees here. Mastering Torts, for the purpose of your exam, is mostly about memorizing the elements of the torts you cover and any defenses applicable to them.

You'll probably begin by learning the intentional torts: assault, battery, false imprisonment, intentional infliction of emotional distress, trespass, and conversion, and the defenses to these torts, including self-defense, defense of others, defense of property, consent, privilege, and necessity. From there, you'll address "negligence," the mother of all torts. During your treatment of this subject, you will discuss (1) the duties of care owed by professionals, business and property owners, homeowners, drivers, and parents; (2) what, specifically constitutes a breach of those duties; (3) examine the difficult subject of causation—including actual and proximate cause, and the foreseeability of the injuries produced by a particular act or omission; and (4) learn the potential defenses to a negligence action, including contributory and comparative negligence, and assumption of risk. You will then discuss the various theories of damages, and the interplay of insurance in a negligence action.

Later in the semester, you will address the subject of strict liability torts—torts which impose an absolute duty of safety on the defendant, including the harboring of wild or known dangerous animals, and the perpetration of ultra-hazardous or dangerous activities and their associated defenses.

Time permitting, you may delve into one or more of the "specialty torts." Among them, you might study products liability—examining when commercial manufacturers and vendors can be held liable for product-related accidents, and what defenses apply in such actions; public and private nuisance and their defenses and remedies; and the torts at the junction of constitutional law, including defamation (including libel and slander), invasion of privacy, and misrepresentation, and the related defenses to these torts, including consent, truth, and privilege.

In summary, torts is a rich and wildly interesting area encompassing a wide array of subject matter. Its cases often read like tragic comedy and are among the most entertaining in all of law.

Property

The course in first-year Property is a strange amalgam of the past and the present-day. The course couples obvious, almost inaccessible nods to ancient English traditions (see, e.g., the Rule Against Perpetuities and the Rule in Shelley's Case) with modern day landlord-tenant, real estate, and personal property issues that many of us may have experienced in our own lives. The result, once you get past the arcane language and theory, is a largely black-letter and practical body of doctrine that many students enjoy because of its ready application to everyday life.

The course generally begins with a nod to merry old England, and a lengthy treatment of "estates in land" including the different types of present possessory estates and possible future interests that a person can have in a piece of real property. During this part of the course, you will learn about the effects that death and failing to heed your forefathers' wishes can have on your ability to receive and retain an estate, and the effect that sloppy drafting can have on who takes possession of your land after you die. Amazingly, much of this arcane stuff still applies today, which unfortunately means that most of it will also be fair game for both your final exam, and the bar exam.

Enjoy.

You will then take up the next broad topic in first-year Property: landlord-tenant law. During this immensely practical segment of the course, you will learn about the creation and enforcement of leases, the duties of both landlords and tenants, and the remedies that each have at their disposal upon a breach of those duties, the law of assignments and subleases, the law of fixtures, and the assignment of tort liability between landlord and tenant.

From there, you may pause for a couple of weeks to discuss the only marginally related area of personal property (read: possessions other than land). During this segment, you will discover who has legal rights to lost or mislaid property, what a "bona fide purchaser" is, and who has the "more significant" right to a piece of property that was lost by person A, found by person B, stolen by person C, sold to dealer D, and bought by person E, when person A sees person E wearing her "lost" ring and demands its return.

Later in the course, you will reach real property's boundary with real estate law when you take up the subject of easements, covenants, profits, and servitudes, or, in a phrase, the different active and passive rights that a person, a corporation, the city, or the public may have on the land of another. You will learn what language is required to create these interests, how they are passed with the land, how and when other people are adequately notified of them, and how these interests manifest themselves in everyday life. You will also discuss the concept of adverse possession—the way that someone who lives on a piece of your land for long enough can actually gain legal title in it.

From there, you will move into "conveyancing," or how to pass title in land from one person to another through land sale contracts, deeds, and wills. Among the topics you will address in this section is how to conduct a title search to assure that the piece of land you are buying or receiving is free from encumbrances, and how to properly record the interest you receive to protect it from later fraudulent conveyances.

Finally, if time allows, you may touch upon the area of natural rights incidental to land ownership, including mining and mineral rights, and oil, gas, and riparian (water) rights.

If you use a good hornbook or commercial outline to get you through the more arcane subject matter, property can be an interesting and highly practical subject. Many people who have gone on to specialize in landlord-tenant law, real estate, or oil and gas law trace their initial interest in their specialty subjects to their course in first-year Property.

Depending on what law school you attend, criminal law and procedure may be taught as one course, or as two separate courses. For purposes of this explanation, I will treat them separately.

Criminal Law, the stuff of movies and prime-time television, is a favorite of most law students. The cases are interesting, the subject has an obvious place in everyday life, and accordingly, the underlying theory is accessible and readily applicable.

The study of criminal law typically begins with a philosophical discussion of the different theories and purposes for punishment. You will likely discuss the purpose and origins of the "Model Penal Code" (a codification of substantive criminal laws promulgated by the American Law Institute), and how it compares and interacts with the various state criminal codes. From there, you will learn about the general elements of criminal conduct, namely the *actus reus* (culpable physical action or inaction), and *mens rea* (culpable mental states).

With an understanding of the underlying theory, you will launch into a study of the crimes themselves. You will learn the different types of homicide, and the physical actions and mental states required for each of them. You'll address attempt crimes, and the physical acts and mental states required to constitute attempt. You'll then learn the principles of exculpation, including self-defense, protection of property, law enforcement, justification, duress, intoxication, diminished capacity, and insanity. You'll also learn about accomplice liability, and the physical acts and mental state required for culpability. You'll then run through the alphabet of other crimes and their required elements, including offenses against the person (criminal assault and battery, mayhem, kidnapping, false imprisonment, and the sex offenses), offenses against property (larceny, robbery, embezzlement, false pretenses, extortion, receipt of stolen property, and forgery), and offenses against the home (burglary and arson). Throughout your coverage of criminal law, you'll read hundreds of cases from different jurisdictions which will both help to define the boundaries of the different crimes, and raise fascinating theoretical questions about the theories underlying the criminal justice system. Without a doubt, criminal law will be one of the highlights of your first year curriculum.

Criminal Procedure, often called Constitutional Criminal Procedure, is largely a study of the Fourth and Fifth Amendments, and how the adversarial clashes between criminal defendants and law enforcement officials have played out in the courts. The course typically features extensive coverage of Fourth Amendment law centering on the relationship between the warrant clause and the reasonableness clause, and includes topics like when the police can search homes, cars, and people, what constitutes probable cause, and what is required to obtain search warrants. You'll learn about eavesdropping, and wiretapping, and when these activities are permitted. Fifth Amendment law protections against self-incrimination, involuntary or coerced confessions, and improper witness identifications are usually studied in depth, as are the Sixth Amendment rights to counsel and trial by jury. In each of these areas, particular emphasis is commonly placed on Supreme Court decisions, and how the different courts (Warren court, Burger court, Rehnquist court) have approached these subjects philosophically.

Depending on your professor's particular focus, you may also take up trial-related subjects including the roles of the police, the prosecutor, the grand jury, bail and pretrial release, discovery, plea bargaining, sentencing under the Federal Sentencing Guidelines, and the development and recent curtailment of habeas corpus rights.

Whether it is offered as part of the first year criminal law class, or as an upper-year elective, Criminal Procedure always generates passion and excitement among students, and, when properly taught, is usually one of the most popular classes in the law school curriculum.

Constitutional Law

Summarizing Constitutional Law in a few paragraphs is a nearly impossible task. At its broadest, Constitutional Law is about how the United States Constitution, as the "Supreme Law of the Land," (1) establishes an organized framework which equally distributes power to the three branches of government (legislative, executive, and judicial), (2) describes the general plan by which public affairs are to be administered, and (3) lays out the fundamental principles which are to regulate the relationship between the citizen and her government.

So how does this play out in the first year course?

Nearly every first year Constitutional Law course opens with a discussion of *Marbury v. Madison*, the case which established the function of the judiciary and the nature of the Supreme Court's authority as the ultimate interpreter of the Constitution. From there, discussion typically moves to the relationship between the states and the federal government through the commerce clause, the spending clause, and the federal government's power to tax. While much of this treatment will be historical, the principles underlying the commerce clause and the spending clause and the powers they provide empower congress with the constitutional pathway which produces much of the federal legislative action that happens today.

At some point during the semester, there will be a clear break in the doctrine as you move from the discussion of the structure of government, to a discussion about individual rights and liberties. This "second half" of the first year Constitutional Law course typically begins with a discussion of the Bill of Rights, the post–Civil War amendments, and the circumstances surrounding their adoption. Due process of law, equal protection rights and levels of scrutiny for racial, ethnic, and gender preferences, and constitutional restraints on private conduct will be among the many interesting topics you'll discuss in this section of the course.

Depending on time and the interests of your professor, you may touch on the First Amendment freedoms of religion and expression to a limited degree, although these subjects are usually saved for an entirely separate course or courses on the First Amendment given as upper-year electives.

Constitutional law is one of the most complex, fascinating, and intimidating subjects taught in the first-year curriculum. It is, however, the essence of American law, and provides the often unseen, but ever-present framework underlying every other subject in law.

Administrative Law

Although neither a mandatory part of most first-year curricula, nor a required upper-level course at most law schools, Administrative Law plays such an important role in the way our society functions these days that I'm writing this section with the expectation that before long, it will be a required course. Required or not, you should take it during your first year so you have at least a rudimentary understanding of how the complicated administrative system works and fits in to the three branches of government.

Administrative Law, at its essence, is the study of the rules, regulations, orders, and decisions promulgated and issued by administrative agencies to help them carry out their regulatory powers. In the introductory course, however, you will not be studying the specific rules and regulations promulgated by, for example, the Environmental Protection Agency, or the Food and Drug Administration. Instead, you will study how administrative agencies came into being, and how, despite the tremendous protestations about separation of powers and lack of direct political accountability which continue to this day, the legislative branch was allowed, in the name of "efficiency" and "economy," to get away with delegating so much of its power to these agencies.

Your study of administrative law will engage these issues as they were decided by the United States Supreme Court. In addition, you will learn about the controls exercised over these agencies by the other branches of government. You will learn the framework for agency rulemaking and adjudication, the process by which judicial review can be taken from agency action, and what damages are available against the federal government and its officers when an agency oversteps its bounds.

You need only peruse your law school course catalog briefly to grasp just how important a role administrative law plays in the landscape of American law. Environmental law, oil and gas law, food and drug law, energy law, securities law, labor law, tax, and trade are only a few of the areas of law influenced heavily by administrative agencies. Best get this subject under your belt early.

CHAPTER 8

Getting Out of the Gate—
Applying the Lessons of Futures Past

Where there is no vision, people perish.
—PROVERBS 29:18

IMAGINE that law school is a horse race. On the first day of classes, the professors pass out the syllabi, the gates spring open, and the horses (that's you) burst forth from the cages. In a real horse race, however, the thoroughbreds charge forward on a beeline course down the track toward the finish line. In law school, however, when the gates open, the first-year students charge out of their cages and spray out in any number of directions in a zealous but aimless charge. Not surprisingly, after fourteen weeks barreling off in the wrong direction, many of these hapless 1Ls cross the finish line exhausted, frustrated, and completely confused. Worse yet, many of them end up bombing their first-semester exams—and their dismal results hang on their necks like albatrosses for the rest of their law school careers.

Your job is to do everything in your power to make sure this doesn't happen to you.

How?

Truthfully, it begins with a change of mindset. An admission that the glory days of high school, where you could walk into a test without studying and get an A anyway, are over. An understanding that you spent your last miracle in college when you partied the semester away but crammed successfully enough during the last three weeks of the semester and reading period to perform well on your

111

exams. In law school, there are no miracles, and there aren't any gifts. At the end of the road, it's just you, an empty bluebook, three hours, and a class full of competitors looking to force you down the obligatory curve, in order to get the spot on the law review, the judicial clerkship, or the plum job in the shining city.

> If I could do it all over again, I would have taken an entirely different approach to my study strategy during those first few months. I would have been more diligent about keeping up with the reading, forced myself not to get bogged down in the minutiae of cases, started using commercial outlines sooner, and started making my own outlines right away.
>
> —Carolyn

People can sugarcoat it all they want, and believe me, they'll try—but at the root of it all—if your law school employs a mandatory curve as most do, the reality is this: Somebody is going to get the A's and somebody is going to get the C's. You're either the predator or the prey. As the next chapter will discuss, this situation doesn't give you license to be an asshole to your classmates, but it should light a fire under you. You're in a new reality now. Heed this warning: If you approach law school like it's an extension of college, when grades come out, you'll find yourself in a hole that you may be digging yourself out of for the rest of your law school career.

Here's what you need to know to get a clean start out of the gates.

Case briefing—their way

If you were to talk to ten law students about the best way to study law on a daily basis, you'd probably end up with ten different answers. Some students will, no doubt, tell you that you can do well in law school by simply reading commercial outlines and hornbooks and not actually reading cases at all. My experience suggests that this is true to some degree. Commercial outlines and hornbooks are an extremely important element in your studying process. I wholeheartedly endorse their use, and I will teach you how to use them for maximum benefit in the next section. Before you start relying too heavily on commercial outlines, however, you need to learn and develop the core skills of the lawyer—how to sift through facts, glean the law from carefully written judicial opinions, and synthesize the law.

On the other hand, many law professors and some students take the opposite extreme, suggesting that "real students" should be purists—embracing the struggle for understanding by simply reading the assigned cases over and over again until clarity comes, and briefing every case on their own, without using commercial outlines. That advice is equally bad.

> *Never* brief a case. The entire first semester, I typed up elaborate briefs of each case while I read. Don't do that.
>
> —Allan

Somewhere in your orientation materials, a professor from your law school probably sent you an article on "how to properly brief a case." Read that article carefully, and do the sample case brief if one was provided. What you're doing in that exercise is learning the rudiments of a process. You need to know how to walk before you can run, so follow their directions. Put down the name of the case, and learn how to write the citation in proper form even if you don't know what it means yet. Write down the procedural posture—or, in other words, how the case got to the court it's in. List the relevant facts, frame the question presented carefully, and answer it. Add a few lines to flesh out the court's reasoning, and most importantly, provide yourself with a hook. Why was this case significant? What did this case contribute to its area of law?

I'm not providing you with an example of a sample brief for two reasons. First, unless your law school practices some unorthodox, alternative teaching style, you'll get an assignment to brief a case in your orientation materials. Second, you won't be using this method much longer. You *must* learn it, however. This is not a place to cut corners. The more time you put into learning how to brief a case properly, the faster and more skillfully you'll be able to brief cases my way.

Do the orientation brief now, without looking at the sample provided.

Now compare what you've written to the model your professor provided. How'd you do? Chances are, if you took it seriously, your brief is twice as long as it needs to be, contains a slew of unnecessary facts and reasoning, and probably took you over an hour. Sound about right? Don't worry. Things are about to change dramatically for the better . . . but you had to do at least one case out their way in order to recognize just how much better!

Case briefing—my way
(The five-step plan to success)

You already read Chapter 6, so this shouldn't be news to you. Two nights before classes begin, you should have a syllabus, a textbook or textbooks, the *Law School Confidential* recommended hornbook and/or commercial outline, and a three-ring binder for each of your law school classes. Now pick a subject, grab your syllabus, and let's get started!

STEP ONE: Start each night with a lesson from your commercial outline

One of the most critical secrets of law school success is being able to put the hundreds of cases and case excerpts (often called "squibs") you'll read for each law school class in some kind of context. The most efficient way to do this is to start with the commercial outline. Why reinvent the wheel struggling for countless hours to create a context when someone has already done this for you? I'll let you in on a little secret.

> If I could do it all over again, I would focus much more on the "black-letter" law—the holding and how each case advances the ball in that particular area of the law—because that's what's important at exam time. I tended to focus too much on facts because I was terrified I would look stupid in class if I couldn't remember what a case was about.
>
> —Keith

Law professors generally scorn commercial outlines. Some even ban them from their lectures. But the truth is, for your purposes in law school, there is not an enormous difference between a well-constructed commercial outline and a good hornbook. In fact, some offerings—like Professor Joseph Glannon's highly recommended *Civil Procedure* from Little, Brown's *Examples and Explanations* series—is a hybrid between a commercial outline and a hornbook. In any case, you're looking to put each night's reading in context, and consequently, each night's reading should start with a read through the relevant section of the applicable hornbook. Here's how you do it.

Grab your syllabus and determine what pages in the textbook your professor has assigned for tonight. Go to the textbook and see what the general topic heading is. If you're having trouble determining what it is, don't forget to check the table of contents at the front of the book. When you've determined the general topic area—write it down.

Next, flip through the span of pages the professor assigned, and write down the name of every case that appears. There will be "major cases"—the ones that are excerpted in edited form—and "squibs"—the cases that are mentioned and discussed in a paragraph or two in the professor's linking text between major cases. Be sure to write down the names of these squib cases, too, as they often provide important interstitial development between the major cases that can greatly assist your understanding. Once you have your list of cases for the night in that subject, put the casebook aside (for now) and consult one of the recommended commercial outlines. Go to the index in the outline and find the pages where the cases you've listed are discussed. Chances are, the cases will be grouped together in a section not unlike the one in your textbook. Read the section of the outline for understanding, marking the holdings of your listed cases, and any explanatory text discussing how the cases affect each other, with a highlighter. Don't try to memorize things, or write anything down yet. Just read and highlight. What you're looking for is an overview of the night's reading in that subject—a context in which to put the cases you're about to read. To employ a metaphor—think of the law as a series of somewhat linear lengths of chain. Each case you read adds another link to the chain, and is dependent on the cases that preceded it to illustrate the development of the law. That's the magic epiphany you're striving for in each of the subjects you'll study in law school—to be able to follow the cases, link by link down the chain, until you finally grasp the big picture of how all the cases in the chain work together to govern a particular area of law. This is a somewhat simplistic notion of the law, but it will work for now.

> The key to academic success in law school is good outlines. A huge mistake I made in law school was refusing to use outlines from former students and commercial outlines like Gilbert's and Emmanuel's. **Using these outlines is an integral part of studying for law school**! It is not against the rules. But for some reason, I wanted to prove that I could do well on my own. And all I did was put myself at a disadvantage to everyone else by not using all of the resources available to me. After my first semester, I learned.
>
> —Steve

So what do you do if an assigned case isn't discussed in your commercial outline? One possibility is that the case is of minor importance—in which case, it's probably in a squib, and thus, you can take its holding at face value from that squib and move on. If you're really stuck on that case, you can always go to the law library and consult some of the other hornbooks in the subject area to see if they covered it, but my recommendation would be not to worry about it. We're using the outline right now for an overview, so complete coverage is unnecessary. Use the outline for what it can give you, and move on to briefing the actual cases, discussed in the next section. Getting 100 percent coverage of cases discussed in your textbook in your commercial outline is rare. Don't worry about a missing case or two. The question to ask yourself is, do you know what you're going to be reading about tonight, and do you have some sense about how the law has developed in the area? If you can answer yes to these questions, you're ready to proceed.

STEP TWO: Brief in Technicolor

If you followed the instructions in Chapter 6, you should have an ample supply of green, red, yellow, blue, and orange highlighters on hand. Open up each of your casebooks to the inside front cover and reproduce the following key inside:

GREEN:	facts
YELLOW:	critical legal reasoning
RED:	holding; court; judge; procedural posture
BLUE:	important precedents cited and their holdings
ORANGE:	important dissenting remarks

From now on, you'll be briefing your cases in your casebooks, in color, as you go along. Here's how to do it:

First, skim the case completely from beginning to end. Just read. No pen, no highlighter, nothing. Force yourself not to get too bogged down in minutiae. Just get a sense for how the case is organized, what the case is about, what the holding is, and how much good supporting reasoning is provided. Resist the urge to mark anything. An average-sized case should take you ten to fifteen minutes to get through.

When you've finished skimming the case, you're ready to start briefing it. Remember the one cardinal rule about this method of case briefing—highlight *sparingly*. Mark the court, writing judge, procedural posture, and holding in red, the most relevant facts in green, the most persuasive or historically important reasoning in yellow, significant case precedent in blue, and any notable reasoning in the dissent in orange. If you find yourself passively painting the text as you go, rationalizing that you'll come back to this later, you're missing out on the benefit. Force yourself to read, highlight, and mark the text actively and critically—bringing out only the most crucial aspects of each case.

When you've finished, skim back over the case and write a word or two in the margins next to each highlighted section to flag important concepts. For example, in a contracts case, you might write "consideration" next to the part of the case where consideration is discussed, or "three part test" next to the place in a constitutional law opinion where a three-part test is applied. Just a word or two here or there to trigger your memory. That's all you need.

Finally, go back to the top of the opinion and draw yourself a simple picture to remind you what the case is about. I don't care that you got a C+ in seventh grade art, just draw a picture that will trigger your memory. No one else will see it but you.

So what's the benefit to this method? There are several. The first is time. This method saves a lot of time that you'd otherwise spend copying passages of an opinion into a notebook or typing them into a computer. The words are already on paper in a safe, organized, and bound volume. Why recreate the wheel? Spend the time you save by not having to write out your briefs analyzing and thinking about the law. Figure out how each case fits into the framework you discovered in the commercial outline.

> I agree with Keith. Spend more time figuring out the black-letter law. The professors tend to emphasize the methodology (i.e. how to think about the law) and don't emphasize the black-letter law. However, when it came time to take exams, I found that the key was the black-letter law . . .
>
> —Pat

Critics of my method will argue that people don't remember things as well when they highlight them as they would if they wrote them down, and that studies have shown that highlighting encourages passive study and postpones learning and commitment to memory. They're right—and that's why briefing in technicolor is only a part of your overall study method. You'll have at least two more passes through the material—the first in class when the material is discussed, and the second, when you're constructing your own outlines for each class. You'll be writing those yourself—and that final step will help to really crystallize and structure your understanding of how the law fits together. But we're getting ahead of ourselves. First, go ahead and do your first case brief for class following the method I just discussed and come back when you're done.

Finished? Great. Now quickly flip back through the case. You should see a lot more black-and-white unmarked passages than you do highlighted sections. Do you? You *must* resist the urge to highlight too much, because at the end of the semester, you'll be coming back through the material looking for the major points—and you won't have the time to reread everything! Highlighting too much will make you your own worst enemy when it counts the most. Less is more!

Okay, so I promised you that there were several benefits to my system, but so far, I've only told you that it saves time. What about the other benefits?

Flip back through the case again. If I were to ask you to stop on a dime and tell me the holding of that case, how long would it take you to find it? Go ahead—find it. Look for red. Got it? Great! How long did it take you? Five seconds? Congratulations. You now have a very effective shield against the fear and paralysis caused by the Socratic method.

How?

An example:

You're sitting in Contracts at 9 A.M., and your first cup of coffee is just starting to raise the fog. Then suddenly, and completely without warning, it happens.

"Ms. Reader (that's you)," the professor blurts out, "what happened in the case of *Hadley vs. Baxendale*?"

You're overcome by fear and start to panic. You didn't even have your book open yet. You did your contracts reading two days ago. A dead silence falls over the classroom as you furiously flip to the right page. There, staring you in the face, is a picture of a mill wheel with a line through it. Now it all starts to come back to you. In the next moment or two, you've found the green highlighted text, and you're ready to recite the facts.

"Uh . . . there was a mill, and the crank shaft broke. The mill operators sent out the crank shaft to have it fixed, but the delivery of the new shaft was delayed, resulting in lost profits to the mill operators because the mill couldn't function while they were waiting . . ."

"Not exactly eloquently stated, but good enough Ms. Reader . . . and what did the court hold about those lost profits?"

She wants the holding. Just look for the red highlighting and read it.

"Umm . . . the lost profits weren't reasonably foreseeable as a consequence of the breach of contract, and shouldn't have been taken into consideration in estimating the damages."

"Excellent, Ms. Reader. What was the disposition of the case?"

"The disposition of the case?"

"Yes, Ms. Reader. What did the court decide to do?"

Oh-oh. Didn't highlight that, did you? Don't ever forget to highlight the disposition of the case (affirmed, reversed, remanded, vacated, etc.). It's part of the holding, so it goes in red too, and it's almost always in the last three lines of the opinion before any dissents. For those of you playing along at home, the answer is that a new trial was ordered. It's right there in the last paragraph.

Highlighting in technicolor goes a long way toward improving your performance in the Socratic sweepstakes because you'll never totally freeze up. All of this assumes, of course, that you've prepared for class the night before (or earlier). If you're staring at twenty pages of unmarked text the day you're called on, it's not going to be pleasant for you.

STEP THREE: Supplement your notes and tab your statutes in class

Yet another benefit to briefing in technicolor is the ability to concentrate more intently during lectures. Personally, I hated taking notes in classes—there were always gaps in the notes I took, and while I was distracted by the necessity of getting everything down, I would always miss important comments made during the lectures.

Not anymore.

By briefing this way, you'll already have marked 90 percent of the material the professor will bring out during the lecture. No need to frantically write down holdings, procedural postures, or important reasoning—you've already captured it.

Sure, there will be a few things the professor points out in class that you won't have marked out in the text, and that's why you should bring a set of highlighters to class and simply mark those passages in the casebook in the appropriate colors as the professor hits them. You may also want to date the cases as the professor discusses them such that, at the end of the semester, you'll know what cases the professor discussed in class and on what days. That way, if you need to clarify a point, you'll know what day to consult in your friend's notes. I also liked to star the passages that the professor noted were particularly important.

The same goes for statutes, rules pamphlets, and advisory committee notes. Time is usually short in the law school exam room—so one of the biggest favors you can do yourself before you enter the exam room is to have your permitted materials as well organized as possible. There is no reason, in a Civil Procedure or Contracts exam, to waste precious time flipping through your Federal Rules pamphlet or the U.C.C. aimlessly looking for a particular provision.

Go to your campus bookstore or nearby office supply store and purchase a few sets of stick-on "flags" that you can write on. Bring them to class with you every day, and every time a professor discusses a particular rule or code provision, highlight the relevant portion of the provision, write anything the professor says about it in the margin next to the provision, and then flag it in the statutory compilation with a stick-on tab with the number of the provision and a brief description written on it. This way, come exam day, if the section is implicated on your exam, you'll not only know exactly where to find it, but you'll have an instant index of everything the professor said about the provision right where you need it.

Finally, most professors like to make a summary comment or two about a case or statute—often putting it into context with the other cases and statutes you've studied or placing it in a particular historical or political context. You'll want to capture those comments—but don't write them down on looseleaf paper or in a notebook—put them right in the margins. That way, you'll have everything in one place! It will make outlining simpler, and once you are out of law school, after your notebooks and loose-leaf paper are long gone, those notes will still be right there at your fingertips.

The final advantage of this method of case briefing, though, is how much it will increase your concentration. When you get into class, look around during the middle of the lecture. As the professor goes over a case, most of your classmates will have their heads down, writing furiously, trying to capture every word. They won't succeed, so they'll get frustrated and confused—distracted from the critical conveyance of information going on in class. They may even mishear things and record misinformation in their notes. Later, they'll spend countless hours trying to reconstruct and decipher these notes—if they even use them at all.

You, on the other hand, will be watching the professor—intent on the discussion and stopping only to highlight a few passages here and there and make a few marks in the margins as class progresses. You'll have already captured the critical material, so you'll be free to concentrate on what the professor is saying or eliciting from your classmates. Learn the material instead of trying to record the class in your notes.

Try it. The benefits of this approach will be readily apparent.

STEP FOUR: Write your own outlines

This is unquestionably the most crucial step in the learning process, and also the hardest step, because it requires the most discipline. Every day after class, for every class you had that day, you need to consolidate your knowledge into a concise but comprehensive outline summarizing that day's material. Here's how to do it.

> Every semester, my friends and I would say, "this semester we'll start outlining our notes right away and that way, we'll be done by reading period and we can just study." And every semester we would fail miserably and spend the last few weeks in utter hell literally living at the library.
>
> —Bess

Go somewhere quiet where you can spread out your materials and plug in your laptop. Start just as you did last night—by typing in the names of the cases you read in chronological order. Be sure to include the name of the court and the date of the decision to aid understanding and avoid possible confusion. Now, taking each case one at a time, refer to your casebook and, after scanning for green highlighter, plug in one to four sentences of the most relevant facts. Anything more, and by the end of the semester, you'll have produced a new casebook. You may want to set off these facts in italics to make them more easily distinguishable.

Next, go back to the casebook and, after looking quickly for red, plug in the holding. You may want to set this off in bold to distinguish it from the facts, or skip a line between the facts and the holding. Force yourself to make the holding as succinct and clear as you can.

Next, go back to the casebook and see if the professor had anything interesting to say about the case historically, politically, or contextually. What, if anything, did you scribble down in the margins? Skip a line after the holding and plug it in.

Finally, go back to the commercial outline where you started last night and remind yourself of what it had to say about the case. What did you highlight? Did the outline help to put the case in a framework by linking it to the cases that preceded and postdated it? Did the outline make any other remarks that your professor didn't? If so, add these notes from the commercial outline right after your professor's comments.

Do this for every case you covered, in every subject you had that day, during *every day* of the semester. It will probably take you about an hour, on average, to update your outline for each class. Assuming that you have three classes a day, that means that you'll be spending three hours every day developing your class outlines. This is absolutely crucial to your mastery of the material, however, and it is by far the most valuable time you'll spend studying. If you keep to this schedule on a daily basis (which requires a great deal of discipline), at the end of the semester, you'll have a 60–120 page outline for each of your classes which will represent, in one neat, concise package, everything you need to worry about for the exam.

> If I had it to do over again, I would have kept reviewing material from earlier in the semester as the semester wore on. I kept up with my reading and always went to class, but nevertheless found that by December, I had forgotten virtually everything we learned in September.
>
> —Joel

When you get near the end of the semester, we'll address the fifth and final step to the plan, where we'll take your outlines and distill them down into a series of case-chain "maps"—the deadliest weapon in the armory for conquering law school exams. We'll get to that in Chapter 12. For now, though, you job is to religiously develop your outlines for each class. Force yourself to do it every day, and keep up, as the end-of-semester benefits of your discipline will be enormous.

Determining your work schedule

It is vitally important to your success in law school that you develop an effective routine in the very early days of first semester, and stick to it. In law school, time is your most precious commodity, and it is critical to your success that you learn to manage it wisely. A brief look at the schedule that awaits you makes it obvious why this is so.

The average law student will take four classes per semester, and have three lectures on any given day. Assuming that each class lasts one hour, that's three hours of in-class commitment every day. Pursuant to the strategy we just discussed, when you get out of class, you'll need to spend approximately one hour per subject consolidating last night's highlighting in your casebooks and commercial outlines, and anything you added to them from today's lectures, into your outlines. That's three more hours. Then there's tonight's reading. Assuming that you have three classes tomorrow, and an average reading load of twenty pages of cases per class—at a reading rate of ten pages per hour, that's another six hours. Three hours in class, three hours of outlining, and six hours of reading and briefing for tomorrow's classes equals twelve hours of work. Throw in an hour for lunch, an hour for dinner, a couple of hours for your afternoon workout, and you're looking at a sixteen hour day.

Even if you spill some of your outlining hours over into your weekends, as you'll almost certainly have to do on occasion, it should be extremely obvious that you don't have much time to waste! Your daily schedule will look something like this—the schedule that I eventually settled on:

7–9 A.M.	breakfast/read for class three
9–10 A.M.	class one
10:30–11:30 A.M.	class two
11:30–12:30 P.M.	lunch
12:45–1:45 P.M.	class three
2–4 P.M.	workout/break
4–6 P.M.	outline classes one and two
6–7 P.M.	dinner
7–11 P.M.	read for classes one and two
spillover to weekend	5 hrs outlining for third class each day

Obviously, you can move things around as needed, but the take-home message from this illustration is that there really aren't a lot of free hours available in each day. If you choose to sleep late in the morning, you'll have to either cut your workout down, stay up later to make up the hours, or push more of the outlining off until the weekend. You can't put it all off, though, because that's fifteen hours, and you need six hours on Sunday to read for Monday.

Find a schedule that works for you and stay dedicated! You're going to fall a bit behind here and there, but struggle every weekend to stay current. Every now and then you'll catch a break when a professor gives a shorter reading assignment or fails to get all the way through the material you prepared for that day, and you'll end up with bonus hours you can use to stay as close to caught up as you can. You must, at all costs, avoid the crush at the end of the semester. If you arrive in December nearly on schedule, you'll have a tremendous advantage over your classmates—and you may be able to avoid the crippling stress that many of them will succumb to as exams near . . . which means better grades for you. You have to get through all the material—and it's now or later. Do it now.

A word about study groups

Some people swear by them, others won't go near one. I never consistently participated in a study group because I found them frustrating. People often showed up late, and without their promised materials prepared. We wasted a lot of time gossiping about classmates, bantering about professors, and planning meeting times. When we finally did get down to work, the focus of our discussion had to be divided among everyone's questions—which meant that we spent considerably more time going over things I already knew than on things I needed clarified. Given the tight schedule I just illustrated for you, I found study groups to be more of a hindrance than a help, and if you stick to my system, you probably won't ever need one anyway.

That said, many people like to bounce ideas around with others, and to have someone around to test their understanding of the material. If you're one of these people, you might try to find a study "partner"—someone you can count on to do the reading, keep up with outlining, and discuss the law with you. Finding some-one like this can also be very helpful in forcing you to stay on schedule. I did this, and it worked out well. There was always some-one there to discuss the material, but no bureaucracy, fewer dis-tractions, and no time wasted discussing things we both knew.

It's your choice—but think it through very carefully. Once you commit to being in a study group, you can't change your mind without angering the other members of the group and at least potentially damaging those friendships and your own reputation. This is an issue to consider in the first few days of law school, because once school starts and these groups begin to form, you'll need to decide right away whether you're interested in participat-ing.

CHAPTER 9

The Unspoken Code of
Law School Etiquette

*So it is that the gods do not give
all men gifts of grace . . .*
—HOMER

LAW SCHOOL is a kind of intellectual boot camp. It is likely to be as strenuous and draining as anything you've ever experienced in your life. With this new experience comes a new set of social norms—a canon of ethical behavior to govern your behavior and social interactions during the next three intensely competitive years. The problem is, in most schools, the canon is unspoken. It's something you have to figure out as you go along—which can be extremely stressful, deeply humiliating, and even permanently destructive depending on which mistakes you make, and when and how you make them.

Consider this chapter to be your "Federal Rules of Proper Law School Behavior"—a codification of the dos and the don'ts collected from your *Law School Confidential* mentors. When these rules are followed, you end up with a school where class materials, knowledge, and understanding are generally shared freely among students, where in-class discussion is vigorous but respectful, and where the study of law is made just a little bit more humane in the process. When the rules aren't followed, you end up with places (if you've done your research, you know the schools I'm referring to) where needed books disappear from the library shelves, every word spoken is contested and challenged, and the educational experience seems to degenerate into cannibalism.

Regardless of what school you go to, becoming familiar with these rules will help to ease your assimilation into the confrontational, competition-laden law school culture, help to ensure that you remain in the good graces of your classmates, and consequently, assure that your law school experience will be as civil and collegial as possible.

THINGS YOU SHOULD DO

It is your duty to follow the honor code

At some point during the summer or during your law school orientation, you received a copy of your law school's honor code, or code of ethics. If you haven't already done so, read it from cover to cover and make certain that you understand the expectations it places on you. Some of the things in there are probably pretty harsh, but they're in there for a reason.

There's a reason why most law schools make you a culpable party if you see someone hide a book, lie on a resume, or cheat on an exam and fail to report that student to the dean. That reason is called civility. Law school is competitive enough. With a mandatory curve forcing a large percentage of the class, most of whom are used to getting A's all the time, to get B's and C's—and with those grades perhaps causing rejection by law journals, judges, and employers—and ultimately taking money out of people's pockets—most law school student bodies exist in an uneasy, if not perilous equilibrium. All it takes is one well-known case of a person successfully cheating his way to success to throw off the balance and create an atmosphere of "every man for himself."

On the other hand, if cheating is reported by students, thoroughly investigated by the school disciplinary board, and severe punishments are meted out and announced to the student body, the equilibrium is strengthened. At a place where everyone has an equal chance to succeed, and where cheating carries a supreme price (normally suspension or expulsion and a permanent letter in your files sent to all future employers), an atmosphere of civility and cooperation can flourish.

Permit me an example. During my years at Penn, I represented my class on the disciplinary committee. In my first semester on the Committee, we heard the case of a student who had been turned in by a fellow classmate for using a commercial outline in an exam where the use of such outlines had been expressly forbidden by the professor. The student (who, by the way, had gotten an A on the exam) admitted using the outline, knew that it was cheating, and defended his choice by referring to the pressures he felt to do well. The committee gave the student an F in the course, expelled him for a year, and ordered the "letter of reckoning" placed in his file for all future employers to see. We then announced our decision to the student body.

The result was remarkable. After the decision was made public, more than two dozen students in my class approached me before first semester exams to clarify which materials were permitted and which were forbidden. Everyone wanted to be sure they were in compliance with the code.

A level playing field was assured.

Unfortunately, which result ultimately prevails really depends on the attitude of the student body as it is passed down from upper-classmen to 1Ls from year to year. The deans and professors aren't going to catch the cheaters in the majority of cases. You are. Or you'll turn the other cheek and ignore it, and the cheating will go unpunished to the detriment of everyone and the atmosphere of the school as a whole.

At some point during orientation, the dean will probably make some high-minded speech about how you must keep people who are willing to cheat in law school out of the profession by reporting them. He'll say that if they're going to cheat here, they'll cheat to win in practice too, and bring disgrace upon the profession. He'll probably also talk about reporting cheating to preserve the law school atmosphere of civility and cooperation—a point which I've just addressed and I think is an extremely valid argument. But for those of you who still aren't convinced and are out there shaking your heads saying, "I'm not going to rat out a friend," I'll appeal to your basic, utilitarian instinct. Do you want to let that person next to you get away with using notes in a closed-book exam and push you down the curve? Positions on law reviews are routinely decided by fractions of grade points. Whether you make the law review substantially affects your chances of getting a judicial clerkship, and significantly affects your employment opportunities. One grade can matter. The cheater knows that, or he wouldn't be taking the risk.

Don't let him get away with it.

A final word on the subject. Make sure you understand what obligations the honor code puts on you. If you're unclear about what you're allowed to bring into an exam, ask each of your professors to clarify the rules. Make sure you know what constitutes plagiarism in law school—and whether your professors intend the rules of plagiarism to apply during your written exams. This is particularly relevant in long take-home exams. Be sure you understand the rules of proper citation and attribution when writing papers and journal articles. You will be expected to know what the rules are—and you may pay a high price for your ignorance.

Lastly, no situation you're in is so desperate that you have no alternative to cheating. If you ever find yourself in the position (and most of us have) where you feel so overwhelmed and outgunned that you start rationalizing with yourself about cutting corners—stop. Take a night off. Go see the dean. Extensions can be given. Exams can be postponed. Maybe all you need is the dean's reassurance that everyone feels the way you do. Just don't cheat, and throw away all that you've worked so hard for. The pressure is real—but it's passing. The consequences of cheating and getting caught, however, will in all likelihood be permanent.

Share your class notes, hornbooks, and outlines with anyone who needs them

I didn't say you have to put posters up advertising the fact that you have the best Civil Procedure outline known to man and that you'll gladly make copies for anyone who asks—but if someone in your class needs a hand, be willing to provide it. The operative rule here is, "what goes around, comes around" and there's nothing wrong with building up some "favor equity" in your classmates. You never know when you'll miss some classes and need notes, or fall far behind and need to borrow an outline to catch up. Resisting the urge to be cutthroat will earn you a solid reputation among your classmates, win you some friends, and make your law school experience much more enjoyable. Finally, take the time to notice when the person sitting next to you is missing. If she is, and there's a handout or revised syllabus distributed in class that day, pick up an extra copy for her, slide it into your notebook, and give it to her in the next lecture. Do your part to make the law school atmosphere more cooperative.

> The reality is that law school attracts competitive people, and the way the system is set up really encourages people to be competitive. My father, who was a partner at one of the biggest law firms in New York, used to say, "hierarchies don't select for nice." That may be, but my feeling is, life is short, and the world is a much more pleasant place when people are nice to one another. Be decent to people. Don't belittle others to make yourself feel better, and don't refuse to help someone because you think you'll do better if they do poorly.
>
> —Carolyn

Despite what the cynics might suggest, I agree with Carolyn. Sharing class materials never cost me a grade in law school. Try taking the collegial approach. I think you'll agree that the benefits far outweigh the negligible risks to your GPA.

Phrase in-class comments as questions—not statements

Assume, for the sake of example, that the topic of the day in Torts is proximate cause, and your professor has just given you the famous hypo about the guy in San Francisco who accidentally spills a drum of gasoline down a hill. The gas flows down the hill past a service station where a spark from a mechanic's torch ignites a raging fire that destroys the service station. Assume that after a confusing Socratic exchange, it is established that the gas spill was the proximate cause of the fire, and that the guy on the hill is found negligent and responsible for the damage to the service station because the potential damage to the service station was foreseeable (a requirement of proximate cause). Now assume that you have no idea what the professor is talking about, because you can't understand how a fire at a service station that far away could possibly have been foreseeable to our hero on the hill, (trust me, you wouldn't be alone in your confusion on this point), so you decide to try and clear up the point. You raise your hand, and the professor recognizes you to speak. Observe the following subtle, but significant difference in phraseology, and the different effect it will have on the professor and your classmates:

The wrong way to make a point

"Yes, Mr. Reader?"

"Well—I don't think it's foreseeable to the guy on the hill that his gas spill would cause a fire that far away—especially since it was the spark from the mechanic's torch that ignited the fire."

You've raised a good point—and no doubt, it's one that a lot of people in the class were probably thinking about. But there are probably also a few people in the class mumbling under their breath about you at this point. You know why? Because they don't care what you think—they just want to know what the law is! If you make enough of these "I think" or "I don't think" comments over the course of the semester, people will start resenting you for taking up their class time with your opinions. People will start rolling their eyes at you when you raise your hand, whispering to each other as you speak, and not listening to the comments you make, because they'll assume that you're just babbling on expressing more of your opinions again.

I know your intentions were good. You were just trying to clarify the point, right? Well how about doing it this way instead?

A better way to make the same point

"Yes, Mr. Reader?"

"Professor, I don't understand this. I'm confused as to how it's foreseeable to the guy on the hill that his gas spill would cause a fire that far away—especially since the spark from the mechanic's torch ignited the fire. Can you explain that?"

Now your classmates are nodding in consensus with the confusion raised by your question instead of muttering under their breath because you expressed your opinion. They're paying attention and waiting for the professor to clarify his point in response to your query. They may even come up to you after class, reassure you that they had the same confusion, and thank you for raising the issue during the lecture.

Understand that when you express confusion and ask the professor a direct question—she's more likely to break the Socratic dialogue and respond with a direct answer rather than another confusing hypo. People like direct answers in law school—and they'll appreciate your taking class time in asking the question and eliciting a clearer answer. Your opinion, though, they can do without.

Remember that.

When you're speaking, speak up, and when you're not, shut up!

Even if you're not the type to speak out in class, at some point, you, too, will be a winner in the Socratic sweepstakes. Like it or not (and most don't), when your day comes, the rest of the class has to be able to hear you in order to learn from the responses you give the professor. The soft talker is not welcome in law school. Your classmates are going to have a tough enough time deciphering your comments as it is. Don't make them struggle to hear what you're saying. Speak up!

On a related note, when you don't have the floor in the lecture, close your mouth and open your ears. Talking to your friend next to you about how much you disagree with so-and-so's political views, how attractive so-and-so is, what exactly it was the professor just said, or what you're doing for the weekend is rude. It's rude to the professor (and he might just embarrass you to make that point), rude to your classmates around you who are trying to listen to and take notes on the in-class exchanges, and on top of that— it's against your own interests. While you're busy prattling away, you're missing what's going on in class . . . and you can't afford to do that.

When referring to cases or statutes, provide page or section numbers

This is an often unspoken, but major pet peeve of many students. When you refer to cases or statutes while making comments in class, either in response to a professor's question, or in asking one of your own, always provide page numbers and paragraph or section references so that everyone else can follow along with your comments. One of the realities of law school is that you'll all be teaching each other through your comments and questions. Offering page and section references when asking questions or making comments communicates a spirit of collegiality to your classmates, and fosters a more cooperative atmosphere in the classroom.

Reign in your electronics

Many law students take notes in class on a laptop computer. Not all laptops are made alike, however. Random buzzes, beeps, quacks, or whatever other sounds your laptop makes can be extremely distracting to your classmates. If you're going to take your laptop into lecture, disable your sounds ahead of time, and make sure you have a fully charged battery so you don't have to scuffle around to change it in the middle of the lecture. It is also considered proper to check with the people assigned to the seats around you to determine whether your typing bothers them. Some people just can't concentrate with all that clicking going on. If you encounter objections, see the professor and ask to have your seat moved. You're the one making the noise—so it's *your* problem.

One last point on electronics. For heaven's sake, turn off your cell phone when you're in a lecture. There is no quicker way to draw the ire of the professor and your classmates than to have it ring on you during a class. No law student is so indispensable that he needs a cell phone in class. Get over yourself and leave the phone at home.

Maintain a sense of humor

Law school can be a deadly serious place, and there's no better way to cut through that atmosphere than by slipping in a well-placed witticism, or poking a little fun at yourself during Socratic questioning. You don't want to force it in there heavy-handedly, but if the professor gives you the opportunity, go ahead and let it fly. Remember, you're paying for the flogging you take every day. The least you can do is attempt to enjoy it.

THINGS YOU SHOULDN'T DO

Resist the urge to make unsolicited, tangential, or politically charged comments during lectures

Sometimes, trying to do the "right thing" in law school makes you feel like you're walking through an unmarked minefield. On the one hand, law is essentially about policy decisions, and policy decisions beg to be argued about. So why, then, am I counseling you to try and hold your tongue?

Every section in every law school has at least one "talker"—a person who egregiously violates this rule. Within a week or two, everyone in your section will have identified who this person is. It's a blowhard who speaks before he thinks his points through carefully. It's the knee-jerk liberal or the gun-toting conservative whose comments are known before they're uttered. The people who feel that no lecture—in fact, no topic of discussion—is complete until they've offered their opinion to the class.

You know what? People really don't like that. Especially not in law school.

Don't be "that guy."

It starts innocently enough one day, very early in the semester. You get engaged in a discussion that you know something about. You raise your hand and the professor acknowledges you. You speak strongly, and make some good points. It feels good. People seem to be listening to you. Your confidence increases, and as the days go by, you find that you have a lot of things to say. Soon, however, your classmates begin to wonder why you think that your opinion is important enough to express three or four times per class, every class, every week. Shortly after that, they'll stop listening to you. If it gets bad enough, you may even hear audible groans the moment you put your hand in the air.

"I really disliked it when the same people spoke in class over and over," Carolyn recalls. "There were some people who seemed to take every opportunity they could to express their political views or general ideas about the world. It really made me angry when people took up class time to express these views when they had nothing to do with illuminating the doctrine we were all trying to learn."

Elizabeth agrees. "Those who were to be respected the most were those who spoke the least. There is at least one person in every section who could not let a class go by without hearing themselves talk. You will identify him or her quickly as the person who raises his or her hand every time a professor asks a question, or even when the professor doesn't ask a question, and often gives a long-winded, politically charged response that is often completely off-base. In one of my classes, our frustration about this was validated one day when this person raised his hand, as always, and the professor said, 'Anyone? Anyone? Anyone else?'"

So what, you say? You're an individualist, and you don't care what other people think? Fine. Just don't go asking to join your classmates' study groups, or to borrow their notes or outlines.

There are two other corollaries to this "rule." First, don't ever try and "show up" a classmate during a lecture. If a classmate is struggling with the answer to a question from the professor, and the professor asks if anyone else knows the answer, don't be the guy who shoots his hand up to prove how smart he is. No one likes a "know-it-all," especially when it comes at the expense of a classmate. If you're going to challenge what a classmate is saying in lecture, be civil and polite. Don't lead with an opening like, "That's ridiculous!" or "That's completely baseless." Instead, lead with a question like, "But isn't it true that . . ." or "But I thought that . . ." Remember that you're trying to trigger a worthwhile conversation about the issue, not trying to make it personal. Second, if you're having a problem understanding a particular concept during a lecture, it is perfectly acceptable to raise your hand *once* and ask for a clarification of the point. Chances are, if you're confused, others are, too, and they'll appreciate your efforts to get the issue resolved. If the professor stops to explain the issue, and you still don't understand, however, don't belabor the point in lecture. Wait until after class, and then follow-up with the professor, either at the podium, or during his office hours. Remember that the purpose of the lecture is not to resolve your personal difficulties with the material, and people will start to resent it if you try to turn the lecture into your personal tutorial.

Don't boast about your study habits

Another readily identifiable "annoying person" in law school is the one who leans over before lecture three weeks into class and tells you that she was up until 4 A.M. working on her contracts outline, which is already two-hundred pages long. Similarly, there is no need to tell anyone that you're one-hundred pages ahead in your Civ Pro reading, that you put in one-hundred hours on your Legal Writing appellate brief, or that you had tea and a fantastic philosophical discussion about *mens rea* with your criminal law professor yesterday afternoon. People just don't want to hear it. If you loved the topic you were working on enough to stay up all night with it, good for you.

Just don't tell anyone else.

"People like that used to really make me roll my eyes," Elizabeth recalled. "I had a classmate who took great delight in trying to unnerve her fellow students before exams by saying things like: 'Did you study the latest revisions to the Uniform Commercial code? No? Really? (gasp for breath) Oh well, I guess you still might pass.' "

Safeguard your reputation

Yeah, it's a euphemism, and you probably know what I'm getting at here, but in case you're really a wonk, let me spell it out for you. Your social life at law school will be . . . well, put it this way: Remember high school? Bingo. Except you don't have to sneak around to drink, you have your own place, you don't have a curfew, and sex probably isn't a big mystery anymore.

On the other hand, you're back in an environment with two-to three-hundred people who take all the same classes, and are forced, by necessity, to spend almost every waking hour together. You'll see these people every day, like it or not. You have a locker again. People will be cliquey and catty just like they were in high school. And even though sex probably isn't a big mystery anymore, people in law school will still whisper and gossip as if it were.

Before you enter law school with the intent to make up for the opportunities lost when you were a dork in high school, remember this: It's a really small environment, with very little privacy. In the day-to-day world of law school, with the long, grueling hours of tedious work and frequent feelings of hopelessness, people get worn down, and seek comfort in different ways. With nothing but law to discuss otherwise, gossip spreads quickly. A couple of early mistakes can earn you a reputation for the duration, and a damaged social reputation can easily carry over into the academic environment, and on into your future as a lawyer. Exercise discretion.

> In law school and in your legal career, your reputation is your most valuable asset. Once you've lost it, it's really, really hard to earn it back, and you may never be able to outrun it either. You never know where the road ahead of you will lead to, and the legal community is smaller than you think. The people you mistreat today might be in the position to remember those acts one day.
>
> —A mentor

Oh—and no, it's never a good idea to get involved with a professor.

Adhere to your school's recruiting guidelines

The National Association for Law Placement (NALP) disseminates, through your placement office, a list of guidelines for students to follow during recruiting season. Students enrolled at member law schools are required to adhere to these guidelines, which regulate how many employment offers a student can keep open after certain dates in the recruiting season. The purpose of these guidelines, of course, is to keep the recruiting process moving and to free up job opportunities for other law students. In addition to the NALP Guidelines, your school may have its own set of rules about recruiting—like, for example, whether you are allowed to put your class rank and/or grade point average on your resume.

It is essential that you inquire about these rules and guidelines in advance, and be sure that you adhere to them throughout the recruiting process. If your school does not compute class rank and GPA, and forbids you from computing your own GPA and putting it on your resume, don't even think about doing it. Schools that do this are typically trying to prevent employers from comparing their students on the basis of numbers alone. You ought to appreciate this effort. Once one overly competitive student computes a GPA and includes it on a resume at a school that bans this practice, employers will start asking every student at that school about their GPAs, and why theirs weren't included on their resumes. Needless to say, if you are discovered doing this, you will face stiff penalties from your school, and even stiffer ones from your classmates.

The same advice applies to keeping too many employment offers open after stated deadline dates. A recent NALP rule allowed you to keep three offers open after November 1, and only one after December 1, but check with your placement office to be certain of the current rule. Obviously, no one can keep track of every law student's open offers, but there is almost never a reason why you can't whittle your choices down to three by November 1. Remember that somewhere out there, there is another law student waiting to hear from the firms you turn down.

Imagine that student is you.

Avoid all post-mortem discussions about exams

Law exams are, by their very nature, anxiety inducing. More often than not, they test the gray areas of the law, and force you to apply the law you learned during the semester to "reason out" an outcome to the exam questions. In most cases, there isn't going to be one "right answer" to a law exam question.

When the exam is over, there will be winners and losers. Some people will feel great about their exam, others will feel like hurling themselves off the nearest bridge. The funny thing is, there is often no correlation between how you feel about an exam when it's over and the grade you ultimately receive. There are just too many variables involved to be able to accurately predict your grade. If you feel like a winner, that's great. Work off your euphoria on your afternoon run, or in the nearest bar. If you feel like you've been beaten up, take solace in the fact that, unless you left your exam book blank, your grade is unpredictable.

One way or the other, you may feel an overwhelming urge to "check" or discuss your answers to the exam with your classmates in the exam room or hallway immediately after the exam. Resist every temptation to do this. It is a major no-no of law school etiquette.

Why?

Because nothing good ever comes of it. No matter who you talk to, either you, or the other person is going to end up feeling bad. Because there is typically no "right answer" to a law exam question, people can arrive at acceptable, full-credit answers in very different ways. How are you going to feel when your classmate reveals the brilliant public-policy argument he threw in, or the directly-on-point advisory committee note he found in the back of the *Federal Rules of Civil Procedure* which enabled her, in two paragraphs, to answer the question that took you ten pages to reason out? And how is she going to feel when you start talking about an issue raised by the question that she didn't even notice?

See what I mean? Nothing good ever comes out of discussing exams after the fact. When an exam is over, it's over. There's nothing you can do about it anyway, so why dwell on it? All you're going to discover is that your classmates had things in their answers that you didn't include, and it's going to upset you. They're going to discover that you had things in your answer that they didn't include, and it's going to upset them. Soon, everyone ends up feeling that their performance "could have been better," and then people start fretting about how much damage their omissions will do to their grade in the course.

Furthermore, some people just *hate* discussing exams after they're over, and they'll get very upset with you for talking about exams in their presence. Don't ever start in on a discussion of exam answers before you've identified whether you're talking to one of these people. If you absolutely *must* share your thoughts about an exam, do it with an equally willing group of people away from the exam room.

Never discuss grades

Finally, we come to the number one rule of law school etiquette, which I've saved for last for purposes of emphasis. Never, never, never discuss your grades in public. Not even if people ask you about them.

Why?

Again, because nothing good can come of it. If you have better grades than the person asking, that person is going to be made to feel badly. If she has better grades than you do, you might be made to feel badly. And of course, all of this depends on whether you're both telling the truth.

University of Pennsylvania Dean of Students Gary Clinton (who wrote the foreword to this book) once told me, "there are a lot more students walking around here with straight A's than there are students walking around here with straight A's." Don't play this game. The correct, and only answer when someone asks about your grades is, "I don't discuss grades."

Period.

CHAPTER 10

The T-Minus One Month Checkpoint: How to Arrive Ahead of the Competition

In fair weather, prepare for foul.
—FULLER

THE MOST IMPORTANT THING that you can do in law school on a day-to-day basis is maintain your focus. With thousands of pages of reading to complete during the course of a semester, and four months to get through before you're ever held accountable for any of it, it's all too easy to spin your wheels. At one point or another, you'll find yourself over reading and overanalyzing individual cases, spending more time on the subjects you like at the expense of the ones you don't like, and worst of all—excusing frequent lapses in your studies by deluding yourself with the thought that you have "plenty of time" to catch up. The fact is, in law school, there's no such thing as "plenty of time." Let this chapter be your wake-up call—the last checkpoint separating you from disappointment on exam day

In most schools, November 1 is the target date—putting you about five weeks away from your first set of law school exams. Since most law schools administer their first set of exams in December, I'll assume that fact for the rest of the chapter. If you happen to attend a school that schedules exams after winter break, or only at the end of the year, however, this chapter is no less applicable to you. You can use this chapter now, as a measure of how well you've maintained your focus and kept up to date during the first two months of the semester, and come back to it again when you're five weeks away from your first set of exams.

So how are you doing? Starting to feel the pressure mounting? Have you noticed that the library is getting more and more crowded? Have you fallen behind? Are you feeling overwhelmed?

Don't worry. All of those feelings are par for the course during your first year of law school—and everyone is feeling the same way, even though they're not admitting it openly. Let's see where you are, though, so we can evaluate what you need to do during the next five weeks in order to prepare you for those exams!

Remember, your goal is to arrive in your last week of classes with up-to-the-minute class outlines. If you're like most students (I'd say about 98 percent), you're not caught up and up-to-date today. You've tried your best, but the pace set for you in Chapter 8 was tough. There were days when your reading took longer than expected . . . days after you broke up with your significant other when you were too distracted to stay focused on your work . . . and days when you were just too tired and fed up to outline. That's okay. The key now is to start fresh from here. You have a month until exams, and you know what your goal is. You must get those outlines finished—and it's time to decide how you're going to get there from here. Find the heading below that is most appropriate for you and follow its directions.

I've missed a couple of classes, a couple of reading assignments, and I'm two weeks or less behind in outlining for each class

Good news! Compared to the rest of your classmates, you're in pretty good shape! Most of your classmates are farther behind than this at this point, and many of them aren't ever going to catch up. Don't get complacent, though.

The first thing you need to do—this weekend—is get those missing class notes from a friend, and make up your reading assignments. Stay in Friday night and Saturday until you get that done. As for your outlining, it's time to do some simple math. Figure out exactly how many classes behind you are on each outline, and, budgeting one hour per class, figure out how much time it's going to take you to make it up. You have four weekends left with Friday nights and Saturdays unscheduled. Plan your make-up time on these days, and force yourself to stay disciplined so you don't slide further behind. You're almost there! Come finals, you're going to be in a relatively painless position with plenty of time to take sample exams, taper your studying, and rest up properly in order to be in optimal condition when your exams arrive. You may even get Thanksgiving weekend off if you really focus! Have that as your target—and if you're caught up by Thanksgiving, take the three days off to relax knowing that you're in perfect position as you approach your endgame strategy.

I've fallen way behind in my outlining—what do I do?

Listen closely. All the reading and color-coded briefing that you've been doing isn't going to do a thing for you if you don't find a concise way to structure it. Law school isn't like college—just doing the reading isn't going to be enough. There's too much of it, and the distinctions tested are too subtle to rely on the memory of what you read twelve hundred pages ago to carry you through. It's time to take some fairly drastic measures to ensure that you arrive on December 1 with four complete outlines of your own creation. The process of creating your own outlines is the very best way to struggle through the material and get it organized in a way that you can understand. If circumstances warrant it (and they're beginning to in your position), you might have to cut back on everything else that you're doing in order to ensure that you get the outlines done—and that includes actually reading all the cases.

Yes, you read that correctly.

I'm not endorsing you to cut corners on a regular basis, and I'm not suggesting that you'll learn as much from the experience (you won't)—but if it comes down to a choice of skipping reading or not finishing your outlines, my recommendation is to finish your outlines, regardless of what your professors, or anyone else may tell you. You *must* have a sense of the big picture—how all the law fits together—at the end of the semester, or you're just not going to perform the way you want to on your exams. It really is that simple. Here's how to extricate yourself from the hole you've put yourself into in order to still be in decent shape come exam time.

> You have to realize that the key to being successful is not necessarily being prepared for class, but rather focusing on your outlines and on learning the black letter law in preparation for your exams. Don't worry about being prepared for class.
>
> —Pat

The first thing you need to do is to figure out exactly how far behind you are. Remember—plan for one hour of outlining per class for each day behind you are in that class. How many hours will it take you to catch up? If you're three weeks behind in your outlining for each class—that's four classes times three days a week for each class times three weeks times one hour per class to outline, or thirty-six hours total. At nine hours a day of outlining on top of the rest of your workload—that backlog will consume the final four Saturdays of your semester—including the one during Thanksgiving break.

I think you can see for yourself that if you're any farther behind than this, something's going to have to give in order for you to stay on schedule. If you are, pick a class to jettison. Make it one of the classes for which you have a good commercial outline that can pull you through on its own. If I were in your position (and I was), I'd probably pick Torts and rely on Gilberts to carry me through the rest of the semester. Stop reading for that course and use the extra two hours you gain three times a week during the month of November (two hours times three times a week times four weeks, or twenty-four hours) to catch up on your outlining. Those hours will buy you two weeks of outlining in each of your four classes. Add to that the hours from the Saturdays you have left (four Saturdays times nine hours a day, or thirty-six hours), and you have three more weeks of outlining for each of your four classes. That's five weeks of outlining—nearly half the semester—for each class. If you're farther behind than that, you really need to be reading the next section.

Panic button

I'm sure you have your reasons for being in this position, but you need to realize the dire nature of your circumstances at this point. This far behind in your preparation, you're in considerable danger of registering a potentially irreparable semester, unless you take some affirmative steps, now, to right your course.

The first thing you need to do is figure out whether whatever has distracted you up to this point is still a distraction for you. If you've been troubled by family problems, illness, financial issues, or other personal matters that continue to plague you, it's probably time to schedule an appointment with the dean of student affairs at your law school. He may offer to postpone your exams, or suggest that you take a voluntary leave-of-absence, straighten out your problems, and start fresh in the spring term. Yeah—you might have to graduate a semester later than your classmates—but that's a hell of a lot better than taking four horrendous grades on your first semester exams and paying the price in lost opportunities for the rest of your law school career. Too much rides on your first-year grades. Don't gamble with them.

If, on the other hand, whatever problems you were having have been resolved and you don't want to talk to the dean about getting a postponement (or if he denies your request), you need to decide *today* what method of damage control you're going to adopt to try and salvage the semester. It's too late for you to start writing your own outlines, so you're going to have to proceed on faith. The following method should be enough to earn you some form of "B" in your classes—and while B's aren't exactly going to wow employers, earn you a seat on the law review, or qualify you for a judicial clerkship, they will keep you in the middle of the pack somewhere and prevent your law school career from falling into an irreparable shambles. Let me hasten to add that this method is for emergency use only. I do not endorse its use for routine study.

Read Legalines to catch up,
and find four good student outlines
for your courses

Something has to go—and if you're trying to save your grades this semester—it has to be your daily reading assignments. There is a set of commercial outlines called Legalines, which are essentially Cliffs Notes for law casebooks. They boil down the long cases into simple, one or two page briefs that you can easily skim in a couple of minutes. Get the edition of Legalines specific to each of your textbooks and read the cases you've missed. At least you'll get the most important facts, the holding, and some basic reasoning from this.

Next, try to find someone in your class who sympathizes enough with your predicament to be willing to give you copies of the four outlines he or she has prepared for the classes. If your reasons are compelling enough, there might be someone compassionate enough to bail you out. In that case, simply take over, starting today, where those outlines left off, and force yourself to stay current for the rest of the semester.

More likely, though, you'll have to settle for the copies of last year's (or older) outlines circulating among the 1Ls in your class. Upperclassmen are usually willing to allow you to photocopy their old outlines—so find a 2L you know and ask. Be sure that the person you ask had the same professor and used the same casebook that you're using. If you can't find an old outline that satisfies these criteria, go back and use the first method. Using an outline for a different professor, or tracking cases from a different casebook will only confuse you. Don't do it.

Assuming that you do find appropriate outlines, spend several days reading each one carefully. Note the different sections it is broken up into and study the sections separately, examining the holdings of the individual cases and how they "flow" together to create the governing law in a particular area. If it helps you to focus, highlight the relevant parts of the outlines in the appropriate colors as if you were reading the cases directly.

This method will not provide you with the same depth of knowledge and understanding of the material, but this late in the game, you don't really have time for depth. What you're looking for is a basic knowledge of how the material fits together so you'll be able to apply the law you've learned to a new set of facts with a slight distinguishing "twist" or "wrinkle." On your exams, the professor will be evaluating how you analyze those facts based on the law and underlying social policy you learned during the semester. Shoot for the basics.

You're not likely to get many A's using this method—you simply won't have enough knowledge of the policy and reasoning underlying and driving the holdings—but you will probably be able to avert disaster. Given your situation, expect to get B's, and feel fortunate to have escaped your predicament without irreparable damage.

Regardless of your situation, you now know what you must do during the next month to get ready for exams. Remember, the goal is to arrive on December 1 (or a week prior to the end of the semester if your school uses a different exam schedule) with four complete outlines of your own creation—one for each of your classes. In Chapter 12, we'll discuss the fifth and final step of outlining "my way"—how to turn your outlines into concise, one-page visual "maps" of the law which will help you to spot issues, red-herrings, and take you step-by-step through your first semester exams in the most painless way possible. In order to be ready to map, however, your outlines must be finished—so get to it!

WHAT ELSE DO I HAVE TO DO BETWEEN NOW AND EXAMS?

Acquire old exams

Spend the dead time between classes this week in the law library making photocopies of at least three old exams and model answers in each of your subjects. Do the best you can to find the actual exams that your professor has administered in the past, as every professor has a different exam-writing style, and different preferred areas of focus. If your professor is a visiting professor or new to your school, use your ingenuity, the Internet, and/or the telephone to find copies of the exams she administered at her prior law school. If you do this, you might even catch an unsuspecting professor administering an identical exam in her new law school. This has happened in the past, and needless to say, the advantage of having worked through the exam and reviewed the model answer in advance is immense.

Resist the urge to work any of the exams, or even to read any of the model answers, until you've finished outlining. Much about your success in law school turns on confidence, and you don't want to undermine your confidence by prematurely addressing an old exam before you've learned all the material it covers. You'll only scare yourself. Wait until Chapter 12. At this point, you've budgeted adequate time to practice sample exams there.

Clarify exam rules with each of your professors

No later than the first week in November (or a month before your exams), talk to each of your professors before class and ask them to address his exam restrictions with specificity. Will it be an in-class exam, or a take-home? How many hours will you have to complete it? Will the format be multiple-choice, short-answer, essay, or some combination? Will the individual sections be timed, or will you be responsible for your own pacing? And most importantly, *what materials will you be allowed to bring with you into the exam?*

Force your professor to be extremely specific in this area—will commercial outlines be permitted in the exam? What about hornbooks or outlines written by other students? Can you bring in a copy of the U.C.C., the *Federal Rules of Civil Procedure,* the *Federal Rules of Criminal Procedure,* or the *Model Penal Code?* Can those materials be tabbed and annotated by you? Is it okay if you've scribbled notes in the margins?

Forcing your professor to specify exactly what is allowed and what isn't accomplishes several things. First, it prevents your professor from surprising you at the end of the semester by telling you that your exam is closed-book. Second, it alerts you to the materials you'll be allowed to bring into the exam room so that you can prepare them adequately (see Chapter 12). Third, it puts everyone in the class on a level playing field, and prevents the confusing and patently unfair scenario on exam day where some students bring no supporting materials into the exam, while others bring an entire library of resources with them. Finally, it clearly establishes, beyond doubt, the ground rules for purposes of the honor code. If the professor specifically says "no commercial outlines," and in the middle of the exam, you notice that the guy next to you is using an outline composed of photocopied pages from a commercial outline, he's clearly and unquestionably cheating—and you have an ethical obligation to report him to the administration. As I've said before, if the ethical obligation doesn't grab you (though it should), with the aid of that commercial outline, that guy is likely to kick your butt on the exam, force you down the curve, and cost you many hard-earned opportunities that you've worked for legitimately.

Send query letters to potential employers

Yes, now. Recruiting season for 1Ls begins on November 1, and many firms make hiring decisions in December immediately after they've completed their 2L recruiting season and have a better sense of what their needs are. Needless to say, if you wait until winter break to get your letters out, the pool of scarce opportunities for 1Ls with law firms may be significantly reduced.

Thus, on the first weekend in November, you need to address this reality by compiling a mail merge and getting your query letters out. Remember that resume you worked up during the summer? It's in your filing system. Pull it out, and you are ready for the next chapter.

CHAPTER 11

Making Your Summer Plans:
How to Win the 1L Recruiting Lottery

The die is cast!
—SUETONIUS

AROUND NOVEMBER 1, just at the time when you are becoming increasingly unable to take on more responsibility, you'll receive your first package of introductory materials from your school's career planning and placement office. Around the same time, placement officers and upper-level students may also start conducting informational question-and-answer sessions about first-year legal employment—often including one or more hiring partners from local law firms as panelists. All of a sudden, you have another giant monkey on your back. You'll start hearing about "summer associateships" with law firms, "internships" with judges, and "externships" with public service organizations. How do you make sense of it all?

At this stage of my law school career, I seriously considered spending my 1L summer at my old job as a counselor at an overnight camp in the New Hampshire mountains. I figured that the rest and balance the experience had always provided would be ideal after the rigors of the first year. Several practicing lawyers I consulted heartily supported the idea and lamented the fact that they hadn't been clever enough to come up with such a plan themselves. In the end, however, I got a summer-associateship at a law firm, and took it—and it proved to be the wiser choice.

Why?

When you enter the real recruiting market as a 2L, the screening interviewers and hiring committees you'll be dealing with are going to carefully scrutinize what you did with your first-year summer. They're going to ask you questions about it, and they're expecting to see something law-related. While you may occasionally find a new-age interviewer who will be supportive of your choice to spend your first-year summer hiking the Appalachian Trail or working with kids, most will immediately suspect that you couldn't get a job, or didn't have enough interest in the law to pursue one. Yes, it's unfair. Yes, it may be completely untrue. But that's what many of them will think—and it will make it harder for you to get the job you want in the 2L market if you haven't had some form of real-world legal experience during your first-year summer. That's just the reality of it—so you best be aware of it now.

Because most schools subscribe to the general guideline prohibiting 1Ls from using campus recruiting services until November 1 (ostensibly because they want you to "settle in" to law school and worry about figuring out how to learn the law for a couple of months before you spend the next two-and-a half years trying to get a job), come November 1, the process will really start to kick into high gear. Fortunately for you, most of your classmates will be too overwhelmed with how far behind they are in their studies to make any affirmative efforts to secure 1L employment until after the end of first semester exams. This presents you with an opportunity, if you're prepared to take advantage of it.

First, a reality check. Unless you go to Yale or Harvard, securing a paying position in a law firm after one year of law school is extremely difficult. Many firms just don't find it economically feasible to spend the exorbitant amounts of money you'll be paid in salary only to have you run off somewhere else during your second summer and then sign on with that second firm out of law school. Many of these firms also deign to waste time accommodating the limited scope of legal knowledge and "rookie mistakes" so common to 1Ls. Thus, unless you come from one of the very top shelf law schools, the odds are against you. The strength of the legal market at the time you're applying will largely determine how successful you'll be. Of course, that doesn't mean you shouldn't try—just don't brand yourself a failure if you don't manage to secure one of these plum jobs during your first summer.

"Finding a paying 1L summer job is very, very hard," Steve notes. "Unless you have good connections, be prepared to put in a lot of hard work. If you are in the position financially where you can take a job that doesn't pay, then it gets a little easier. The best advice I can give is to be persistent. I sent out over five hundred resumes in order to find the job I eventually got. I started by sending them to all the big firms in New York, Philadelphia, and Washington, D.C. When that didn't produce any results, I started targeting smaller, specialized firms in those cities. After that failed, I started looking to larger firms in smaller cities. Eventually, I went to the small firms and solo practitioners in the smaller cities. I didn't get a job offer until mid-May, after finals had passed, when a solo practitioner in Wilmington, Delaware finally offered me a paying job. As it turns out, most people didn't think to send resumes to solo practitioners, and mine was one of the only ones he saw.

I ended up with a great job that summer that gave me not only an income, but some great experience, since the work I was doing with a solo practitioner was much more in-depth than the work summer associates at large firms saw. In the end, it was all about persistence and perseverance: There is a job to be had out there somewhere, it's just a question of how many resumes you'll need to send out in order to get it. For me, it was five hundred. But I got my job."

The Firm

A paid summer "associateship" with a law firm is definitely the position most coveted by the majority of law students contemplating summer job options. As I've just mentioned, however, these positions are extremely scarce, and frequently taken by 1Ls from the nation's top five law schools. Every year, however, there are other students who manage to get these positions. So how can you be one of them?

I mass-mailed my resume to firms in D.C. and Boston in November, making sure to hit all the firms that had posted openings on our Career Services bulletin board. I got forty rejection letters for each positive response, but all you need is one good interview. Focus on a city or cities that you have some connection to on your resume. I got *all* my 1L callbacks from D.C., where I had lived and worked previously. And if you have *any* connection you think might be useful, use it.

—Joel

Most law firms complete their 2L recruiting in the late fall, and impose a final deadline of December 1 on the candidates to whom they've extended summer associateships for the following summer. In other words, as of December 1 each year, almost every law firm knows how many of its summer associate slots have been filled, and how many vacancies they have. Many of the large law firms save one or two spots for 1Ls, but the rest of the positions they ultimately offer to 1Ls derive from unclaimed 2L positions, or a radical uptick in the legal market which has generated an unexpectedly heavy volume of work. What this means for you is that if you want one of these positions, your resume and cover letter needs to be floating around at these firms *before* the December 1 deadline, ready to be snapped up when a space comes open.

You won't have grades yet—at most schools, grades aren't released until late January or early February—and although some of these firms will wait to see your first semester grades before they offer you a position, others will take chances and hire you on the strength of your undergraduate resume. Needless to say, if you can secure a job before your first semester grades come out, it will take a lot of pressure off, and make those first semester grades somewhat less crucial in their importance. The only way this can happen, however, is if you get your resume to these firms before December 1.

So, you ask, how do you find out where to send your materials?

There's a fantastic resource disseminated to 2Ls called the *National Association for Law Placement* (or "NALP") *Directory of Legal Employers.* There's almost certainly a copy in your law library and several in your placement office—but in the unlikely event that you can't find one—almost every 2L will have a copy that they're probably finished using now, so borrow one!

The first thing you have to do is figure out what cities you'd like to explore, or ultimately, to practice in. The NALP directory contains a section listing firms by city—so look up the firms in each of those cities. Find the ones that practice the areas of law you're interested in learning more about, and then check each firm's chart to determine if they've ever hired 1Ls before. While a track record of hiring 1Ls isn't mandatory, many firms have policies against hiring 1Ls and won't even read your materials—so why waste the postage? Conversely, by examining these charts, you can easily locate the firms that *have* hired 1Ls in the past and ensure that each of these firms gets your resume.

Once you've targeted all of these firms, if you want to take a chance at a few firms with no prior record of 1L hiring, you can always add them to the list. Once you've finished with the NALP directory, however, your list is far from complete. Perusing the NALP directory should have produced a list of fifty to a hundred possibilities in at least three large cities. Now it's time to think closer to home.

Think of everyone you know who is a lawyer. Your girlfriend's mother, your next-door neighbor, Uncle Louie in Chicago, *everybody*. Make a list of these people and get their addresses. Do your parents have a lawyer? Did they ever use a lawyer for anything? Do they *know* any lawyers? What about your grandparents, uncles, aunts, cousins, friends, or your parents' coworkers? Do they *know* any lawyers? With so many lawyers around these days, it's a safe bet that most of these people can name at least one lawyer in the area. Get their names and addresses.

It doesn't really matter whether the lawyers they know work for a mega-firm, a small-town firm, or toil alone as solo practitioners. You have an "in" with these lawyers—a personal connection. If the lawyer your parent/relative/friend knows can't offer you a job for the summer, he's a member of a bar association and undoubtedly knows many other lawyers who might be looking for help.

Network shamelessly! You have to be willing to pull out all the stops, to call in every favor, and pull every string within reach to get one of these jobs. Hey—your classmates will be doing it, and the fact is, the spoils of this game usually go to those people who are the most creative in their networking, and the most persistent and dogged in their efforts. I'd say at least eight of every ten people I know who got firm jobs during their first summer got those jobs by networking through someone they knew. This is no time for moral posturing. Gather these names and addresses, add them to the list, and be sure to personalize their letters to highlight your connection. When writing letters to people you know or have been networked to, always close with the line: "Any assistance or suggestions you can provide would be greatly appreciated." People like to help, and if they can't help you directly, they might be able to point you to someone else who can.

Once you have your completed list of names, firm names, and addresses (try to get the list to at least a hundred possibilities), learn how to do a mail merge on your computer or ask the people in your placement office to teach you how to do one. For the big firms that you culled from the NALP directory, direct your query letters to the named recruiting coordinator or hiring partner. If a personal connection has directed you to someone at the firm, send the letter directly to that person and be sure to personalize it (e.g. "Our mutual friend, Harry Helpful, suggested that I contact you").

When writing these letters, remember your audience! First, this is no place for flash, so save the fancy fonts, resume folders, and chic denim paper for your casting interviews in case law school doesn't work out. When dealing with law firms, twenty pound white bond and a plain font is the only way to go. Be brief! There's no reason to write a tome, since the construction of these cover letters is almost boilerplate.

Introduce yourself, state what school you attend, and make your request in the first paragraph. In the second paragraph, explain why the firm and city you selected is of particular interest to you. Add a concluding sentence or two in the third paragraph, and you're done. Straight to the point, and nothing fancy. A sample cover letter follows below. The selections in parentheses should be added only if you are networking to a known person at the firm:

Thomas One El
101 Law School Way
City, State, Zip Code
Phone
E-mail address

Mr. Larry Lawyer, Esq.
Weemake, Bigcache LLP
1 Federal Street
NY, NY, 10010

Dear Mr. Lawyer:

My name is Thomas One El and I am a first-year student at the XXX Law School. I am seeking a summer associate position with Weemake, Bigcache (and I am writing at the suggestion of our mutual friend, Harry Helpful, who suggested that I contact you).

Although it is early in my law school career, I'm interested in becoming a litigator and pursuing my interests in civil rights and employment litigation. I'm particularly interested in your firm because of its reputation as specialists in these areas of the law. I'm also from New York City and look forward to returning there to practice law after graduation.

Enclosed, please find an updated copy of my resume and my undergraduate transcript from XXX University. My first semester grades from law school will be available in early February. If there is anything further I might provide, please do not hesitate to contact me. (Any assistance or other suggestions you might provide would be greatly appreciated.)

Respectfully,

Thomas One El

If you used a mail merge, when you have all the letters personalized and printed, double-check to be sure that the name and address headings match the greeting line. Make certain that the letters contain no typos or printing errors, and be sure that the right letters end up in the proper envelopes. Make a chart of all the firms and contact people to whom you sent queries so you can log the responses as they return. Then send the letters off and get back to the important business of your first semester workload.

The rejection letters should start flowing in as soon as two weeks later. Don't be surprised by the number of these "ding letters" you get back. A 1 to 2 percent success rate is considered successful, and I've known people who sent out hundreds of letters before eventually landing a summer position.

Some firms may respond by expressing interest, asking you to send your first semester grades when they become available, and reserving judgment until after they've evaluated those grades. At these firms, your first semester performance will determine whether or not you are invited to interview. Other firms, however, may call you directly to offer an interview for the position. If and when that good news comes, refer yourself to Chapter 17 which addresses everything you need to know about law firm interviewing.

A final word about applying for firm jobs. Remember that getting one of these positions as a 1L is against the odds. Once you send your letters out, you'll receive a blizzard of rejection letters in response. Many of my friends made light of this humiliating experience by papering the walls of their dorm rooms and apartments with these letters, or having competitions to find the most obnoxious, callously written rejection letter. Your batting average will be abysmal, so be prepared for that. You may get a hundred rejection letters. You may get all rejection letters. Still, it only takes one "yes,"—one door of the hundreds you knock on—to make you one of the select few 1Ls that actually find first-year summer employment. Rest assured that finding this job is the hardest it's going to get for you in law school—but if you do find it, you'll have a crucial foothold that will dramatically increase your chances of success in next year's recruiting season and beyond. Fighting this battle is worth every ounce of effort you put into it.

"I realized early on that I probably wasn't going to get a firm position, and after realizing this, I looked for an interesting job in the legal field that would be challenging and would give me something to talk about in a job interview the following fall," Pat recalled.

"Use whatever connections you have, and spend as much energy as it takes to get a job in the legal field, whether it is paid or unpaid," Carolyn agreed. "It is very important that a 2L be able to talk about her first summer legal experience at interviews during the fall of the second year."

"I was too cavalier about my first year summer job, because I didn't think it mattered that much," Keith noted. "As a result, I ended up interning for a criminal law judge even though I had no interest in ever practicing criminal law. In the long run, my resume would have been more impressive had I taken the time to find a summer job in an area of the law in which I hoped to practice or at least wanted to explore."

Interning for a judge

Many federal judges (both circuit and district) bring on an intern or two during the summer season to help with their caseloads. Many state supreme court justices, and state appellate and trial court judges also "hire" interns during the summer months. Although wholly voluntary (meaning that you're on your own for *all* expenses, including travel, and will not be paid anything), federal and state court internships are, nevertheless, highly competitive. In the more popular courts, or with better known judges, fifty to a hundred applicants may be vying for the one or two available intern positions. Other judges get no applicants at all. It's best to apply for these positions by February 1, and it's best to cast your net wide.

Start by trying to figure out which *type* of judge you're more interested in working with. Consult Chapter 22 on judicial clerkships for a full account of the differences between clerkships in each of these chambers. While you shouldn't limit yourself to any one type of judge, you should have a working knowledge of the differences between internships in the various courts—and mention your interest in the particular internship you're applying for in your cover letters. In other words, in writing to a district court judge, you might add a line mentioning your interest in working with the entire span of a case, from pretrial motion practice, to mediation, to *voir dire* and actual trials. Conversely, in writing to an appellate judge, you should highlight your interest in working within the narrower confines and intricacies of appellate issues and the intellectual challenge of resolving gray areas of the law.

The point is, internships in different courts are very different and will make many different demands on you. Knowing what these demands are and the differences between them, and identifying them in your cover letter will make you a much more attractive candidate.

So how do you start?

As usual, I'd start in your school's placement office or law library. Look for any good directory of federal judges. These directories are usually organized by circuit and state, and provide the names, mailing addresses, and (depending on which directory you find) even short biographies of all the federal judges in the United States and the territories.

List the names and addresses of every federal circuit judge and federal district judge in your home state, and in the state and judicial district (if applicable) where your law school is located. These chambers will be especially fertile ground because in choosing interns, judges frequently favor locals—residents of the state or students at a nearby law school.

Next, get a directory which lists all the state supreme court, state appellate court (if applicable), and state trial court judges in your home state and in the state where your law school is located. Although finding this directory can be a bit trickier than finding one which lists federal judges, your placement office or law library should either have a resource providing these names on hand or be able to get one in short order.

By the time you've finished listing these judges, you should have more than fifty names on your list. To round it out, choose one or two other states to which you have some connection, like the state where you did your undergraduate work—or a state where you have interest in practicing after graduation. For example, if you've spent every summer since childhood vacationing in Wyoming—apply to the judges in Wyoming and mention this connection in your cover letter. Do not underestimate the power of local ties. If you go to a top twenty law school on the east coast, and randomly send a letter to a federal district court judge in Wyoming—your application is likely to be greeted with the reaction, "Why is this guy applying to my chambers in Wyoming? He must be doing a massive mail merge . . . I'll save the position for someone more appropriate." On the other hand, if you send this letter to Wyoming, and explain that the reason you're applying is because you spend every summer there, love the state, and are considering the possibility of settling there, you stand a much better chance.

Once you've compiled this list of judges, separate the names by the type of court they preside in (federal circuit, federal district, etc.). When you have the judges categorized this way, further subdivide them by state. Each separate pile will need a differently personalized letter—one which stresses your interest in the kind of experience particular to that kind of court, and states your connection to the state where that court sits. If you share any common ground with the judge (same law school, same undergraduate school, love of birdwatching, etc.), you'll want to work that into your letter as well. You're looking for any edge you can get that will distinguish you from the masses.

Incidentally, it is not disingenuous to tell one judge that you're fascinated by appellate work, and another judge that you're interested in learning the ropes in state trial court. Judges understand the high hurdles posed by the first-year employment search, and they're not about to hold your disparate interests against you. As long as you don't tell every judge that you write to that the "only thing I've ever wanted to do in my life is intern in your chambers," you're on solid ground. You need to cast your net wide this year. Don't fret about it.

So what should your query letter look like? All the basic rules about correspondence sent to law firms apply equally to correspondence sent to judges. Again, the letter is almost boilerplate, other than whatever personalization you can add. It's a three paragraph letter. In your salutation, remember that United States Supreme Court and state supreme court officers are called "justices" while all other judges in the state and federal courts are called "judges." In the first paragraph, introduce yourself, your law school, and state your purpose. Express your interest in the type of work particular to that court, your connection to the state, and any common interests shared with the judge in the second paragraph. Close by referencing your enclosures, and end with a conservative salutation. Simple and to the point. No frills. An example follows below:

Thomas One El
101 Law School Way
City, State, Zip Code
Phone
E-mail address

Hon. Gavel A. Blackrobe
Federal Courthouse
55 Court St.
Concord, NH 03110

Dear Judge Blackrobe:

    My name is Thomas One El, and I am a first-year law student at the University of XXX Law School. I am seeking an internship in your chambers for the summer of 2000.

As a future litigator, I am particularly interested in learning about the breadth of federal trial practice, from pretrial motions and mediation to *voir dire* and evidentiary issues. I am developing strong research and writing skills during my law school's full-year Legal Research and Writing course, and would love to have the opportunity to develop and hone them further in the context of such an internship. Given my family's ties to the state and my strong interest in hiking and other out-door activities, I am particularly interested in returning to New Hampshire to practice after graduation from law school. Accordingly, I am focusing my job search on opportunities to return to New Hampshire this summer.

Enclosed please find a copy of my current resume and undergraduate transcript from XXX University. My first-semester grades will be available in early February. If there is anything else I can provide, please do not hesitate to contact me.

Respectfully,

Thomas One El

Note the important information conveyed by the letter. In paragraph one—the name of the law school you attend. If it's a nationally-known school, the judge's alma mater, or an in-state school, you'll likely catch the judge's eye. In paragraph two—your justification for applying to his court, your connection to the state where the court sits, and any commonalities shared with the judge (here, hiking and outdoorsmanship, which could be a common interest shared with the judge or a justification for coming to New Hampshire). In the final paragraph, I've worked in the name of my undergraduate school. Again, if it's a nationally-known school, the judge's undergraduate alma mater, or an in-state school, it will help.

Make a chart of all the judges to whom you send letters so you can easily track responses when they arrive. Judges are busy interviewing and selecting law clerks during February and early March, so don't expect too many responses until late March or April. That's why it's so important to cast your net wide. You don't want to come up empty in late April and have to scramble to find something else to do.

Working for a public service organization

A common misperception among first-year law students is that, should you choose to volunteer your time with a public service organization, you'll have your choice of places to volunteer, and can wait until the last minute to make the arrangements.

Think again.

Service organizations, like law firms, deal with real people and real problems. These organizations frequently feature tightly knit and highly energized work environments, and they tend to be very careful about whom they hire. As with law firms and judicial internships, the most popular public service internships—particularly those with the Department of Justice, the U.S. Attorney, state district attorneys' offices, or any well-known national organizations—are going to be highly competitive. Accordingly, query letters for these placements should be sent no later than winter break to ensure the best possible return.

So how do you know what options are available, and how to apply? Again, your first stop should be your law school placement office. They will likely have binders containing lists of public service organizations offering internships, including contact names, addresses, required documentation, and deadlines. If you have a favorite professor, you might also want to ask him to recommend a good service organization for a summer internship.

Once you've compiled a list of contact names and addresses, you'll need to formulate individual query letters for each organization. Avoid using a boilerplate letter and mail merge for these letters—as each of these organizations will be a distinct entity with a different mission that you should address individually. Follow paper and font guidelines as with firm and judge queries, but the text of these letters can be made more personal, expressing the reasons for your interest in the particular organization, your endorsement of their mission, prior related work you've done, etc. There is no one "proper" way to write a query letter to a public service organization. Let your feelings be your guide.

Occasionally, you may find an organization which offers "stipends" for some positions, while other positions in the same organization are strictly voluntary. You'll want to make it clear which position you're applying for, and should you decide to apply for both positions, do so in separate letters sent under separate cover. It's hard to make a convincing case that the organization should give you a stipend, if, in the next paragraph, you make it clear that you're willing to work for free.

Working for a public service organization can be an immensely rewarding experience, both emotionally and intellectually, if you find a placement you're interested in and take an active role in seeking the kind of work you want. In the right situation, you will be given important and challenging work with immediate consequences on human lives.

Researching for a professor

In the weeks just prior to spring break, professors will begin deciding how to spend their summer months away from the classroom. Many professors will sign deals around this time to write a hornbook, edit or contribute to a casebook, or begin work on a law review article that they intend to write during the summer. Many of these professors will need research help and some will be willing to pay for it. If you don't see any signs around the law school by the end of February, ask your favorite professor if he, or one of his colleagues, needs help for the summer. If he isn't writing this summer, chances are, he'll know someone in need of help and can direct you to that person.

The opportunity to work for a law professor carries with it a number of benefits beyond whatever stipend is offered. The experience will likely offer you the rare opportunity to establish a close, one-on-one relationship with a law professor—a relationship which may help you to discover an intellectual curiosity in a particular area of the law, provide you with ideas for a "note" or "comment" if you make the law review or another journal, provide you with an important source for recommendations, and even give you a mentor on the faculty (something that few law students have, but nearly everyone wishes they had).

Research positions are probably the most overlooked opportunity for 1L summer employment, typically because they are perceived as the least prestigious option. Don't be guided by the misperceptions of your classmates, however. It's a position that may open more doors for you than any of the others.

Working it

Remember the take-home lesson from this chapter: Obtaining employment as a first-year law student will be difficult, and any of the positions discussed above will provide you with valuable experience to ground the knowledge you'll soak up during your first year. Just about the only rule of thumb to follow is to do *something* law-related. Accordingly, you may want to send query letters for many or all of these different positions. So how do you "work it" to afford yourself the maximum opportunity to get the position you desire?

If you're interested in law firms, those query letters should go out the first weekend in November. If you're on top of your course work and can also afford to work up letters to public service organizations at that time—all the better. These letters, however, can also be safely sent out during winter break. Follow those letters with query letters for judges by February 1. Finally, start asking professors about research positions in February. Be persistent, and be resilient.

"I sent out a mass mailing to no avail," Allan recalls. "After that, I got bogged down with schoolwork and didn't start looking again until April or so, which was definitely too late. The best advice I can give a 1L would be to apply to firms and judges as soon as possible. As soon as you are allowed to start applying, you should do so."

"And be persistent," Pat adds. "I called up so many places telling them that I wanted to do volunteer work, but this didn't produce any job offers. I was amazed that after a full year of law school I couldn't even give my time away! But I kept at it, and the persistence eventually paid off in the spring."

Remember, all you need is one positive response.

CHAPTER 12

Your First Semester Endgame

The true test of any man lies in action.
—PINDAR

THERE IS LITTLE disagreement that your initial first-year law examination is the single most unnerving experience you will face in your law school career. Sure, you've taken exams before, but chances are, you've rarely, if ever faced a situation where a single four-hour examination will be the sole determinant of your entire semester grade. The experience will be unfamiliar, the setting can be very intimidating, and unscrupulous classmates may even try to rattle you to throw you off your game—a confluence of factors which can be a recipe for disaster.

We pick up the story one week prior to the end of your first semester—which, for most of you, should be around the first week of December. If you've been keeping up with the preceding chapters, you should at this point have a completed outline (minus the final week of lectures) for each of your classes. We're now in the endgame—the critical time of the semester which ultimately decides who gets the A's and who doesn't. Things should have started getting crazy some weeks ago, but the insecurity and the levels of stress among your classmates should be reaching fever pitch right about now. For you, this means only one thing . . .

It's time to find an off-campus location to study

That's right. It's time to leave. Take what you need with you and then get yourself out of the law library, and out of the law school. Now is the time to seek sanctuary in your secret spot in the stacks of the undergraduate library, at the table in the never-visited map room, or even in your own apartment if you can stand being cooped up there all the time. Just don't hang around the law school!

Why?

Because anxiety is contagious, and you don't want to catch it.

Permit me a story.

During my first year of law school, as I've mentioned before, I lived in the graduate dorms at the center of the law student floors—basically right at ground zero for first-year anxiety and stress. I had created what I thought was the ideal sanctuarial work environment—incense burning, a collection of Windham Hill instrumental music playing in the stereo, and a steaming mug of tea at my side—and I was being very productive.

Then, it started.

The phone rang—parents inquiring about my progress and wishing me well, friends calling to chastise me for being out of touch for months, and to finalize plans for our annual Christmas-week ski trip, and classmates calling to ask questions, ask for notes, or just to bitch about the whole thing. Then came the knocks at the door from classmates looking for notes, outlines and study aids, or friends on different study schedules looking to take a study break. Then, there was always the game on TV which required a "score check" every thirty minutes or so, and, of course, every time the computer beeped in with a new e-mail message—well—it had to be answered promptly, right?

All of this distraction, however, was nothing compared to what happened a night or two later. It was just before midnight, and I was at my desk working on Civil Procedure. Suddenly, there was a blood-curdling shriek from the hallway just outside my room. When I opened the door to investigate, I found one of my class-mates slumped against a wall just down the hall sobbing, and on the edge of madness. As soon as she saw me, she ran over to me, clutched at my arm, and started babbling almost incoherently between sobs about jurisdiction, going on hysterically about last year's exam (which I hadn't looked at yet), and assuring me that she was going to fail.

So much for my little sanctuary. I could feel the blood rushing to my head, and my mouth ran dry. After talking to my frenzied classmate for a couple of minutes, I was completely stressed out myself. I didn't understand half of what she was asking me about.

After she left my room, I called a friend downtown, packed my books and some clothes, and moved out of the dorm, not to be seen again until the beginning of the spring semester.

Avoid the center of the maelstrom at all costs—because once you get infected with anxiety, it's very hard to get rid of it.

"The panic point for me in the first semester was Thanksgiving break," Steve recalls. "Everyone said Thanksgiving was when things got serious, so I knew that I had to be ready for the post-holiday crunch. Despite that, when I returned from break, the pressure was there instantly. There were only a couple of weeks left until finals, and you start realizing how little you know . . . not just in the sense of what has been covered in the courses, but in the sense of what finals will be like. No matter how laid back you are, there's no way to avoid feeling pressure, and you can't help but panic a bit. The thing is, there is no way to overcome the pressure and panic. You just have to work through it and cling to the thought that in a month, it will all be over."

"Try not to worry too much," Allan notes. "Go at your own pace, and don't let other people's study habits affect you. Once you've decided on an approach, stick to it."

Elizabeth agrees. "My most effective strategy was keeping to myself. I avoided study groups, avoided people who were panicking, and played by my own rules."

Okay—so you're somewhere else—away from your classmates and most potential distractions. Now what?

Now it's time to get busy with the fifth and final step of my five-step briefing method that I taught you in Chapter 8. This week, you'll be distilling your outlines down to single-page "maps" or "bullet outlines" of the law you covered during the semester. This way, you can see exactly how the law developed and how it all fits together.

"My theory about law classes is that there are three "stages" one goes through in preparing for an exam," Carolyn explained. "Stage one is getting a superficial understanding of what the law is—like you could get from just reading a commercial outline a couple of times. Stage two is where you lose the forest for the trees by working through the detail and complexities of the cases in the area of law you are studying. Stage three is where you put it all together— you have an understanding of the detail and complexity of the case law, and you know how it all fits together. Obviously, it is ideal to be at stage three when you take an exam, but it is better to be at stage one than to be at stage two.

The classes I did the worst in were those in which I got bogged down outlining and obsessing about details. When this happened, I would get into an exam and forget even the most fundamental black letter law in the subject area. If you find yourself in this position a week before an exam, recognize that you are trapped at stage two, force yourself to stop outlining, and simply work through a completed outline. Master that outline and then work through some practice exams with it," Carolyn suggests.

Mapping out the law

At this point, you're probably thinking—*What?* I've just spent the last three months writing these masterful outlines and now he's telling me that I need to distill them down to the point where I might not even get to use them?

Absolutely. Know why?

Your outlines for each class are probably between 60 and 120 pages long, and aren't in a format that you can glance at quickly to spot issues or to easily see how the different lines of cases fit together. Putting these outlines together, however, has forced you to synthesize and organize the cases you read into a comprehensible structure that you'll later be able to use and apply to the hypotheticals of new facts that you'll find on most of your exams. Naturally, writing these outlines has also forced you to understand the doctrines better and has given you a level of knowledge that you never would have had simply by reading the cases and going to lecture.

Your experiences up to this point have given you the raw materials. Now, however, it's time to hone the tools you need for serious exam success.

Find your first semester classes on the list below, and take note of the tools I recommend that you put in your arsenal for that exam. Then read on for complete instructions on how to create those tools for yourself.

Civil Procedure	map and bullet points
Contracts	map and bullet points
Torts	bullet points
Property	bullet points
Criminal Law	bullet points and map
Constitutional Law	map
Criminal Procedure	map
Administrative Law	map
Labor Law	map

How to create a "case map"

Tape together six sheets of blank, white $8\frac{1}{2} \times 11$ paper to create a large, foldable blank map. Grab an outline for a class listed above that requires a map. Flip through your course syllabus, the outline, or the table of contents of the corresponding casebook or commercial outline to determine how the material is organized. For example, your Contracts outline is probably most broadly divided into five separate sections covering (1) offer; (2) acceptance; (3) consideration; (4) damages; and (5) equitable remedies. Consequently, your case map should be divided into separate case chains for each of these areas, with lines and arrows connecting the various sections of the chains as required. Go through your entire outline carefully, placing each case and its holding into its proper place in the chain. Limit yourself to a case name, date, court, a single line stating the holding of the case, and a number citing you to the page number in your outline where the case is discussed. **Do**

not rewrite your outline on your map. Your map is visual, the outline is substantive. These two resources must work in conjunction, so there's no reason to try to make one the substitute for the other.

Creating a bullet outline

A bullet outline is most useful for classes where general principles can be succinctly stated in a series of elements or steps—and where the development of the doctrine is somewhat less important than the ensuing result. Introductory Torts, for example, is a largely black-letter subject. In preparing for your Torts exam, it is generally more important to know that the elements of negligence are: (1) a duty of care; (2) breach of that duty; (3) causation; and (4) damages, than it is to know details of the cases in your casebook that illustrate the particular tort. In Torts, "theory" is primarily relegated to questions of risk-allocation and damage calculation. Most law school Torts exams, thus, usually consist of (1) some multiple choice or short answer questions addressing the elemental requirements of different torts, and (2) a large "issue spotter" essay where you need to identify and evaluate as many torts as possible in the allotted time. If you attend a law school that emphasizes theory, your Torts exam may also feature a theoretical essay at the end. To perform well on an exam like this—it should be clear that having a list of torts and their individual elements will be more helpful to you than a map of the development of the doctrine.

Accordingly, for an exam like Torts, Property, or Criminal Law (if it is taught without Constitutional Criminal Procedure), we'll develop bullet point "checklists" in lieu of a case map. These checklists will function the same way as a map—helping you to spot issues and address each of the elements of each tort. So how do you develop a checklist like this?

Once again, start with the index of your casebook or a good commercial outline. Using Torts as a continuing example, go through the index and first make a list of all the torts you covered in class. Under each tort, make a list of its required elements. Once you've done this, go through your outline and add in any clarifying information or illustrative examples discussed in the cases or lectures for these elements. For the tort of "negligence," then, you'd start by listing the tort and its elements (duty of care, breach of that duty, causation, and damages). But you won't stop there. Under the "duty" element, bullet out what you learned about what constitutes a "duty," and when you have a "duty." Under causation, bullet out what you learned about the doctrines of proximate cause, and "last clear chance," and the law of the "intervening actor." Under damages, you'd list the different theories of damages, and mitigating factors like contributory and comparative negligence. Remember—you're not trying to recreate your outline. A bullet outline is purely for recall and issue spotting. Cross reference pages in your outline to point yourself to more detail so you'll have it at your fingertips if you need it.

Taking sample exams

Once you have all of these materials prepared and assembled for a class, you are ready to start taking sample exams. Try to take at least one exam under real testing conditions, so you'll get a sense for the timing required. Whenever possible, take a sample exam for which the professor has made a model answer available. That way, when you finish, you actually have something to which to compare your answers. This brings us to a critical point, however. Do not expect to address everything that you'll find in the model answer. The model answer is just that—a "model." Typically, it is either an amalgam of the best student responses or an answer written by the professor with unlimited time and resources and his mastery of the subject at hand.

Don't "freak out" if you missed an issue or two. Instead, ask yourself how confident you felt answering the exam questions. Did you have a good idea of what the questions were getting at? Did the issues seem to "jump off the page" at you while you were reading the question? Did you identify and discuss most of the key issues? That's what you're looking for at this point. Don't forget to use your maps, checklists, and your outline during the exam. It's meant to be a realistic trial run.

Don't worry too much if you find things in the sample exam that your professor didn't cover this year—or even if you find things in the model answer that seem to be dead wrong compared to what you learned in class—particularly if the exam and model answer are several years old. The professor may have changed the focus of the course, and the law may have changed too. Rely on your current outlines, not on what you read in a model answer.

> The classes in which I had the greatest success were those classes in which I had prepared my own outline, taken time to review the outline and become familiar with it, and then taken time to do practice exams using the outline, so I could get comfortable using it.
>
> —Carolyn

Finally, remember that a sample exam is just that—a sample. It's a non-counting dry run. Don't be rattled by the experience. The only exam that counts is the one that you'll take in class.

Review sessions

To go or not to go. That is the question.

The answer depends, in large part, on your personality. Start with the premise that you will learn more substantive law by going to your professor's office hours and banging out all of your questions there than you will ever learn in a review session. If you want substantive questions cleared up—go to office hours, not to a review session. You go to a review session to attempt to steal the exam from the professor.

No, you read that right. If you go to a review session and listen carefully, you can often glean critical information about the structure and content of the exam—which can substantially simplify your preparation. Typically, during the review session, some eager student will ask the professor to discuss the format of the exam. By this time, your prof has probably already written the exam, so she'll inevitably be commenting on the actual exam you're about to take, and she may discuss it in some specificity. Listen carefully to everything that comes out of the professor's mouth about the exam—particularly her responses to students' questions. Little throwaway phrases like, "yeah, that's important," or "good question," or any in-depth analysis the professor undertakes during the review session may tip you off to material implicated on the exam. Conversely, if a student asks a question about a particular area of the law and the professor responds, "don't worry too much about that"—that should immediately translate "forget it, it's not on the exam." Pay particular attention to anything the professor writes on the board during a review session—as it is likely to be important to the exam, and write down any hypotheticals she covers, as they may closely mimic exam questions.

> Know your professor. Is there some theme she has mentioned
> again and again throughout the semester? If there is, there's
> an excellent chance you'll see it one more time—on the exam.
> —Joel

Finally, listen carefully to any suggestions the professor makes about how to structure your exam answers. If she tells you she prefers the answers to be written in black pen, be sure to write in black pen. If she tells you to print and skip lines, do it. I once had a professor state in a very sparsely attended review session that he preferred "essay" questions to be answered in outline form, with lots of letters, numbers, and bullet points, because he had an answer key he was working from and it made it easier to check off points in an outline than points in prose text. Interestingly, he mentioned this **only** in the review session!

In the average law school class, fewer than half the students will attend the review session. Needless to say, that gives you a significant advantage if anything significant comes to light—and remember the mantra of this book—success in law school is all about getting a little bit of an edge.

So, if this is true, you ask, why don't more students attend them?

First of all, most students are too far behind in their exam preparation to spare the time to go to a review session in the final week of the semester. Others have been frustrated by past sessions that didn't actually function as a "review," or where they couldn't get their questions answered because other students monopolized the questioning. In other words, these students went to the review session for the wrong reasons and ended up disappointed. However, if you go to a review session looking for exam hints, you'll rarely leave without gaining some insight.

In my mind, the *only* valid reason for not attending a review session is if you know that you are overly anxious about the subject and will be unable to sit through other students' questions without panicking. Remember that much of success in law school is about confidence, and the worst thing you can do before an exam is sabotage your confidence. If you fall into this category, try to remember that most people who ask questions are confused—and don't listen to anyone except the professor. If you follow this advice, you should be able to overcome your anxiety.

The final hours

A few final words about pre-exam preparation. Don't discuss your preparation with anyone except a study partner or the members of your study group. Nothing will bring on self-doubt and paranoia faster than finding out that you have taken a different approach to preparing for an exam than your classmates have. There's no telling whose methods are better, and since you're the one using this book, forget about everyone else. Trust my advice, and trust yourself.

On the eve of an exam, gather all the materials you'll be taking into the exam room in one place. Be sure you have your exam ticket, photo identification, a watch, and a sufficient supply of pens. If the administration allows you to bring food and beverages into the exam, bring a PowerBar (or the like), a couple of rolls of Life-Savers, and a bottle of water—each of which will give you a little boost when you need it most. You want to be as calm as possible on the morning of your exam, and the last thing you want to be doing is scurrying around looking for things.

Finally, and perhaps more importantly, stop studying around dinnertime the night before your exam. Acknowledge that you'll never master all the material. Think about how far you've come with the doctrine and how much you've learned about the subject since the beginning of the semester, and then go do something fun and relaxing to take the pressure off. Take a long walk, grab a workout, or go to a movie—just don't study. Don't drink to excess or take anything to help you sleep, since you don't want to be groggy in the morning. Go to bed a bit early, and try to make peace with yourself knowing that you've done all that you could possibly do.

Exam day

The big day has come.

Get up a little earlier than usual and collect yourself. Force yourself to eat a good breakfast. You'll be surprised how draining a four hour exam can be, and you'll need the resources.

Get to the exam room at least twenty minutes before the exam is scheduled to start and scope out a good seat if you're allowed to choose your seating. The best seats in an exam are the seats that minimize distractions—typically the seats in the front and back corners of the exam room, and the seats farthest away from exit doors. Gather up a supply of bluebooks and scratch paper so you can use one bluebook per essay response and so you won't need to get up during the exam when every minute counts. Spread out your materials to make them easily accessible. Relax, and above all, don't talk to your classmates about any substantive law, or eavesdrop on any such discussion. Block it all out. When ten minutes remain before the start of the exam, take a precautionary bathroom break to stave off any need to leave the exam room during the next four hours.

The exam itself

Perhaps the most important piece of advice I can give you about taking a law school exam is to **budget your time.** The most common and most destructive exam mistake made by first-year students is spending too much time on any one question, and coming to the end of the exam with only ten minutes left to respond to an equally weighted final essay. Do not let this happen to you. Be disciplined! The second important rule of first-year examsmanship is that you need not spend all of your time writing. In fact, you shouldn't. These two rules, working in concert, can help to ensure that your exam-room performance is as relaxing and productive as possible.

When you first get your exam and the proctor gives you the green light to begin work, take a deep breath, sit back, and read.

Just read. Let the questions wash over you, and let your subconscious mind begin working on the answers. When you've read through the entire exam once, determine how the points are allocated between questions, determine the order in which you want to attack the questions (remembering that there is no requirement to do them in order), and then physically write down on the exam itself at what time you have to move on to the next question. For example, for a three-hour exam with twenty-five multiple choice questions worth one point each, five short answer questions worth five points each, and two essay questions worth twenty-five points each—you should devote forty-five minutes to the multiple choice questions (or slightly less than two minutes each), forty-five minutes to the short answer questions (nine minutes each), and forty-five minutes to each essay. You must *force* yourself to stay on this schedule no matter what. When your time on a particular section expires, wrap up and move on.

Continuing with the same example, and assuming a three hour exam that begins at 9 A.M. and that you're taking the sections in the order given above, write 9:45 at the top of the multiple choice section, 10:30 at the top of the short answer section, 11:15 at the top of the first essay, and 12:00 at the top of the second essay. Start working the multiple choice questions. Bang them out in order and skip any that you can't answer. Remember the technique you used on the LSAT and cross out any clearly wrong responses as you read them so you won't waste time re-reading wrong responses on your second pass-through. Remember that you have less than two minutes to respond to each question. At 9:45, guess on any questions you have not yet answered, and move on to the next section, regardless of how many questions you have left. Begin attacking the short answer questions, remembering that you have only nine minutes to spend on each question. Don't fall into the trap of spending fifteen or twenty minutes on the really tough question you're almost certain to find in this section. It's a trap for the unwary—designed to keep people from getting to the essay questions, and thus, to make the grades easier to distinguish from each other. Hit and move on. Include as much relevant information as you can, but when the nine minute interval has expired, force yourself to keep moving. Remember that no one will get the full number of points on the exam, so you won't need full credit on every answer to do well.

At 10:30, decide which of the two essays you want to deal with first, and re-read it. As you read, spot issues and mark up the text of the question accordingly. When you've finished doing this, take a deep breath, sit back, and carefully read the paragraph(s) at the end of the question where the professor lays out the question(s) he wants you to answer. Take time to think about and sketch out a brief outline of your response to the question(s). It is perfectly acceptable to spend the first fifteen to twenty minutes of a forty-five minute essay reading the question carefully, spotting the issues, and organizing your response. A well-thought out, well-organized response will almost always outpoint a rambling, disorganized answer with crossouts and arrows drawn all over it.

Use headings whenever possible to help guide your professor through your response, and don't waffle or equivocate. If the question requires you to take a position, take one—and remember that on most law school exams, it's not the position you take, but how you *defend* that position with applicable law and policy, that determines your grade. If you must equivocate, or if the outcome of a question is seriously in doubt, take what you perceive to be the stronger position in your heading, and then add a sentence or two of potential alternative outcomes at the end of your response. Adopting this structural approach to answering essay exams will make your exam read more clearly and look more professional— attributes which almost always translate into higher grades.

> Remember to go through your analysis in logical steps, from beginning to end. The order in which you present your ideas is more important on a law school exam than it ever was in an essay or on a term paper. Include only those facts and issues which are relevant, but don't exclude basic principles because you think they are too obvious.
>
> —Elizabeth

A couple of final pieces of advice. First, answer *only* the questions the professor asked you to answer—don't waste your time with extraneous issues or go off on a tangent for the sake of getting more of what you know down on paper. Chances are, if it's not on the professor's grading sheet, you're probably not going to get credit for it. Finally, if you perceive a problem with the question or must make any assumptions prior to giving a response—be sure to note your assumption at the top of your response to make the professor aware of the perceived ambiguity.

But wait . . . my exam is closed-book!

There are very few compelling arguments favoring the administration of a closed-book law exam. With the exception of think-on-the-fly evidence questions in a deposition or in trial, you will almost never have to respond to a legal question without the aid of some resources. Consequently, in a perfect world, closed-book exams should rarely be given. Occasionally, however, you will run into a hard-headed professor who doesn't conform his teaching to the realities of legal practice. Faced with this circumstance, your preparations should be identical to your preparations for an open-book exam, with an additional day or two budgeted into your study time to allow for mnemonic development and memorization.

Rest assured that students' answers on a closed-book exam will be of a significantly lower quality than the answers given in an open-book exam where case names and other information is accessible. Don't dismay if you draw a blank on a case name, or if one of your mnemonics fails you in the exam room. Don't be a prisoner to memorization. When all else fails, remember that you wrote outlines and case maps and spent a long time working with the doctrine before you memorized anything—so think back to the general themes of the course and the way the law developed and work from there.

The "doomsday scenario"

It's virtually a guarantee that you will face the doomsday scenario at least once during your law school career. For me, it happened during my first-year contracts exam. The three essay (each with multiple parts) exam was slated to last four-and-a-half hours. I had prepared my own extensive contracts outline, and knew the cases from the class cold—but I did not prepare the bullet outline that would have spared me this brush with disaster. I got the exam, read over the three essay questions, and began to outline the first question, but quickly got stuck. I moved to the second essay, worked through part of that one, and got stuck. Now, about forty-five minutes into the exam with nothing to show for my effort, I began to panic. I moved to the third essay, read it, and couldn't even spot an issue in it. With classmates writing furiously all around me, I sensed the walls beginning to close in around me, and felt a lump rising in my throat. I checked, and rechecked, and re-rechecked the time, and went back to the first essay, but after flipping through my outline, I couldn't resolve my mental block.

A full ninety minutes had passed, and I still didn't have a word written down in a bluebook. I was looking at certain failure, and with this growing realization, I became incapable of even reading the words on the paper in front of me. We're talking a complete mental meltdown. Then, I made the move that almost certainly saved my skin on the exam.

I got up and walked out.

Yup. Left the exam hall, went to the bathroom, took some deep breaths, and splashed some cold water on my face. I imagined skiing in Colorado over winter break, and inhaling the crisp winter air. Knowing that I was facing a disaster in progress, I calmed myself down, rechecked the time and realized that I had two hours and fifteen minutes left to answer all three essay questions—or forty-five minutes per question. I then reentered the exam room, sat down, pushed my outline aside, and resolved to just write down what I knew.

Two hours later, I had written what I felt was the bare minimum on the three essays, and left the exam room feeling thoroughly beaten and humiliated—but at least I had managed to beat the mental block and get *something* down on paper for each essay. Outside the exam room, there was panic and distress in the air, as exasperated students expressed their dismay at the difficulty of the questions. It seems that I was not alone in my confusion. My spirits were somewhat lifted by hearing this, but I was still gravely concerned about reeling in a C or worse.

When grades came out, however, I was pleasantly surprised to discover that my resuscitation efforts had earned me a B on the exam—hardly a stellar grade—but a pretty good "save" considering the dire circumstances I found myself in. As bad as the situation seemed at the time, it proved not to be the end of the world.

I share this story with you to arm you for your inevitable confrontation with the doomsday scenario. If an exam has you on the ropes, remember this story, and don't be afraid to take a walk to clear your head and refocus your resolve.

THE PERFORMANCE SELF-EXAMINATION: PART ONE

Immediately after you take each exam, no matter how tired, fed-up, or anxious you are—you need to force yourself to sit down for a few minutes and indulge in the following exercise.

In the table that follows, fill in the name of each of your first semester classes in the space provided, and then, as soon as you finish an exam for a particular class, answer each of the questions in the table in the column for that class. Be as complete and as honest as possible. Put your responses right here in the book, in the spaces provided. Spill over into the margins if you need to. Remember this is your book—and you only do law school once, so scribble at will.

After you've taken all of your exams, the notes you put here will be a testament to your preparation for, and execution of each particular exam. Then, when your grades come out next semester, you'll put those into the chart and be able to compare how you did in each class to the way you prepared in the hopes of making some distinctions about what worked and did not work for you.

First Semester Performance Evaluation (Part One)

Name of Class				
Grade received				
Number of lectures skipped				
Statute/code/ rules based class or case law based class (e.g. tax (code based) vs. Con Law (case based)				
% of reading assignments completed on time				
Duration of class period and time of day it met				
Professorial style (Socratic/lecture)				
Male or female professor?				
Seat location (front/mid./ back)				
Did you sit next to friends or other distractions during class periods?				
Brand of comm. outline/hornbook used				
Did you use the commercial outline as directed by Chapter 6 of this book?				
Did you participate in a study group?				
Number of times you went to office hours				

FIRST SEMESTER PERFORMANCE EVALUATION

Did you attend the review session?				
Did you make your own outline?				
Did you make your own bullet point outline, map, or checklist? Which?				
How many sample tests did you take?				
Was exam open or closed book?				
Was exam essay, multiple choice, or mixed?				
Was exam a take-home or in-class?				
How did you spend the night before the exam?				
How many hours of sleep did you get the night before the exam?				
Did you wake up feeling well-rested?				
What did you have for your pre-exam meal?				
Did you eat or drink anything during the exam?				
Where did you sit in the exam room?				
Were you bothered by any distractions in the exam room?				
Did you take a bathroom break to clear your head?				

FIRST SEMESTER PERFORMANCE EVALUATION

Did you take time to read the questions carefully and outline a response before you began writing?				
Did you organize your exam answers well with headings, letters, and numbers as in a memorandum?				
Did you write in blue or black pen?				
Did you skip lines and write on only one side of a page?				
Did you print, type, or write legibly?				
Did you have problems with time?				
Any other thoughts				

Now for each class, consider what you brought with you into the exam room. What did you depend on the most? The least? What did you never look at? What *would* have been helpful to you if you had it in the exam room? How might you have been better prepared for the exam? Should you have known more policy and theory? More case names? Should you have spent less time with individual cases and more time on the big picture? Write down your responses to these questions in the space below.

CLASS ONE: _____

_____

_____

_____

CLASS TWO: _____

_____

_____

_____

CLASS THREE: _____

_____

_____

_____

CLASS FOUR: _____

_____

_____

_____

Good.

Now you have a permanent record of things while they are fresh in your mind. When your grades come out, come back to this chart, put them in at the top of each column, and try to make some distinctions based on your results.

For now, though, go home and relax. Have a good time. Indulge yourself in the holidays, the company of friends and family, bad television, trashy novels, sun, skiing, or whatever else suits you. Don't dwell on your exams—they're history now, and there's nothing you can do to change them. You'll take part two of this performance self-exam on the day your grades come out.

CHAPTER 13

Looking Behind and Looking Ahead: Assessing the Damage and Charting the Course for Your Second Semester

An error gracefully acknowledged is a victory won.
—GEORGES GASCOIGNE

So YOU SURVIVED your first semester of law school. You arrived home craving nothing more than sleep and several days of mindless television, but instead, were forced to tolerate Uncle Bernie's incessant questions, and your mother's annoying references to "my son/daughter, the budding lawyer." But somewhere, alone in the dark, however briefly, you probably found yourself smiling in tacit recognition of what you've just accomplished. Although the worst is only half over, you're a survivor. Whether you're anything more than that will be determined by a slip of paper with four letters on it that you'll receive sometime in late January.

Your grades.

The only commemoration of the war you waged against yourself and your classmates during your first semester of law school. The fruit of nearly four months of arduous labor. The cold, hard truth.

So what do you do if the news is bad?

First of all, we need to discuss what standards we're using to evaluate performance. This is not college, and although law schools definitely still practice grade inflation, getting straight A's in all four first semester classes is a very rare occurrence in most law schools. The majority of students receive a mix of grades. Starting with that as the realistic standard, let's evaluate *your* first semester grades.

Every school uses a different grading system, and inflates grades to varying degrees. Some schools use a strict B– mean, while other schools scale up to B or B+ mean. You may already know what the mean grade at your school is, but if you don't—look on the walls near the registrar's office for the compiled grade distributions from last semester's exams. Specifically, check the grade distributions in the sections taught by the professors you had. Almost every law school compiles these grade distributions section by section to assess the reliability of grading between sections, and to assure that one first year professor is not grading radically easier or harder than another. As I discussed earlier, to encourage this result, many law schools employ a strict bell curve for first year grades, assuring that each section has twenty percent A's, forty percent B+'s, and forty percent B's and B–'s, or some such arrangement. If you can't find the distributions posted anywhere, ask the registrar for the information.

So what does it look like? Where are your grades compared to the grades of the people in your section? Glance at the headings below. Determine which one is most applicable to you, and read on.

I got straight A's, mostly A's and B+'s, or I am ahead of the curve in most classes

If your first semester grades fall into this category, you are now in the pole position in the race to secure a job during your 1L summer, a seat on the law review or one of the other journals at your law school, and the plum interviews with employers next fall. You are also at a huge psychological advantage given that you found a formula that worked at getting you the grades you want and deserve. Congratulations on your outstanding results, but don't rest on your laurels. The hallowed halls of law school are littered with the broken dreams of students who got off to great starts after their first semester, but then became cocky or complacent.

Flip to the middle of this chapter and take part two of the performance self-evaluation. Try to concretize the formula you used to achieve success in the classes where you met with success, so you can go back to that formula again and again this semester, and on into the future.

HOW TO SPIN THESE GRADES: Frankly, you won't need to spin anything. You're in position to attract maximum attention from employers looking to hire 1L help. Be sure to send a photocopy of your grades and a brief cover letter to any employers you contacted back in November that haven't already rejected you. Prepare to get some favorable attention. Remember to practice humility, and not to discuss your grades with your classmates. When asked, just say, "I did okay."

I got a mix of grades, some ahead and some behind the curve

If you got a mix of grades, perhaps something like A–, B+, B, B, you are part of the perplexing group that includes most first-year law students. Ahead of the curve in one or two classes, dead at the mean in a class or two, and behind the mean in the last class, you wonder what caused the discrepancy in your results.

That's precisely what you need to find out—and that's what we'll be doing in part two of the performance self-examination later in this chapter. In the meantime, however, don't worry too much. You're probably right in the middle of the pack, within striking distance of making law review with a good second semester, and with grades that aren't going to scare off potential 1L employers. Spend some time with the performance self-examination. In your position, with a mix of grades, you have the most to learn, and the best opportunity to draw distinctions between strategies and approaches that worked for you, and those that didn't.

HOW TO SPIN THESE GRADES: Because a combination of grades is very common, they won't hurt your chances of getting summer employment—they just won't get you any additional attention. If you went to an outstanding undergraduate institution (like an Ivy League university or its equivalent), graduated with an excellent GPA, and have a strong resume, wait for potential employers to contact you to request grades. It's possible that some employers will hire you on the strength of your undergraduate record without waiting for your first semester grades. Since your grades aren't anything to be ashamed of, send your transcript immediately to any employer that requests it.

If, on the other hand, you went to a second or third-tier undergraduate school, or had an average undergraduate record, you may want to be a bit more proactive and send your grades out to your top choice potential 1L employers without waiting for them to contact you. The operative rule here is this: getting a 1L position is extremely difficult. If you think your first semester grades improve your overall record, send them out right away. If they detract from a sterling undergraduate record, wait until employers solicit them.

One grade is widely disparate from the others

Hopefully this means three A's and a B-, but even if it means three B's and an A, you are in a great position to learn something about why one class worked out so differently from the others. Go to the performance self-examination later in this chapter and compare your preparation for the disparate class with the others in an effort to make distinctions to help you in the future.

HOW TO SPIN THESE GRADES: If you got three A's and a B- (or a close equivalent), you had a bad day. You misread, or mistimed a question. The professor tricked you with a tough question. You are almost certain to be asked, either this year in a 1L employment interview, or next fall in 2L recruiting about "What happened?" in the disparate class. Don't run and hide from a bad grade. Embrace it, and discuss it candidly. Few law students escape law school without at least one low grade. Almost every law firm recruiter will have a war story of his own. Tell yours, and laugh about it.

If, on the other hand, you have one very good grade and three mediocre ones, is it because you were really interested in the subject you did well in? Is it because late in the semester, you figured something out about law school, and applied it in that class with great results? Figure out a way to show a potential employer that you learned something from first semester, and are excited about the distinctions you made. People know that first semester can be a very difficult period of adjustment. If you can show both that the experience didn't destroy you, and that you are actively pursuing ways to improve, you might impress an employer enough to take a chance on you.

All grades at or below the mean

You are probably somewhat depressed about this outcome, and, after all the work you put in during the first semester, that's understandable. But did you really put in the time? Were you really disciplined? Did you follow the advice of the earlier chapters in this book, by preparing your own outlines, staying current in your reading, and not missing classes? Or did you party too much, spend too much time with a new love interest, or underestimate how hard you really have to work to do well? When you complete part two of the performance self-evaluation, spend some time thinking about how you spent your first semester, day by day. Be honest with yourself. Did you really put in your time? Get your exam responses and look them over. Compare them to any model answers the professor might provide.

If, after honest introspection, you really feel like you worked as hard as your classmates did, you followed the advice given in the previous chapters, and you are at a loss, it's time to take the next step. Make appointments and talk to each of your professors from last semester. Ask them for their advice on ways you might improve your performance. Do not allow your bitterness or embarrassment to stop you from turning this seemingly negative experience into a positive chance to learn something. Speak candidly to each professor. Ask each of them for their advice. Although one or two of them might brush you off, chances are you'll find one or two of them who will want to help you. Listen carefully to what they say, and write down any suggestions they make. By opening up to a professor, you might establish the rapport necessary to turn one of these professors into a mentor.

HOW TO SPIN THESE GRADES: I have to be honest here. Getting four B's (or worse) during your first semester puts you into a bit of a hole. Those grades aren't going to attract 1L employers, and they're going to make it pretty hard for you to grade onto the law review, even with a sterling second semester.

So should you just pack up and go home?

Of course not.

First of all, you need to spring into action the day you first find out about these grades. Chances are, you'll get your grades first by calling the automated grade retrieval system or looking them up on your law school web page. These grades, however, are still unofficial, and can occasionally be changed if errors in the curve, or errors in grading are subsequently discovered. It will likely be a couple of weeks before you receive "official" notice of these grades from the registrar.

In the meantime, call in every favor you can. If anyone you know well works for a firm that you've queried, particularly in your hometown or home state, it's time to make a frontal attack on that firm with everything you have. Call them immediately to determine the status of your query. Offer to come up and interview at your own expense. Make them refuse you on the phone before you give up. If you are asked about your first semester grades, tell them that you'll be getting official notice from the registrar in a couple of weeks. This may buy you the critical time you need to get the firm to make you an offer. What you're hoping for is that they'll hire you on the strength of the personal relationship you have with the person there, on the strength of your undergraduate resume, or because they have a need they are impatient to fill, without seeing your first semester grades. If the firm wants to wait to see your first semester grades, there is nothing you can do about that. Although this should go without saying, under no circumstance should you ever lie about or misrepresent your grades.

Grades are critical, and without good grades, you have a much more difficult task to secure 1L summer employment. Don't give up, though. Somewhere out there, there is a judge who will bring you on as an intern, or a public service organization or a professor in need of free research assistance. Keep asking around. Use the professors you talked to as networking resources. Go to your career placement office and ask for advice.

When you do get an interview for a position, don't apologize for your grades, and don't hide from them. They're out there, and you're going to be asked about them. Have a well thought-out response ready. Explain what you learned from first semester. Tell the interviewer about the distinctions you've made, and how you're applying them to improve this semester. Be self-deprecating, but be confident. It is, after all, only one semester. If your credentials were impressive enough to get you into law school—you still have a proven track record to build on.

"In college, I had become accustomed to a steady stream of A's and A minuses with an occasional B, but in my first year of law school, I got a steady stream of B's with an occasional A or A minus," Joel notes. "I was unhappy, but I don't have many words of wisdom here except to say that law school is hard—it's full of smart people, and the curve is generally steeper than the curves in college. Don't be defined by your grades, and don't think that your occasional answer in class or your comments in study group aren't worth making because you didn't get straight A's during your first semester. Your grades are not you—they're just your grades."

THE PERFORMANCE SELF-EXAMINATION (PART TWO)

Go back to the table in the last chapter and write in the grade you received for each of your classes. Whether your grades were perfect, perfectly awful, or anywhere in between, you have something to learn from the following exercise. Answer the following questions as truthfully and completely as possible.

If there were differences among your grades, look at the different variables in the table and highlight any differences between the classes you did well in and the classes you struggled in. What do you notice about the classes you did well in? What did you do differently in the classes where you faltered? Answers to these questions might not be immediately obvious. There might not seem to be any correlation. That's part of what makes law school so frustrating—sometimes, it just seems like the grades are handed out randomly. But perhaps there is something hiding in this chart you've just filled out. Look for any distinctions you can draw. Remember that to succeed in law school, you only need to be a little bit better than everybody else.

Don't get too caught up on your grades, though. The exams are subjective, there is no exact formula for grading them, and often there is not much of a difference in performance between one letter grade and another.

—Allan

So now, you face a new semester, clean textbooks, and a fresh start. Take one more look at the chart you filled out in the last chapter and remind yourself what you learned and the new approaches you are going to bring with you into the new semester. Don't fall into the same traps that caught you last semester!

"I stopped briefing cases and concentrated on doing all the reading and making some notes in the margins," Allan states. "I think this system was much more efficient. You get used to reading cases and what you're looking for, so you absorb a lot more."

"Second semester, I picked the two classes I really wanted to 'master,' and decided early on that I wanted to prepare my own complete outlines for those classes. I prepared outlines for both of these classes and shared them with my study partner in exchange for his outlines for the other two classes. This system worked really well," Carolyn notes.

"My biggest lesson after first semester was that my writing style needed to change," Elizabeth adds. "If you were an English major or a history major, or a major in a similar subject, yours may need to change too. I discovered that I could no longer write in a flowery, free-flowing style. Legal writing is crisp, brief, and to the point."

So what are the things you are going to change about your approach to the new semester? Write them in the space provided below so you can refer back to them and so you don't forget what they are.

_____

_____

_____

_____

You may have the choice of one or two elective courses during your second semester. If you do have such a choice, choose wisely. In law school, you have a limited number of credit hours at your disposal, and you can't afford to waste any of them. Every choice should be made for a reason, so before you take a course, ask yourself what purpose the course will serve in your "grand scheme." This is a good time to begin thinking what approach you want to take to the rest of law school. To get a head start, jump ahead to Chapter 16 and read about the different philosophies you can take to your upper years in law school.

"I took a practical skills type of class rather than another big doctrinal course. This was a good strategy for me, because it was a change of pace from the rest of the first-year offerings," Joel recalls.

"I tried to take the courses with the professors I heard were the best," Alison adds.

Finally, with a semester of law school under your belt, you may start to feel restless and drawn toward doing some public service work, or participating in some of the various extra-curricular activities at the law school or in the larger university community. My advice is to wait a few weeks until you get a feel for whether your schedule is actually any lighter this semester. Remember this is still the first year of law school, and grades remain crucial. During the recruiting season next fall, employers will be scrutinizing your second-semester grades, both to look for trends, and to determine whether you were able to adjust and improve your performance after one round of exams. This is not the time to over-commit to anything except your studies.

> Although I felt okay about my grades, I was bored with law school and the whole scene made me depressed and unhappy for most of second semester. I was sure that I didn't want to be a lawyer. Obviously, that would change later on.
>
> —Alison

There will be plenty of time for public service work and other extra-curricular activities during your upper years of law school. In the first year, your first priority, indeed your only priority, should be getting the very best grades you can. If, after two or three weeks of class, you really feel that you have a couple of free hours a week to commit to an activity, then go for it. Anything more demanding than that should be deferred until next year.

CHAPTER 14

First Year Endgame:
Succeeding in Exams and the
Law Review Competition

There is a tide in the affairs of men,
which, taken at the flood,
leads on to fortune.
—SHAKESPEARE

ALTHOUGH IT SEEMS like only yesterday, it has been nearly a full semester since your first set of grades arrived. Whether the news you received that day was positive, positively abhorrent, or somewhere in between, another opportunity is coming.

What are you going to do differently this time? Look back at the performance self-evaluation you completed at the end of last semester. Hopefully, you have been implementing any distinctions you were able to draw from that comparison with respect to study habits—but what additional distinctions can you draw about exam day itself? Compare the classes where you did well with the classes where you didn't. Where are the differences?

Assuming that you feel you were equally well prepared for all of your exams, you need to try and give yourself a little edge. Did you get more sleep the night before the exam where you did well? Did you eat a better breakfast? Did you eat something during the exam to stave off fatigue?

What did you rely on in the exam room? Where did you sit? Did you print in pen, and structure your exam answer like a legal memorandum, with headings, letters, and numbers? What else can you see as potential differences between the exams where you scored well, and those where you didn't?

I developed the "Performance Self-Examination" after my third semester of law school. Among the distinctions I made when comparing my first three semesters' grades, I noticed that I got better grades on pure essay exams (exams without multiple choice sections), on exams where I sat in the very first or very last row, or in the corners (where distractions from other classmates were significantly minimized), on exams where I relied on the case maps I developed, on exams where I relied heavily on Emmanuel's and Little, Brown's *Examples and Explanations* study aids, and on exams where my essays were printed or typed, double-spaced, written on one side of the page, and organized in legal brief format with headings. I did best on open-book and take-home exams.

I can almost hear your skeptical groans from here, thinking that I've gone completely off the wall, that these findings are just coincidental, and that I'm wasting my time and yours highlighting these differences.

Well, maybe, but once again, I remind you that success in law school is all about finding and capitalizing on the little distinctions that will make you just a little bit better than the person in the seat next to you. It may be coincidence, but I never got worse than a B+ in the six classes where I used case maps, never got worse than a B+ in the seven classes where I sat in the back corners of the exam room to shield me from in-class distractions, and got a B+ or better in five of the six classes where I used the relevant Emmanuel's commercial outline throughout the semester.

On the other hand, my worst grades in law school came on multiple choice exams, exams where I failed to follow the timing suggestions the professor provided, and exams (during my first semester) where I did not have a bullet point outline or casemap in addition to my outline.

Great, you say. So I'll sit in the back corner of the exam room and follow some of the other suggestions in this book. But how can I avoid taking a multiple choice exam?

Glad you asked.

Take a look through your course selection book next time

you're picking courses. See if you don't find at least a couple of sections of the same class taught at different times by different professors. Now read the course descriptions. Chances are, you'll find at least a couple of courses where you'll have the choice between a take-home final and an in-class final, or a multiple-choice final and an essay final. At least three times that I can remember during my law school career, I chose one section of a course over another section based entirely on what kind of exam was to be given at the end, with great results. Of course, this should not be the only factor you consider when choosing classes, but it is something to consider.

In most law schools, at the end of the second semester, often immediately following the conclusion of the last first-year final examination, you will be confronted with a great challenge.

If at any point during your first year of law school, you've found yourself wishing you could start over again with a clean slate, kicking yourself for not working harder during your first semester, or feeling like you've bought yourself a non-exchangeable, non-transferable seat in mediocrity class that you're never going to be able to escape from, then this is the answer to your prayers. An opportunity, for one week, to wipe the slate clean—to forget about the grades you've posted to date, and stand on a level playing field once again to confront the "Great Equalizer."

The law review/law journal writing competition.

At most schools the event includes a writing component and an editing component. Although you are likely to be in no mood for such things right after exams, if such a competition is offered at your school, it can be more important to your future than any law school exam will ever be.

In the "bad ol' days," membership on a school's law review was determined by grades alone, and only the true elite, usually the top 10 percent of a law school class, was offered membership. At most schools, however, the system changed as the powers-that-be recognized that many excellent writers and legal thinkers were slipping through a grades-only filtering system. Accordingly, a new system began to emerge, whereby a sliding scale employing a combination of first-year grades, and a score on a writing and editing test, is used to select journal membership.

Our competition was eight days long, right after finals. I started the day I got it and worked diligently, eight to nine hours per day on it, with a half day off in the middle to do something fun and relaxing. My main advice is to start as soon as you get the competition. If you procrastinate for two or three days, there is a good chance that you will either give up, or not do as well as you might have done, since you'll have to work longer hours in the remaining time to make up for it, and there is no way that your twelfth consecutive hour of subciting will be your sharpest. My method worked, as I made the law review entirely on the strength of my writing competition.

—Joel

While these systems vary from school to school, and the exact formulas used are often closely guarded secrets, this is typically how such a system works. The registrar assigns a code number to each student entering the competition, and a copy of that student's first-year grades, with name removed and code number added is submitted to the law review editorial board. A grade-point average or other numerical equivalent is then computed to represent that student's grades, and the coefficient representing the percentage that the law review decides should be assigned to first-year grades is multiplied with the grade point average to determine a "grade value score." Some Law Reviews offer automatic membership to the students with the top five or ten grade value scores without considering performance on the writing competition. Others don't.

The editing portion of the writing competition is typically a grueling exercise in "blue booking"—that is, using the legal style manual (called the "Blue Book") rules to correct an unedited law review article section containing hundreds or even thousands of errors in its text and footnotes, using a large photocopied packet gathering the relevant sections of the original source materials. Your job will be to carefully mark up the manuscript, checking every quote, citation, and footnote for stylistic, grammatical, content, and blue-booking errors.

"I participated unsuccessfully in Penn's journal competition," Carolyn recalls. "Looking back, I realize that I just hadn't taken enough time during the year to become familiar with the Blue Book and the proper rules of legal citation. As a result, I had no idea about proper citation forms, and my heart wasn't really in the competition because I was exhausted after exams."

At Penn, for example, the competition was held in three large classrooms at the law school, which were open from 8 A.M. to 11 P.M. every day for the nine-day length of the competition. Students were free to come and go as they chose, but no materials were allowed to enter or leave the room. As sick as it sounds, most students spent at least fifty hours during that week editing that manuscript.

About 80 percent of the class signed up for the competition. Attrition, however, was a major factor, as the apparent absurdity of the exercise, combined with the levels of frustration and exhaustion in a student body that had just completed the rigors of first year and yearned to escape Philadelphia for the summer, produced a competition drop-out rate of about 20 percent. Other students remained in the competition, but turned in lackluster efforts. A select core of students—maybe 30 percent—churned away day after day, morning to night, in search of the elusive invitation to join the Law Review.

At the conclusion of the competition, the edits were collected and scored, page by page, against a list of the errors intentionally written into the manuscript by the editors. Generally, for every error discovered, you get some fraction of a point, and for every error properly corrected, you get some additional fraction. After all pages are corrected, your entire edit receives a "raw score."

In addition to the editing component, the writing competition, not surprisingly, contained a writing component. At Penn and many other schools, the editors of the law review select a very general topic ("drugs," "education," "crime") and gather hundreds of pages of sources on the topic, including law review articles, legal cases, commentaries, editorials, book chapters, and the like. Your job as a competitor is to develop a thesis, and then write a piece of persuasive writing, usually ten to twenty pages in length and in proper Blue Book form, using only the provided materials as sources. This essay is then graded by the editors for quality of writing, persuasiveness of the argument, grammar, style, content, and Blue Booking, and assigned a "raw score."

Not surprisingly, time is often a factor in the quality of student performances on the journal competition. If your school's competition includes a writing segment, make sure you get to it with enough time to do a good job. It doesn't do you any good to turn in a sterling edit if you turn in a sloppy essay, as Alison counsels.

"I killed myself on the editing part and by the time I got to the writing part I was completely spent and did a very bad job. I made a journal, but I didn't make the law review. I really wish I had better divided my time between the two parts."

"I worked very hard and methodically revised my paper several times before handing it in," Keith remembers. "If I could recommend one approach to the writing portion, it is **revise, revise, revise**."

"I approached the competition like an exam, because it is certainly as important, if not more important, than an exam," Bess adds.

Depending on the particular practices of a school's law review, the writing and editing raw scores might be combined or assigned separate coefficients at this point. For purposes of this illustration, we'll assume that they are kept separate. Each student's grade scores, writing scores, and editing scores are then totaled up, and a rank order is established. It is from this final rank order that journal membership is decided.

To fully comprehend the critical importance of the writing competition, consider the following hypothetical example. Student #1, who we'll call Arrogant Andrea, has the following first year grades: A, A, A, A, B+, B+, B, B—certainly a solid effort, but probably not enough to simply "grade on" to the typical law review. Using the common numerical equivalents (4.0 for an A, 3.5 for a B+, etc.), Andrea's grades add up to a "29" raw score. Student #2, who we'll call Earnest Erin, on the other hand, had a rougher time of it during her first year. Her grades were A, A, B, B, B, B, B, B–, comprising a numerical equivalent of 25.67.

In approaching the writing competition, however, Arrogant Andrea got cocky, feeling that her grades were probably good enough such that a minimal effort in the competition would suffice to earn her a seat on the law review. Her essay earned only seven out of a possible ten points, and her edit, a 122/200. Earnest Erin, conversely, realizing that she was fighting an uphill battle to begin with, wrote the essay of her life, earning a nine-and-a-half out of ten points, and did extremely well on the edit, netting a 178/200.

Assume that the hypothetical law review in question values grades at 50 percent, the edit at 30 percent, and the essay at 20 percent in determining its members, and that the scores are normalized using coefficients to put each of the individual scores on a scale with a top score of one hundred. Accordingly, raw grade scores are multiplied by 3.125, the edit score is multiplied by 0.5, and the essay score is multiplied by 10. Each score is then multiplied by the percentage weight assigned to it by the editors of the law review.

Take a minute to work through the math so you understand what I'm talking about.

Got it? Now, are you wondering what happened to our two competitors? Follow the math below.

Arrogant Andrea's total score is the sum of each (coefficient) times (section score) times (weighted percent of the section) or $3.125(29)(.50) + .5(122)(.30) + 10(7)(.20)$ or 77.61 out of a possible 100 points. Earnest Erin's total score is $3.125(25.67)(.50) + .5(178)(.30) + 10(9.5)(.20)$ or 85.8. Erin gets the seat on the law review.

As the example above illustrates, the law review competition can provide a "back door" to journal membership for those individuals whose grades wouldn't get them in the front door. For the truly determined, this competition can be a one week cure-all to a semester's worth of disappointing grades.

So should you do it?

But why do it? What's so important about being on the law review anyway? Does it just mean that you'll be part of an elitist "club," and have to spend a lot of time doing the same kind of mind-numbingly boring editing that you did in the competition for two more *years*, surrounded by some of the most arrogant, annoying people in your law school class?

Uh . . . yeah, maybe. That really depends on how your law review selects its members. But there are a lot of other reasons why you might want to be on the law review.

First of all, it's a tremendous honor—among the biggest you can get in law school, and everybody knows it. Employers know it, and covet members of law reviews, sometimes providing a sizable "bonus" to incoming associates who were members of their law reviews in law school. Judges certainly know it—as membership on a law review is almost a prerequisite to getting a high level clerkship with a federal district or circuit court judge. Law schools know it—check and see someday how many of your professors made the law reviews at their respective schools. Even clients know it—being able to put "law review" on your resume and your firm biography singles you out for distinction. There is just no ignoring the fact that membership on your school's law review opens important doors for you—and in this business, the more doors you have open to you, the better.

How important journal membership is to getting prime job interviews and offers depends largely on the reputation of the various law schools. Generally, at the top ten or fifteen law schools, it is less critical than it is at other schools.

"At a school like Harvard, journal membership is relatively unimportant to getting the best job offers," Joel notes. "Journal members do very well during interview season, but many non-members also get excellent offers, and virtually everyone who isn't a psychopath or a chronic drooler gets a respectable offer."

Carolyn agrees. "At Penn, journal membership seemed to be only one of many factors that firms considered in deciding whether to hire someone. I don't think that it was overwhelmingly important. But at Penn, we also got to pick the firms we wanted to interview with—the firms weren't allowed to pick us."

"At Boston College, being on the law review was really important to getting the prime job interviews," Bess recalls. "When the school posted the interview lists for on-campus interviews, the lists for the employers all included substantially the same people—all law review and other journal members. This was very frustrating for people who weren't on a journal. You might not make the cut for an initial interview solely because you weren't on a journal because the firms get so many resumes that many of them make the cut based on this distinction."

Everyone agrees, however, that being on the law review, or at least being on some journal is critical if you plan to seek a federal clerkship or a prestigious state court clerkship after graduation.

"Pretty much crucial," Keith notes.

"It's really important in the clerkship process," Joel counsels, "since the process is extremely competitive and most judges were journal members themselves."

"If you're at all interested in getting a prestigious clerkship after graduation, being a member of the law review, or at least some reputable journal at your law school is virtually a prerequisite," another mentor added. "Many judges won't even consider applicants who weren't on a journal."

But what about the substance?

Well, there is also no denying the fact that certain aspects of law review membership are mind-numbingly boring. You do have to cite check and Blue Book professors' articles, which can often be tangles of nearly incomprehensible argument, impenetrable language, and sloppy citation. On the other hand, you get to write a "Case Note" or "Comment" of your own, generally on a subject of your own choosing, and have a chance to get that note or comment published—an impressive credential that again helps you with employers, judges, and clients. You also get a lot of firsthand contact with professors, which can help you establish the rapport needed to find a mentor on the faculty and get the most out of your law school experience. You'll be on the front lines of the law, reading articles espousing the newest legal theories and policy arguments. Finally, with all the writing and editing you'll be doing, you'll be honing your legal writing and editing skills to razor sharpness—skills which will serve you well for the rest of your days in the law.

Law review membership is not for everyone. It is grueling, tiresome, inconvenient, time-consuming, and often incredibly frustrating. To me, however, its benefits far outweigh these drawbacks in the mind of the long-term thinker.

Think very carefully before passing up this golden opportunity.

Finally, before you leave law school for the summer, stop by the placement office and provide them with your summer mailing address. During the summer, the placement office will need to send you a lot of important correspondence regarding recruiting season, and you'll want to be in the loop. If you haven't done so already, you'll also want to order a *NALP Directory of Legal Employers* from your placement office. It is from this directory that you will do most of the research needed to select firms to interview with next fall.

CHAPTER 15

Working for Free or Working for Pay, Your First Summer Paves the Way

The world is always ready to receive talent with open arms.
—Holmes

WHETHER YOU ARE working for a firm, interning with a judge, or doing public interest work, your goal during your first summer is really quite simple. You're looking to make a great impression.

Even if your experience is not all that you hoped it would be (and many first-year positions aren't because in many cases, you have to take what you can get), your first-year position will inevitably lead you somewhere. If you love the position, perform admirably, and prove to be a good fit for the firm or organization where you spend your first summer, your first-year position may lead to permanent employment. This is pretty unusual, however. More likely, your first-year position will expose you to new areas of the law, help you determine what areas of law motivate you, and consequently, will suggest areas of interest to focus on during the upper years of your legal education. Be on the lookout for these things as you proceed through your first summer.

> The most important thing I learned during my 1L summer is how important it is to be able to write well. At Penn, like all 1Ls, I took the legal writing course. The course was pass-fail, though, so a lot of people did not take it seriously. I was glad that I did.
> —Carolyn

"You learn a great deal more about law and lawyering during the summer than you do in school," Bess suggests. "I learned more about the law in ten weeks of a summer job than I learned during an entire school year because you learn the most by doing."

"I did research, wrote memos, and even wrote a few briefs," Allan adds. "Pretty much the same thing I do today as a first-year associate, so it was a good barometer."

"The most important thing you discover is how everything you learned during your first year of law school applies in the real-world practice of law," Pat concludes.

In addition, your first-year position can be very valuable in helping you to make judgments about your affinity (or lack thereof) for a particular city or geographic region of the country, the size of the firm or organization you most want to work for, or, even more broadly, whether you enjoy practicing law at all. As Joel discovered, "I learned that I didn't want to spend a career working in the ultra-political atmosphere of Washington, D.C."

Most importantly, your first summer experience will earn you important contacts in the legal community to support your candidacy for future positions. Whether you realize it now or not, contacts are crucial in the legal profession. Lawyers move around a lot, and chances are, wherever you end up during your first summer, you'll find people who have already been where you want to go who can help you get there.

Of course, to take full advantage of all of these possibilities, you'll need to have your eyes and ears open, do good work, and make people want to help you. Here are some strategies about how to survive and thrive in your first summer position in order to achieve the maximum benefit from it.

For those clerking for a judge

You have two ultimate goals to achieve from your position this summer. First, you want to cultivate the judge as a mentor. Judges are typically seasoned veterans of the legal wars with a wealth of advice to provide to law students—but they don't always just volunteer their advice. You have to ask for it, and the judge is more likely to provide you with his best wisdom if he likes you. Makes sense, right? So how do you make the judge like you? We'll get to that in a moment.

The second goal you want to be able to achieve during your summer internship is to earn the judge's enthusiastic reference. Remember, every judge on the bench once worked somewhere else, and a recommendation to his old law firm to hire you will virtually assure you of success. Similarly, no matter what kind of judge you are interning for, chances are he knows a fair number of people in the local bar association who have the power to hire you. Finally, if you do an exceptional job for the judge and the two of you really hit it off well, you might stand an increased chance of getting hired by that judge for a full-time judicial clerkship after graduation. Although many judges say that they avoid hiring former interns as judicial clerks because of just such an expectation, I know at least three people who are presently clerking for judges they interned with as 1Ls. So the take home message about your judicial internship is to (1) do the best job you can; and (2) try to develop a relationship with your judge. But how do you do that?

At the beginning of your internship summer, you will probably be given a couple of case files to work on. These files will typically be relatively straightforward cases containing one or two discrete issues. Alternatively, the judge or his law clerks may simply give you individual issues upon which you will be asked to draft "bench memos." The judge and his clerks rely on these memos when drafting legal opinions, so the accuracy of your work and the clarity of your writing is of paramount importance. Be certain to read cases carefully before citing them, and always cite check everything before you turn it in.

Depending on the trial schedule in your court, there may also be opportunities to watch trials during your internship. Ask the judge every couple of weeks whether there is something interesting coming up that he thinks would be worthwhile for you to observe. Remember, however, that first and foremost, a judicial internship is an academic position, and you will be expected to help shoulder some of the written workload in the chambers during the weeks you are there. The most respected judicial interns are humble, arrive at the office on time, perform careful research, write clearly and in a well-organized fashion, confer with the judicial clerks and the judge and ask questions when doctrinal questions arise that they don't understand, and generally help to reduce the workload for the chambers. The less well-respected judicial interns view their internship as a "summer off" or take the attitude that since they aren't being paid, they don't have to work hard. These interns typically spend a lot of time surfing the Net, talking on the phone, socializing with other interns, clerks, or court staff, or sitting in the courtrooms watching trials, but complete very little in the way of substantive work during the summer. Needless to say, the diligent intern not only gets more from his experience, but will almost certainly get more in the way of advice and assistance from the judge. Work hard, and consistently prepare high quality work product, and it won't be long before you find yourself in the good graces of the judge. Take the other road, and you'll waste an opportunity.

For those going to a firm

For those of you heading to a law firm during your first summer, you should have one of two primary goals in mind: (1) perform admirably and be personable enough so the firm invites you to return during your second summer (and then, perhaps permanently), or (2) perform admirably, get exposed to the firm's different practice areas, get some good experience, and parlay that into the job you want for your second summer. Although there are a number of subsidiary goals that we'll discuss in a moment, be clear that one of these is the main objective for your first summer in a law firm. A lot of first year students lucky enough to end up with firm jobs during their first summer fail to fully capitalize on the experience, either because they know going in that they're not interested in joining the firm permanently, or because they're not focused on what they need to take from the experience.

We discuss summer associate life in a law firm in detail in Chapter 23. If you will be working for a firm during your 1L summer, however, you should flip ahead and read that chapter before your summer begins. The advice and suggestions contained in Chapter 23 apply equally to 1L and 2L summer associates with the obvious caveat that as a 1L summer associate, expectations of you will be somewhat lower, and you won't be facing the prospect of a permanent employment decision at the end of the summer.

Your subsidiary goals as a 1L summer associate, however, can be much different. During your 2L year, assuming a robust economy, you'll probably experience a "buyer's market" working in your favor and will have some choices about what positions to pursue and which offers to accept. As a 1L, however, if you managed to land a position in a law firm, it might not be the firm you want to end up at. It might not be the right size, they might not practice the kind of law you're interested in practicing, and it might not be in the right state or even in the right region of the country. Nevertheless, there will always be lessons to learn from your 1L position if you are aware of the opportunities to make these distinctions. Accordingly, after you've read Chapter 23 and have a good understanding about how to succeed and thrive as a summer associate in a law firm, and after you've identified which of the primary goals you're working toward, consider the following.

If you think the firm you're at is the place that you'd like to end up after you graduate, make an effort to get to know as many people at the firm as possible. Don't brown nose or walk around pressing flesh like a politician, but take every non-awkward opportunity to introduce yourself to people you haven't met. This includes support staff, associates, and partners. Spend some time with the firm directory and do your best to learn and remember names. Find the associates and partners that do the kind of work you're most interested in, take the initiative to express your interest to those people, and inquire if they have any work that they'd like you to do. If they do, and they offer something to you, you're in business. If they don't have anything at the moment, ask them to remember you when they do, and let them know how long you'll be at the firm.

Remember that it is the people who take polite initiative that get what they want. There is a difference between sycophantic groveling, and a sincere expression of interest in pursuing a line of work. The above strategies constitute the latter, and should be readily employed.

If, on the other hand, you discover that you have no interest in returning to the firm you're at, there is still a lot you can do to make the experience worthwhile. First of all, no matter what firm you're at, there are people with contacts that could prove useful to you. Cultivate these potential contacts by doing a great job on the assignments you are given, being a team player, and learning about the partners and associates at the firm and where they've come from. Ask a lot of questions during the summer social events to get to know these people better. If you've done a great job but decide not to stay, these people will know you, like you, and will be willing to offer enthusiastic endorsements about you to their friends in the places you are more interested in staying long-term. Even in the largest metropolises, legal communities are well connected, and people move around so much that contacts are plentiful. Whether you will have access to these contacts depends on how you come across as a 1L.

You should also use your first summer to explore the city and the geographic area where your firm is located to determine whether or not you want to consider the area in your 2L job search. If you decide that you have no interest in staying in the area next summer, figure out why. Is the city too big or too small? Is it too congested? Does it lack character or culture? Is it too far away from a large metropolis? Not enough young, single people in the area to socialize with? Forcing yourself to answer these questions will help you to eliminate similar geographical areas during the fall recruiting season just ahead.

Next, consider the firm itself. What has made you decide that you're not interested in staying with them long-term? Consider the following list of questions, and/or add your own thoughts.

- Is the firm too big or too small?
- Has the firm seemed poorly organized to you?
- Does it lack the practice areas you want?
- Are the partners and associates hostile toward each other or toward you?
- Did you notice any camaraderie among the partners and among the associates?
- Is the firm too "ol' boysy" for your tastes?
- Has the firm made any effort to provide you with work you are interested in, or have you been more like slave labor to the firm's "dog cases" and scutwork?
- Did you get enough guidance on your projects and enough feedback on your work product?

- Did people at the firm have time for their outside interests and families, or did it seem like the law trumped everything else for the majority of people?
- Is the firm a sweatshop where people seemed to work around the clock?
- Did people at the firm generally seem happy or miserable?

Finally, we come to the big question. What if the reason you don't like the firm is because you just hate practicing law? Does this mean that you should quit law school now, save yourself the rest of your tuition money, and find something else to do?

The answer to this question is necessarily too much an individual choice to be answered generally. The fact is, there are several people involved in this book who, knowing what they know now, would not go to law school if they had it to do over again. There are others of us, however, who would have quit after our first summer, but are now happy that we made it through, and are happily putting our law degrees to good use. If you really despise everything about law school and the practice of law, you have thoroughly explored the different options for legal practice (e.g. firm practice, in-house counsel, permanent law clerk, prosecutor, public defender, public service work), you have thoroughly examined the different ways a law degree can advance other careers (e.g. anything business related, consulting, agenting, editing, and/or writing), and you still see no benefit to continuing, then you should probably take the next step by making an appointment with the Dean of Students at your law school to discuss your future. If you haven't thought these things through, however, don't even *think* about dropping out until you do. You've simply come too far at this point to make a rash decision.

As you proceed through your 1L summer, write down your thoughts and the answers to all of these questions while they are fresh in your mind. The observations you make now will greatly aid your employment search this fall, both by helping you to avoid ending up in a similar place next summer, and by providing you with certain questions to ask about during your screening and callback interviews. Space is provided at the end of this chapter to memorialize these impressions such that they will be available to you in one place when you need them next fall.

For those going into public service jobs

Our discussion in this section must necessarily be general, because the breadth of possible jobs in this category provides innumerably different experiences and challenges. A few things can be said, however, about how to maximize your summer working in one of these organizations.

First of all, display initiative. It is very easy, particularly if you are working in a larger organization like an urban district attorney's office, or a large urban service provider, to get lost in the shuffle. Often overburdened with work and understaffed, these places can appear to be disorganized and frenetic, and if you wanted to, you could spend a large part of your summer sitting around watching things happen around you. Accordingly, in many cases, it will be up to you to step up and take the initiative. Volunteer to help someone on a project, or find out which people are overworked, and ask them to delegate some work to you. Law students who are proactive in this way tend to have great experiences in these positions. Those who wait to be spoon-fed, however, will often go hungry.

Second, cultivate a mentor, and try and get that person to take you under her wing. Summer internships in service organizations can often be less structured than law school summer programs, but popular opinion has it that if you have a good mentor, you'll have a great experience. Find time at the beginning of the summer to sit down with someone within the organization to discuss roles and goals. If no mentor is assigned to you, target one yourself. Be clear on what you would like to do with your summer, and then ask your mentor whether your desires are realistic, and what he or she recommends that you do to have an experience as close as possible to the one you want.

Finally, be a team player and be enthusiastic. As with judicial internships and firm associateships, even if the experience ends up being somewhat disappointing, there are always things you can gain from it. Work hard, do a good job, be sociable, and get to know people and their backgrounds. That way, when the summer is over, if you decide you're not interested in a repeat engagement with the organization, people will be happy to provide contacts for something more like what you're looking for.

It is very easy, if your first summer position ends up being a disappointment, to simply write off the experience, rest up, do as little work as possible, and count down the days until you can go back to law school. As I have tried to illustrate in this chapter, however, it is not good for business. Every experience you have links into something else. The exact pathway may not be clear to you yet, but someday, you might be able to call on the contacts you made at a prior stop. With this in mind, do the best job possible and trust that your efforts will eventually pay dividends.

Thoughts about your 1L summer

_____

_____

_____

_____

_____

_____

_____

_____

_____

PART THREE

The Second Year
They Work You to Death

CHAPTER 16

Charting a Course for Your Upper Years

In life, as in chess, forethought wins . . .
—HENRY BUXTON

AT THE END of your first full-year cycle of law school, if you're not completely confused, disenchanted, or disillusioned, you may be thinking about the best way to dedicate your remaining four semesters. With most of the required courses now out of the way, you'll have the luxury to choose what to take and when to take it. But should you choose the practical over the philosophical? The useful over the interesting? Only the courses you'll need for the bar exam?

How do you decide which approach to adopt?

This chapter proposes and explores several different general approaches to your upper-year curriculum to help you decide which approach best fits your needs. While you will no doubt want to "dabble" a bit in the different courses your law school has to offer, you do have a limited number of credit hours to spend, and only two years to take what you can from the diverse offerings your law school curriculum provides. Deciding on a general philosophical "approach" to help dictate the majority of your course selections will help to ensure that your upper-level years provide you with an enlightening and meaningful educational experience.

When I first went to law school, I thought I wanted to practice international law. I used many of my second-year electives to take things like Public International Law, International Business Transactions, and other such courses, only to decide it wasn't for me. I became more and more interested in litigation, so in my third year, I loaded up on trial advocacy classes.

—Elizabeth

First, some general comments. In planning your upper-year curriculum, remember that in law school, like in college, course formats will vary. Be sure to avail yourself of seminars, and smaller, non-Socratic discussion-based classes in addition to the large, Socratic lecture classes that characterized your first year. If your law school is part of a larger university, don't dismiss the possibility of cross-registering for a couple of classes at the business school or the undergraduate college if doing so will enhance the approach you choose. When you find your niche, explore the possibility of doing a one-on-one tutorial with a faculty member in your area of greatest academic interest. Finally, make every effort to take at least one intensive research and writing experience since these are the skills you'll rely upon most in whatever field of law you ultimately choose to practice.

With this in mind, let's explore the different approaches that you might take during your upper years of law school.

The bar exam preparation approach

I've put this one first, because I think it is the easiest approach to dismiss, and, in the end, is probably the least beneficial strategy to employ. Although you don't know it now, you're going to learn everything you need to know for your bar exam in your bar preparation course. That six-week program will teach you all the "black-letter" law (the "rudiments" of a particular subject) you'll need to "master" each subject covered on your state's bar exam. In law school, however, you learn theory and policy, follow the law through its historical changes, and, in essence, learn much more than you'll ever need to pass a bar exam.

Taking classes in law school solely because you need to know the subject for the bar exam is overkill. By the time you get to the bar exam, you'll have forgotten half of what you learned, and if your law school emphasizes theory and policy over black-letter law (as most of the top law schools do), there's no guarantee that you'll even cover everything you'll need to know for the bar exam.

Take my advice—let your bar review class teach you what you need for the bar exam. Use your time in law school to adopt another approach. You can always take a couple of non-required, broad survey courses (see survey approach below) in frequently tested subjects like income tax and corporations if waiting until the bar review course to see these subjects for the first time is just too unsettling for you.

The survey approach

Adopting this approach depends, in large part, on the vision you have for your future. In large-firm, big city practice, the days of the "lawyer as generalist"—moving effortlessly from a tax question to a torts question to a constitutional law question—are gone. For the most part, attorneys in the large firms that populate the big cities have become specialists in a particular area of law (labor law, real estate, tax, etc.). Many of these lawyers have developed further subspecialties within their area of the law to the point where their entire practice revolves entirely around one or two sections of the Income Tax Code or the Securities Regulations, and the progeny of cases developing from them. On the other hand, law school graduates who flee the big city and hang a shingle in smaller towns or rural areas still need to be generalists in order to put food on the table. These lawyers may still do a will in the morning, a real estate transaction at lunch, and argue a torts case in the afternoon. Those who go to small or midsize firms may find their experience to be somewhere between these two extremes.

Of course, no one expects you, as a beginning second-year law student, to know that Rule 10(b)(5) of the Securities Laws is going to be your bread-and-butter. On the other hand, you'll need to know something about where your interests lie before you start going to recruiting interviews, because you're going to need to seek out firms that have active practices in the area(s) of your greatest interest, and you're likely to be asked, at least generally, what your interests are.

I can see you now, shaking your head and wondering out loud, "but what if I have no idea what area of law I'm most interested in? All I've done is take required courses for a year . . ."

Not a problem. If that sentiment applies to you, then the survey approach is where you belong, at least for this semester. But don't just go into it blindly. Think about which courses you enjoyed during your first year, and which ones you hated, and look for trends.

Did you enjoy the structure provided by working closely within the provisions of the U.C.C. in Contracts and the federal rules in Civil Procedure, or did you prefer the wide open, theoretical concepts of Constitutional Law? Were you more interested in the legal aspects of human drama found in Torts and Criminal Law, or the business-related themes of Contracts and Property? Did you enjoy the research, writing, and oral argument in your first-year Legal Research and Writing seminar? Were you relatively comfortable responding to the challenges of the Socratic method, or does speaking out in class make your stomach turn? Do you see yourself more as a litigator or a corporate lawyer?

Well?

Yeah, I know there were a lot of tough questions in the last paragraph—so take some time right now to think about them. Sketch the classes you liked and didn't like into groups and look for similarities. Take as much time as you need to get a better sense of what your interests are in the law. Don't read on until you've done this exercise.

No, I said don't read on until you've finished the exercise! Did you do the exercise? The next paragraph will still be here when you finish.

Okay. Now that you have some idea where your motivations are, it's time to think about which survey courses you should take this semester.

If your interests were more on the business and/or financial side of the law, look for the general, introductory survey courses in corporations, commercial paper, federal income tax, corporate tax, antitrust, securities regulation, and bankruptcy. Don't even think of taking them all in the same semester, because if you find out your interests really lie elsewhere, you'll be in for the roughest ride of your life. Generally, Corporations, Commercial Paper, and one of the introductory tax courses is where most business law oriented law students cut their teeth. Take two of these courses to start. If your interest in this area is still viable after those courses, you can take the others next semester and then move into the major approach in a couple of these areas during your third year.

If your interests were more in the litigation area, your scope of choices is even wider. Perhaps the first choice to make is whether you're more interested in criminal or civil practice. Keep in mind that while criminal work may seem "sexier" right now, this choice generally narrows your options upon graduation to: (1) state or federal prosecutor (positions which pay much less than the going rate for private practice and are still extremely hard to get); (2) the public defender's office (which generally pays little and may implicate a number of moral issues for you); or (3) specialized criminal defense (which you can do in a firm). If any of these choices interests you, after the introductory courses in criminal law and constitutional law, look for courses in constitutional criminal procedure and advanced criminal procedure, and evidence. If your interest continues after these courses, you can further specialize (see the major approach below).

If your litigation interests are in the civil arena, after the introductory courses in civil procedure, torts, contracts, and property, consider taking the survey courses in evidence, federal courts, First Amendment law, administrative law, labor and employment law, family law, or real estate. When you find an area that you're interested in, you can further specialize (see the major approach below).

> I also tried to mix together tougher, code-based classes like Tax, Commercial Credit, and Securities Regulation with common law classes or classes in a particular area of law that was easier to grasp.
>
> —Alison

While it is possible to stay with the survey approach for the entirety of your law school career in order to get a broad view of the legal landscape, most law students eventually like to graduate with one or two areas of advanced expertise. Accordingly, if you can move from the survey approach to the major approach by the beginning of your third year of law school, you'll be in great shape to launch your career come graduation.

The major or career-focus approach

The major or career-focus approach begins, for most students, with at least a semester in the survey approach—until such time as you are clear about what areas of law you are most interested in pursuing. Once you've made the general decision between corporate law and litigation, and if you've chosen litigation, between criminal and civil litigation, you're ready to specialize.

Why is this helpful to you?

As we've mentioned previously, if you think you're headed for big city or large firm practice after graduation, you'll eventually be asked to specialize—so it's not a bad idea to develop an expertise in law school. Even if you're looking to a midsize or smaller firm, you won't be practicing every kind of law—so develop some more thorough knowledge in the areas in which you're likely to practice. For example—if you know that your life's calling is going to take you to your uncle's five person firm in Peoria, you probably don't need to take too much time developing a specialty in oil and gas law, but you might want to know something about wills and trusts. Perhaps now, you're beginning to understand why I've been preaching about having a vision for your future *before* you get to law school!

It's great if you can identify early on what area you want to practice in, because you can then structure your course load accordingly and begin to build a transcript that your prospective employers will really notice.

—Keith

Although every school is different, a chart of some of the more common "majors" undertaken by today's law students follows below. Of course, there are other possible majors not on this list—but this is a representative sample to get you started. Below each "major" is a sampling of courses you might take to develop your specialty.

MAJORS:

Business/Finance/Commercial Law
- Accounting
- Corporate Tax
- Partnership Tax
- Closely-Held Corporations
- Corporate Finance
- Antitrust
- Commercial Paper
- Mergers and Acquisitions
- Securities Regulation
- Bankruptcy

Constitutional Law
- Administrative Law
- Federal Courts
- Constitutional Criminal Procedure
- Constitutional Litigation (Section 1983)
- Education Law
- Employment Discrimination
- First Amendment
- Conflict of Laws
- Immigration Law
- Any upper level seminar on specialized topics in constitutional law

Criminal Law
- Criminal Procedure
- Constitutional Criminal Procedure
- Evidence
- Mental Health Law
- Death Penalty Law
- Habeas Corpus
- White Collar Crime
- Topics in Criminal Law Theory

Family Law

- Family Law
- Wills
- Trusts
- Estate and Gift Tax
- Estate Planning
- Mental Health Law
- Welfare Law
- Education Law

Health Care Law

- Health Care Law
- Administrative Law
- Antitrust
- Insurance Law
- Law and the Elderly
- Mental Health Law
- Advanced Topics in Health Care Law

Intellectual Property

- Copyright Law
- Patent Law
- Trademark Law
- Computer Law
- Internet Law

International Law

- Conflict of Laws
- Comparative Law
- Comparative Constitutional Law
- Comparative Labor Law
- International Business Transactions
- International Environmental Law
- International Human Rights
- International Trade
- Uniform International Sales
- International Civil Litigation

Labor and Employment Law
- Labor Law
- Employment Law
- Employment Discrimination
- Federal Courts
- Constitutional Litigation
- E.R.I.S.A.
- Sports Law

Public Interest Law
- Federal Courts
- Constitutional Litigation
- Employment Discrimination
- Family Law
- Education Law
- Health Care Law
- Immigration Law
- Welfare Law
- Local Government
- Civil Practice Clinic
- Public Interest Externships

Real Estate
- Real Estate Transactions
- Environmental Law
- Administrative Law
- Construction Contracts
- Land Use
- Local Government
- Zoning
- Federal Income Tax
- Estate and Gift Tax
- Wills and Trusts

Tax
- Federal Income Tax
- Corporate Tax
- Partnership Tax

- Estate and Gift Tax
- International Taxation
- Tax Policy
- Advanced Specialized Topics in Tax

The clinical approach

The clinical approach is designed primarily for those students with a future in litigation. Law school classes can be frustratingly theoretical, and professors often pay little or no lip service to how different concepts play out in real-world practice (in many cases because the professors never *had* any real world practice!). If you are like I was, you're probably sitting out there reading this with no idea about how to draft interrogatories, what you can and cannot ask in a deposition, or what a "speaking objection" is. You took Civil Procedure, you took Evidence, and still, you feel like you would have no command over these subjects in real-world practice.

Sound familiar at all?

If so, you might want to consider making room for some clinical experience in your law school career. A good course in trial advocacy, for example, typically takes you through a hypothetical civil trial from the client interview, through the jury verdict—illustrating the interplay of the rules of evidence and procedure in drafting and responding to interrogatories, conducting depositions, assembling affidavits to support a motion for summary judgment, and the like. You won't get these things in a regular law school course, and without such a course, you could easily graduate from law school with no idea whatsoever about how to handle a civil case in the real world. A course in trial advocacy is a *must* if you're going to be a litigator.

Pro bono or legal aid clinics offer similar, real-world practical experience with real clients with real problems. If you are willing to make a large time commitment, an experience with one of these clinics could allow you (with the aid of a more experienced supervisor) to handle a whole case from beginning to end, affording you exposure to all the intermediate steps along the way. Internships and externships with judges or public service organizations (see Chapter 21 for more information) can provide similar practical experiences to ground your theoretical legal knowledge.

There is much to be said for devoting a semester, later in law school after you have developed a working knowledge of the core litigation subjects, to trial advocacy or a clinical practicum. Doing so will illustrate how the legal system actually works in practice in a way that none of your theory-based classes ever will.

Other considerations

Finally, you may want to take some classes simply because you heard the professor is great. You never know what the professor's love of a subject might do for your own interest in it.

"Just as I would strongly recommend that you avoid taking *any* class taught by a professor who is widely regarded as a bad teacher, I would try to take classes taught by professors who have reputations as excellent teachers," Carolyn notes. I decided not to leave Penn without taking Constitutional Litigation because I had heard how excellent the professor was, and it turned out to be the best thing I did in my three years of law school. Professor Kreimer was one of those rare teachers who, through his own enthusiasm for and knowledge of the subject matter, inspired a classroom full of students to push themselves harder intellectually than they ever thought they could."

"Cross-register once or twice too," Joel adds. "Take a business school or public-policy school class if the schools are good and the subject matter interests you."

"It also pays to take easier and/or more mainstream classes during the first semester of your second year because of recruiting," Steve suggests. "Interviewing for a 2L summer job is very important, and very time consuming. You'll be in and out of town on callbacks, and ultimately, everyone ends up blowing off classes for the first few months to focus on the job search. Sooner or later, though, you're going to have to go back and figure out what you missed, and it's a lot easier to do that if you are taking corporations, where there are ten different commercial outlines and fifty different outlines prepared by former students floating around, than if you are taking the Feminist Perspectives on Intellectual Property Law seminar for which there are no study aides available."

CHAPTER 17

Your Survival Guide to Recruiting Season

Make hay while the sun shines.
—ENGLISH PROVERB

WELL, THIS IS IT.

For many of you, this is what law school has been all about. For well over a year, you've put in the long hours, endured the journal competition, and positioned yourself with an at-least-somewhat calculated employment decision last summer, all with an eye toward this day.

The day it all begins to pay off. Literally.

Whether your law school allows employers to select whom they want to interview, whether it uses a lottery system, or whether you are traveling to a regional recruiting event, there are a number of strategies and tactics that will radically increase your chances of surviving the screening interview. But let's not get ahead of ourselves. First, a word about how this whole process works.

Whether the employers come to your campus, or you travel to a regional "job fair" or similar recruiting event, the process has two stages: the screening interview, and the "callback" or "flyback" interview. The screening interview is usually a twenty to thirty minute one-on-one interview conducted by a single representative of a firm or organization. During the screening interview, you will generally be asked about your resume, your grades, your practice interests, your law school experience, and anything else the interviewer picks up from the materials you submitted. There is a lot you can do to prepare for these screening interviews, and prepare you should, because although a screening interviewer usually doesn't have a fixed quota of students to call back, the number of students invited to the firm for a second round of interviews rarely exceeds 25 percent. To earn one of these prized "callback" interviews, you need to make yourself "stand out" from the crowd.

How will you know whether you've succeeded?

Generally, a firm or organization will call you within a week to ten days of your screening interview to set up a callback (also called a "flyback") interview at the firm (See Chapter 18 for complete details). But we're getting ahead of ourselves again. Let's start at the beginning.

How to decide where to interview

As I touched on earlier, depending on which law school you go to, interview opportunities may be predetermined by employers, decided by lottery, or open to your preference. Given the importance of this process, I would make every effort possible to attend a law school that uses one of the latter two systems.

In schools where employers determine who they want to interview, you have little choice in the matter. If you are selected, you go to an interview. Period. In a school using one of the latter two processes, however, you'll need to research firms and submit a preference list to your placement office—probably during your 1L summer.

You'll do most of this research in the *NALP Directory of Legal Employers*—a compendium of information about nearly every law firm in the United States. The directory contains the mailing address, contact person, and a one-page synopsis of the practice areas and other relevant information about each firm. If you ordered it last spring as I suggested, you should receive it during the summer in time to do this research. Once you have the directory in hand, most of this will be self-evident.

How to prepare yourself for the screening interview

Is there any "magic formula" to guarantee success in a screening interview? Well, a resume including a high grade point average from an Ivy League university and a law school transcript with straight A's during your first year at a top ten law school, coupled with an affable personality, would probably ice it for you.

What, you don't have all of these attributes?

Well relax, because most people don't—so let's talk about what you can do with the record you have to maximize your chances of securing the largest percentage of callbacks from the firms at the top of your list.

Know your audience

Remember when your seventh grade algebra teacher told you that "the only dumb question is the question that you don't ask?"

She was wrong—at least in the context of the law firm recruiting process.

In this game, the only dumb question is the question that is readily answered by a law firm's publicity materials.

Know why it's a dumb question?

Because it makes you look like you didn't give too much thought to the firm you're interviewing with.

Between the NALP directory, your law school placement office, the Internet, the *Martindale-Hubble Directory of Lawyers and Law Firms*, and the telephone, there is very little general information about a firm and its lawyers that you can't find out ahead of time. As soon as you know you have a screening interview with a firm, you should begin the process of gathering this information.

So what, at a minimum, should you know?

I would know approximately how many lawyers the firm has, in what cities it currently has offices, what its practice areas are, and what its specialty areas of practice are. I would find out who the firm's largest clients are. If the firm is large, I would know where the firm ranked in the city and in the country in the annual poll of associates' satisfaction, and where the firm ranked in the annual poll of summer associates. I'd find out the latest information about starting salary, bonus structure, vacation time, partner track, and billable hour requirements, and how those numbers compared to the numbers of comparable firms in the same city. I'd also want to know whether the firm has a multi-tiered partner track. Finally, I would go to the placement office a day or two before the interview, get the name of the lawyer that will be conducting your interview, and then find out a few things about her from Martindale-Hubble. Determine where she went to college and law school, how long she has been with the firm, what areas of practice she is involved in, and what a couple of her interests are. I'd put all of this information down in a notebook or journal, and take it into the interview with me.

Then, I'd formulate at least three questions about the firm that you would like to have answered and that you are reasonably sure are not answered by the firm's other materials, and write them down in the same section of the notebook or journal with room for answers. Things like whether the firm makes an effort to direct specific kinds of work to the associates most interested in doing that kind of work; how easy it is to move between practice groups at the firm; and what kind of training and feedback the firm provides to first year associates. See the section below on "Asking the Hard Questions" for more ideas. You want to have these questions ready when the interviewer asks you the inevitable question, "So, do you have any questions for me?" or to jump right into at an appropriate point in the interview.

Be prompt and polite

You'd think this would go without saying, but firm recruiters have told us that it is not uncommon for law students to arrive late and out of breath to a recruiting interview. Plan to arrive at least fifteen minutes before the time your interview is scheduled to leave yourself enough time to review your notes and your list of questions for the firm you're about to interview with. When the interviewer greets you, be confident! Smile and introduce yourself with a firm handshake. While you will, no doubt, be nervous, remember two things: (1) the recruiter is just a human being like yourself and probably had to endure a similar interview; and (2) first impressions count.

Dress conservatively

Like I just said, first impressions count. While your classmates might think it wonderful that you've maintained your individuality in law school by wearing tie-dye to lectures and following Phish around the country during winter break, the law firm recruiting interview is not the time to wear anything controversial. At least not if you want to get a callback.

If you're a guy, lose the earring and any excessive jewelry. Regardless of your gender, leave the nose ring, and any other unusual piercings at home. Get a conservative haircut, and save the wild ties for another occasion. Finally, refrain from wearing any political pins, emblems, or identifying symbols on your clothing. (Mind you, this is not a value judgment on my part—just advice about how to survive a screening interview.)

For the men, an ironed and starched white shirt, dark tie, and dark suit (*yes* a suit, and *no*, khakis and a blazer is not appropriate) is your best choice. Don't have one? Buy one. You'll need at least a couple of them for work anyway. For the women, a white blouse under a freshly dry-cleaned dark business suit, a pair of tasteful matching shoes, and a conservative necklace and earrings is the proper choice. Any deviations from this boring but professional standard are made at your peril.

So what are they going to ask me, anyway?

Every interviewer is different, but there are only so many *kinds* of things an interviewer can ask you. Questions during a screening interview will generally come from among nine substantive categories: (1) general questions; (2) questions about your background or the experiences listed on your resume; (3) questions about your choice of law school; (4) questions about your grades; (5) substantive questions culled from your writing sample; (6) questions about your substantive legal interest; (7) questions about your interest in the city, state, or region where the firm is located; (8) questions about your interest in the firm; and (9) the "stunners." I address each of these areas, briefly, in turn.

> Be confident but not arrogant. Try to come off as person that the interviewer could tolerate spending seventy-two hours in a row with.
>
> —Allan

General questions can be as broad as, "Tell me about yourself," and as narrow as, "What is the one thing you'd like to be remembered for when you're gone?" Spend some time thinking about what your strengths and weaknesses are, what your proudest accomplishment has been, and what the biggest obstacle in your life has been so far, and how you managed to overcome it. Think about what you'd like to be doing in five or ten years, how you plan to balance work and family, and what your most important value is. There are many more questions like this, but hopefully you have some sense of what is in bounds.

For questions about your experience, know your resume cold, and be prepared to discuss anything on it in detail. Often, interviewers will seize on something you wouldn't expect (like your interest in rock climbing or oil painting) in lieu of the real accomplishments on your resume. Be prepared to address *everything*. The most common question in this area concerns what you did last summer—so be sure you have some insights ready.

Questions about law school may be as broad as, "So, how do you like law school?" Try to resist the urge to say, "Pshaw—it sucks," and instead, come up with something substantive to say about the subjects you like and why, what your biggest accomplishment in law school has been, or how you've struggled to maintain your identity amid the rigors of the schedule. You might also be asked to describe your favorite professor, and why she's your favorite, what your most rewarding experience has been, how you like your classmates, or how you would respond to a particular situation (like seeing a friend cheat in an exam).

So what about grades? Yeah—they can ask you about them, although in my experience and the experiences of the mentors in this book, employers asked about grades less than we thought they would. The most important thing to remember about grades is not to apologize for them, no matter what they are. If you are asked something like, "Wow, what happened in Contracts?" go ahead and chuckle as you remember getting drilled on the final—but then take a deep breath and come back with something like, "Yeah—it was pretty ugly, but you know what? I learned a lot in that course," and then go on to tell the interviewer about what you learned from the experience. Knowing how to diffuse a potentially tense situation with some self-deprecating humor is an incredible skill to have as a lawyer, and will serve you well if you are asked about grades. The fact is, most of the people who will interview you bombed a course or two themselves, and should find your ability to find humor in the situation an asset.

Know your writing sample. This is an often-overlooked area for potential questions—but I got a substantive legal question about my writing sample, and I bombed it. Couldn't even remember what the damn thing was about, much less answer a jurisdictional question relating to it. Didn't get a callback from that firm either. Hmmm . . .

Be prepared to talk about your areas of substantive legal interests—as they relate to the courses you've taken, the subjects you still want to take, and any interests that were triggered by the work you did last summer. You'll also want to tailor your interests to the strengths of the firm you are interviewing with—so if you love First Amendment work, but the firm you're talking to doesn't do any, you'll want to save that one and talk about some of your other interests that the firm does feature. If you can't find any, then guess what? You probably aren't a good fit at that firm.

One of the most critical questions you might be asked will concern your interest in the city, state, or region where the firm's office is located—and you better have a good answer ready, because this question can be a fatal one. If, for example, you grew up in New England, went to high school and college in New England, have family and friends in New England, spent your 1L summer working in New England, and then, out of the blue, are interviewing with a San Francisco law firm—what do you think they're going to ask you about? Why San Francisco? And you know what? An answer like, "I really want to try something different" isn't going to cut it. The firm is going to be looking to see where your ties are. You need a more compelling reason to relocate—like a fiancée from the region, a spouse attending graduate school in the region, relatives in the area, a history with the area (like spending summers there as a kid, or going to high school or college there), or a particular practice group (like high tech start-ups) that is concentrated in the region. Comments about the climate, the atmosphere, the culture, the people, and the outdoor activities can help if they are well thought-out, but they probably won't be enough on their own. So really figure out why you want to be in the city or region of the country that this firm is from, and come up with a compelling answer to this question which is almost certain to be asked of someone in those circumstances. Of course, if you are talking to a New England firm and you fit the bill described above, then you have your compelling reason right there—you're returning home. Just don't forget to make this point clear to the interviewer even if you aren't asked about it.

You may be asked to describe your interest in the firm you're talking to, what made them stand out to you, or how you feel you might contribute to the firm. Here, the interviewer is probing to determine how well thought-out your choices are, and once again, a bad answer can be deadly—so be ready. Preparing a one-page summary sheet on every firm should help you make distinctions about them—but exercise caution here. You don't want the firm's only distinguishing characteristics to be that they have the highest salary and lowest billable hour requirement in the city. Look for practice areas, firm philosophies, or reputation as possible answers here.

Finally, we come to the "stunner" category—the questions that make your jaw drop open and your heart race faster as you struggle to find a suitable answer that is confident, but not cocky, humble, but not meek. Questions like, "Aren't you really just using our firm as a stepping stone to go to . . ." or "I could fill my entire recruiting class with people from Harvard Law School, why should I choose you?" The best thing to say here is to take a deep breath, and make a remark like, "Wow—let me think about that for a moment," while you consider an answer. Don't be afraid of silence. It's better than putting your foot in your mouth. When you are asked a "stunner," it's usually more to see how you'll react to it—so think before you speak.

"At one screening interview, the interviewer came right out and said, 'well I can see from your grades that you're no legal eagle, so why should I hire you?" Carolyn remembers. "Even though the question made me mad, instead of getting defensive, I just sort of laughed off the comment and told the guy that while I got off to a somewhat average start in law school, my grades were steadily improving, and I was confident that they would continue to improve. I also drew his attention to my writing sample as an indication that I write well, and to my resume as an indication that when I commit to something, I get the job done, and done well. I don't think the interviewer really cared about my grades that much. I think he was testing me to see how I would react to his question because he offered me a callback and the firm made me an offer."

When a "stunner" goes over the line

Once in a while, you hear a horror story about a partner (usually one of the older ones) making an off-color remark, or asking an inappropriate question. If this happens to you, again, the best approach is the calm, rational approach. Don't pop off and start condemning the behavior. First ask to have the comment or question repeated to assure yourself that you heard it correctly. If you did, and it is an inappropriate question, it is then perfectly acceptable to respond by saying, "I'm sorry, Mr. So-and-So, but that question is out-of-bounds." Inquiries about marital status, sexual orientation, religious persuasion, ethnicity, political beliefs, and offers from other firms are regarded as inappropriate. If the interviewer makes an off-color remark about race, sexual orientation, religion, or the like, and you are bothered by it, politely call him on it by saying, "Excuse me, Mr. So-and-So, but what exactly did you mean by that comment?" That should be enough to get the interviewer to move on—and will probably be reason enough to get you to look elsewhere for employment.

What you should ask

If you've followed my advice, you should already have two or three questions prepared for each firm based on the research you've done. But what are some other questions you might ask? Ask about plans for the future of the firm, and any potential areas of growth. Find out what factors led your interviewer to decide to work at the firm, and what it is like to work there—including questions about how work is assigned, how much supervision is provided, how projects are staffed, and how feedback is provided. Find out what traits are shared by the best associates at the firm. Ask about what the social life is like, and how satisfied, overall, the interviewer is at the firm. You'll probably only have time for one or two questions, so ask the ones you are most curious about, that are the most critical to your continuing interest in the firm, or the questions that were triggered during the interview but not sufficiently answered.

Many law students struggle with the decision about whether or not to ask the "tough questions" of an interviewer. If a firm's summer associate program ranked last in the city last summer, or the firm ranked very low in the annual poll of associate satisfaction, or the firm recently experienced a "bloodletting" and fired a number of people, or was implicated in an ethical scandal, you're going to want to find out about those things before you accept an offer from the place. You owe it to the firm and to yourself to put those questions to the firm's front-person—and for your purposes, that's your interviewer.

Remember that you are interviewing the firm, too.
—Elizabeth

Although most law students worry that asking these tough questions will be insulting to the interviewer, in the vast majority of cases, the result is just the opposite. Asking the tough questions of an interviewer shows the interviewer that you have done your homework about the firm, and that you are concerned about those things—as you should be. It also shows the interviewer that you are seriously considering the firm as a place of employment. So when the interviewer asks the inevitable question, "So, do you have any questions for me?" ask away. If you are still squeamish, give the interviewer a softball, like, "I couldn't help but notice that you guys ranked last in associate satisfaction last year. I'm sure it won't happen again, but what changes have been implemented to try and improve the situation?"

Don't cower from asking the tough questions.

The things you should avoid

It should go without saying that no matter how comfortable you feel with a particular interviewer, you should never lose sight of the fact that you are still the interviewee. Vulgarity, off-color jokes, and political humor can only get you into trouble in an interview—so avoid these things at all costs. Equally important to remember is never to bad-mouth another interviewer or another firm during an interview, no matter how terrible your experience or impression may have been. You don't know all the players, and you might step on a mine. Finally, stay away from all questions about salary, bonus structure, benefits, and vacation time until after you have been extended an offer by the firm. That's the only time these issues become relevant.

A few horror stories to calm you down

Every now and then, you'll end up with a particularly salty character on the other side of the interview desk, and things will take an unfortunate turn. Maybe it's the end of the day, and the interviewer is tired. Maybe it's the beginning of the day and the interviewer is tired. Maybe the interviewer is tired of being a lawyer. While you'd think that firms would not roll out their nastier characters on these occasions, sometimes the people who make the decisions at these firms don't think like you and I do. On these rare occasions, things like this can happen:

"I was interviewing with a major law firm that has offices all over the world, and the interviewer did not ask me any questions!" Elizabeth recalls. "He just sat there and read my resume while I sat silently in the chair on the other side of the desk. This went on for some time until I finally broke the silence by mentioning that I love Italy and asked what opportunities I would have to work in the firm's Rome office. The guy then looked at me like I was the stupidest person he had ever seen and abruptly told me that no associate would ever have such an opportunity, much less someone at the bottom of the ladder like I would be."

"I had a screening interviewer from a firm in a smaller market which happened to be my hometown close the door, put his feet up on the desk, and say to me, 'now don't try to bullshit me. You know and I know that you're just using this interview as a trial run for something better, so why should I take you seriously?' one mentor recalls with a smile. "I knew this was the firm I really wanted to work at, so no joke, I looked right back at him and without batting an eye, said, 'because if you don't, you'll be making one of the biggest mistakes of your life.' I think he was trying to intimidate me, but I didn't let him. It must have been the answer he wanted, because he made me the offer, and I'm still there today."

And finally, there is this gem.

"I know someone who had an interview with someone who closed the door, started crying, and said 'Don't come here—it's a horrible place that just sucks the life out of you,'" Bess recalls. "Needless to say, he took a job somewhere else!"

CHAPTER 18

Everything You Need to Know About Callback Interviews

"You can fool some of the people all of the time,
and all of the people some of the time,
but you cannot fool all of the people all the time."
—ABRAHAM LINCOLN

IN THE REALM of law firm recruiting, popular opinion says that if you get a callback, the offer is yours to lose. While this is not entirely accurate, the recruiting coordinators and hiring partners we canvassed said that in a typical year, between 60 and 80 percent of the candidates invited on a callback interview will eventually be extended an offer.

So if all is going well, it is September or October of your 2L year, you've been to a bunch of screening interviews, and now you're starting to accumulate some callbacks. Only problem is, you don't really know what a callback is.

So what the heck is a "callback" anyway?

A "callback," or at some schools, a "flyback," is just the fancy name for the second round of law firm interviews. An invitation for a callback interview means that you "won" the screening interview lottery—and that the firm is interested enough in you to fly you to their city, put you up in a hotel, take you out on a lavish "recruiting lunch," and have four to six more attorneys at the firm talk to you.

This process, which usually takes the better part of a day, will culminate in one of two things: an offer of employment during your 2L summer, or a ding letter.

The process begins with an invitation from the recruiting coordinator at the firm to make an appointment to come to the firm for a morning or afternoon interview. This invitation is almost always made by telephone, and can come as soon as the same day that you complete your screening interview. As a result, as soon as you start taking screening interviews, double check your answering machine to make sure that your outgoing message is professional and clearly identifies who you are.

Callback interviews typically take place in the city where the firm is located, almost always at the firm itself. Unless the firm happens to be in the city where your law school is located, that means traveling, but don't worry—the firm will reimburse you for your travel expenses as long as you don't make outrageous arrangements (see section on "fiscal conservatism" below). If the city is far enough from your law school to make traveling back and forth in the same day difficult, you will also be entitled to charge a hotel room, meals, and related expenses to the firm.

When you get to the firm, you will usually be greeted by the recruiting coordinator, who will likely provide you with a schedule of the partners and associates you'll be meeting with, and the times you are expected to meet with them. In the typical callback interview, you will meet with four to six lawyers, probably a mix of associates and partners. Don't worry that you haven't had time to "study up" on each of these people in Martindale-Hubble. They won't be expecting you to know their life histories. The schedule you'll be given by the firm will probably tell you whether the people you are meeting with are affiliated with the corporate or litigation side of the practice, and also may include their areas of specialty or practice group affiliation. If it doesn't, don't sweat it. It makes a perfectly good question to ask during the interview.

In the typical callback interview, the recruiting coordinator will then "hand you off" to the first person on the list. The individual interviews during your callback will be a lot like the screening interview, so if the nine common question areas are not fresh in your mind as you are reading this, you might consider going back to the last chapter and brushing up. When your designated time with each person runs out, he will take you to the next person, and so on, until you've interviewed with everyone on the list. From there, someone you met with will probably ask you to join them, and several other members of the firm, for lunch (if you had a morning interview), or for drinks or dinner (if you had an afternoon interview). Don't be lulled into complacency by this "social time," however. You're still very much under the microscope for these people—just in a different way. We'll address the finer points of handling recruiting "social time" below.

That's the callback interview in a nutshell. Now let's discuss the important things to remember about the different parts of a callback, and develop some strategies for each part.

Scheduling appointments

It is a good idea to schedule your callbacks as soon as possible, both to assure that the day and time you want is available, and to maximize your chances of getting an offer. During hiring season, the hiring committees at most large firms meet weekly or every other week to make decisions about callback candidates. This process is akin to "rolling admissions," and consequently, the earlier you complete your callback interview, the more open slots the firm will have.

When you call the firm to schedule your callback, ask to speak to the recruiting coordinator, and treat that person the same way you would treat a partner at the firm. Be polite and as flexible as possible. Remember that administrative assistants and recruiting coordinators often wield unexpected power in hiring decisions. One negative word about you can sink your candidacy. One former hiring partner I talked to told me that at his firm, the partners paid particular attention to the way prospective associates treated the administrative staff, and the first sign of disrespect or derision guaranteed rejection of that candidate.

When scheduling your appointment, if there is any particular person at the firm you'd like to speak with, or if you would like to meet with the members of a particular practice group or groups, you should indicate that preference to the recruiting coordinator when making your appointment. Firms will almost always attempt to accommodate these requests. If you will be traveling to another city, you may also need to make travel arrangements and overnight accommodations. Before making flight arrangements or hotel accommodations, however, ask the recruiting director at the firm if the firm gets a preferred rate at a particular hotel that they'd like you to use, and whether they would prefer to book your flights or have you do it. Asking these simple questions shows fiscal responsibility, and is always appreciated. As stated earlier, the general rule is that if you cannot make it to the city where your interview is and back to the city where your law school is comfortably in one day, an overnight stay is warranted. If there is any doubt in your mind about the propriety of an overnight stay, consult the placement director at your law school for advice.

Once you know you'll be traveling to a particular city for a callback, if there are any other firms in that city that you had screening interviews with but have not yet heard from, it is acceptable to call your screening interviewer at those firms for a status report. The best way to handle this situation is to (1) tell the screening interviewer that you will be traveling to her city for a callback interview at another firm, (2) that you are still very interested in her firm, and (3) that you were wondering if you could get a status report for scheduling purposes. If a decision has already been made, she will probably tell you what it was. If a decision has not been made, however, the news that "the competition" is after you and that you called to inquire about your status may get you the nod in close cases, so don't be afraid to inquire.

If you have two or more callback interviews in the same city, do everything you can to schedule them on back-to-back days. This will enable all the firms to divide the airfare and the cost of your accommodations, exhibits fiscal responsibility on your part, will save you a lot of unnecessary travel, and will curb the necessity of your missing too many classes. While the thought of jet-setting around the country to law firms may sound romantic and exciting at first, it is an incredibly draining process that will quickly become tiresome after one or two cancelled flights or long airport delays.

Finally, practice fiscal conservatism during your callback layovers. While it is fine to order room service, and unnecessary to restrict yourself to the cheap chicken entree, you should not be ordering the forty-nine dollar twin lobster tails, expensive wines, or entertaining a spouse or significant other on the firm's tab. Cabs are fine. Limousines are not. And if you want a Swedish massage at the hotel after your interview, you'd better pay for it yourself. You might think that since law firms simply expense these charges out, they don't matter. Think again. Some firms don't look these expense reimbursements over, but others do, and you don't know which ones are which. If a firm is watching and your charges look extravagant compared to those incurred by other callback candidates, it could be held against you.

Tackling the callback interview

Be ten or fifteen minutes early arriving at the firm. Travel to the firm by cab unless it is a short walk from your hotel and you know exactly where it is. This is no time to get lost. Dress conservatively, and remove any controversial accoutrements.

> Read the best paper in the city on the day of your callback. I got a lot of questions that I couldn't answer about what had been on the front page of the *New York Times* that day.
> —Alison

As previously mentioned, you will not be expected to know anything about your interviewers individually (unless you specifically requested one or more of them), but that doesn't mean that you can't ask them questions about themselves during the interview! Before your callback, consult the list of questions you had for the screening interviewer at the firm and see if any of those questions is still relevant to ask. Then try to develop two or three additional questions that are firm-specific or practice-group-specific. Remember the two psychological axioms central to the interviewing process. Interviewers prefer the people they like, and the more good questions you ask and the more you get the interviewer to talk about his life and his experiences at the firm, the better that person's impression of you will be. That doesn't mean you should duck his questions and try to ask one of your own. It just means that you'll want to ask two or three good questions of each person you meet with—and you don't need to wait until the end of the interview to do so. If the opportunity presents itself, jump right in with your questions.

But what about those hard questions? The real zingers—like, "Why do you think the firm ranked last in the city in associate satisfaction last year, and what is being done to remedy that situation?" Or "I noticed that the firm is currently involved in a high profile gender discrimination lawsuit. I know you can't talk about the specifics of the case, but can you reassure me about the way the firm views its female associates?" Should you ask these questions in a callback interview?

Absolutely.

If you are interviewing at a firm that has recently received some negative ratings or publicity, they'll be prepared to answer questions about it. Just the same as in the screening interview, if you don't ask about it, the firm might wonder whether you looked at them carefully enough to become aware of the problem, or they may conclude that you were simply too timid to ask about it. Timidity has no place in the practice of law. This doesn't mean that you have to go after the firm with both barrels on a sensitive issue. Simply pose the question frankly to your interviewer and then listen intently to his response. Never be afraid to ask the tough question. Just ask it professionally.

> Be sure to ask a lot of questions about the firm. There are two reasons for this. First, it gives the interviewer a chance to talk, and it is a lot easier for an interviewer to answer questions than to ask them. Since I now work for a smaller firm, I've had a chance to be the interviewer and based on that experience, I can tell you this—the interviewer is not going to like you much if you make her work too hard to come up with questions to ask you. Second, by asking insightful questions, it makes it clear that you are really interested in the firm and have done your homework about it.
>
> —Carolyn

Joel agrees. "Talk to some 3Ls who worked at that firm last summer, and get some questions from them. Your career services office should be able to give you some names. Read about the firm in *The Insider's Guide to Law Firms.* Check out the firm's website."

If you are interviewing with five different attorneys at a firm, you don't need to have fifteen different questions. It is perfectly acceptable to pose the same questions in each interview. In fact, the consistency or inconsistency of the answers you receive from the various interviewers can be quite instructive! As with the screening interview, the only questions you should not ask during a callback interview are questions regarding salary, benefits, and vacation time. Save those questions until after you have been extended an offer.

Finally, if the firm you are talking to is your first choice, make it clear to every person you talk to. Believe it or not, preferences like that count a lot.

How to handle the recruiting meal

If the thought of the recruiting meal conjures images in your mind of that scene from *Pretty Woman* where Julia Roberts's character flings escargot across the restaurant and fumbles haplessly with the silver, you are not alone. For many 2Ls, recruiting lunches and dinners may be among the most formal dining experiences you will have had to date. Here are some general suggestions.

When you sit down, don't forget to place your napkin in your lap. It's an easy thing to forget about when you're on edge. Chances are, people at the table will be asking you so many questions that you won't have time to really look over the menu before the server comes to take your orders. That's par for the course. If one of the partners encourages you to order first, beg off, tell him that you haven't had a chance to decide yet, and ask to choose last. This gives you the added benefit to see what everyone else is ordering. Try to follow the pattern. If everyone else orders an appetizer, a salad, and an entrée, you should feel comfortable doing the same. If no one else orders an appetizer, you should skip it also.

The recruiting meal is what I refer to as the "social testing segment" of the interview. The opportunity to dine with someone gives people at the firm a chance to observe what you are like as a person in a more social setting, including how you treat the wait staff and what your table manners are like!

—Elizabeth

If you aren't immediately certain what you want to order, it is a nice gesture to ask your companions for a recommendation or two. Again this is calculated, but it won't seem like it. People love to be asked for their advice, particularly when you appeal to their taste and experience, so do it if you can.

If everyone else has a glass of wine, you can too, but otherwise, avoid alcohol. As the adage goes, *in vino, veritas*. As a recruit, you may not want too much veritas spilling out during the meal, so watch yourself here.

Remember to be polite to the server. They may be watching for that.

Finally, try to keep asking questions of people during the meal to keep the conversation from lagging. Throw out a question about the city, where everyone grew up, or what people typically do for fun on the weekends. Keeping it light during the meal is fine, but you'll want to make sure you sustain the conversation. Remember, above all, however, that the recruiting lunch is still that—a recruiting lunch. Let someone else tell the questionable joke or make the political slam. You should stay on the safe topics and refrain from heading into dangerous territory (politics, religion, firm bashing).

Finally, when the meal is over, be sure to make a general comment to everyone thanking them for having you.

When the callback is over

If you have the opportunity, ask the recruiting coordinator when you might expect a decision. Be sure to keep all your receipts together and send them to the firm with any paperwork they gave you for reimbursement as soon as possible. If some expenses, like a plane flight, are being divided between two or more firms, make copies of the receipts and put a note on them to indicate how things have been divided. Finally, if you made a personal connection with anyone at the firm, a thank-you note to that individual attorney is appropriate. Otherwise, a brief thank-you note to the recruiting coordinator asking that person to convey your appreciation to the other attorneys you met with will suffice. Yeah, I know. Somebody probably counseled you against sending a thank-you note, right? I think that's bunk. Use some common sense here. It is never a mistake to express your appreciation for another's hospitality, and I'm quite certain I never lost anything by doing so.

Some horror stories to calm you down

"At one of my callbacks, I met with a senior partner who asked me why I was interviewing with his firm," Allan remembers. "I told him I was there because the firm emphasized 'lifestyle' where the associates tended to have lives outside the office. The guy then went off on me, telling me that any large firm, his firm or any other firm, would make me kill myself, and that my expectations were unrealistic."

Fortunately, Allan's story is relatively rare. Most "horror stories" are more like the following:

"It was my first callback, the day was cold and rainy, and I really wasn't feeling well," Alison recalls. "I went through each interview getting more and more nauseous until I could barely keep my head up. All I could think about was how I was going to get through lunch. When lunch came, I left the table and threw up, and the associate I was with had to have his food wrapped up to go. I went home in a cab, half crying, half sleeping, sure that I would never get a job."

Finally, there is this beauty.

"An airline lost the luggage of a somewhat heavy-set friend of mine on his way to an important interview," a mentor recalls. "He had to go to the interview in the khakis he wore on the plane, and a borrowed shirt, jacket, and tie that were too small and looked ridiculous on him. Nevertheless he marched through the interview with confidence, poking fun at his misfortune instead of obsessing about it, and got the job offer. Callback interviewers want to like you. Let them."

CHAPTER 19

The Future is Now:
Using the "Relevance Calculus"
to Choose a Firm

All that glitters is not gold.
—CERVANTES

I F ALL GOES WELL, by the close of the recruiting season, you'll have secured a job offer for your 2L summer. Hopefully, you'll have several offers to choose from. But how do you decide which offer to take?

You'll mine the placement office, *The Insider's Guide to Law Firms*, and the *Law Weekly* citywide firm rankings. You'll talk to your friends to get their impressions. In the end, though, like so many other times in law school, it will be you, struggling, alone in the dark.

This chapter should help.

How to compare starting salaries

First of all, let's talk for a minute about starting salaries. If you are like most of us, actually having money in the bank at the end of the month is probably a foreign concept—so the very real possibility that you might be making more than $100,000 next year has probably blown your mind. Before you get smitten by dreams of vast wealth and sign on the dotted line, however, it's time for a reality check. Things, you see, are not always as they seem.

The following exercise will allow you to compare and chart out what is going to happen to the starting salaries at the various firms you're considering before you actually get to do much with "all that money" you'll be making. Flip to the "Salary Comparison Chart" in the middle of the chapter. Start by filling in the names of the firms you're considering, and the starting salary at each firm, including any signing bonuses, and travel and bar exam preparation expenses. From there, figure out what tax bracket this salary and whatever other income you might be receiving from investments or other sources will put you in, and lop off the appropriate percent for federal income tax, state income tax, and any applicable city taxes. If you're not sure what percent state income or city tax you'll be subject to, call your firm's recruiting coordinator to inquire.

Now how much are you being paid? Those salaries doesn't look quite as impressive anymore, huh? Look across the board and compare them, however, because differences in state income tax percentages, and the presence or absence of a city tax can make a substantial difference in overall salary value. Circle these values— as these are your after-tax incomes before you spend a nickel on anything. Now enter the billable hour goals for each of the firms, and divide your after-tax salaries by the number of billable hours you are expected to produce. The resulting figure is your after-tax salary per hour. Suddenly, that salary doesn't look so huge anymore, does it?

But now the fun really starts.

Determine the likely rental cost of an apartment for a year in the city where each firm is located. The difference in the cost of housing, alone, from one city to the next, can amount to over $10,000 per year, so take some time to get reasonably accurate numbers here. You may need to consult the real estate section of the city's newspapers, or go on-line and consult a real estate website to determine average rental costs. When you have a number, subtract it from your after-tax salary (the values you circled) for each firm.

Now, are you planning to keep a car in the city? If you are, you're going to pay for it! Determine how much it is going to cost you to park the car for the year, and how much it will cost you to register and insure it. Subtract those costs from what's left.

If you're working in a big city, you're probably not crazy enough to drive to work every day, so you'll probably be taking some form of public transportation, right? Hopefully, your destination city provides commuters with some break on monthly commuter passes. How much are twelve of those babies going to set you back? Yup, you got it. Subtract that from your starting salary.

Now how much are you being paid?

But we're not done yet.

There's a not-so-little matter called a sales tax that you need to consider. Find out if the state where you're going has one, and what percent it is. The average American spends about 10 percent of his salary on taxable consumer goods, so take 10 percent of your starting salary, multiply that number by the percent sales tax your state features, and subtract that result from your starting salary.

Getting smaller isn't it? But we're not done yet.

If you've done any traveling, you probably know that the cost of living can be wildly different from city to city. You have already noticed it in comparing the rents between the cities you are considering, but there are many other less-obvious manifestations of this cost-of-living differential, like food and entertainment costs, that can have a huge effect on your budget, and how much money you manage to squirrel away in any given year. The following methods are not strictly "scientific," but I have found that the calculations that follow can be surprisingly accurate in helping you to "guesstimate" the differences in the costs of living from one city to the next.

First, we'll deal with food. Whether you cook for yourself or are a sustaining member of the local Chinese place, the base cost of food in the city you choose will influence how much you end up paying for things. Accordingly, we're going to go shopping. Visit or call the largest chain grocery store in each city you're considering, and get prices on the following items: a gallon of milk, a half-gallon of orange juice, a box of Cheerios, the per-pound cost of tomatoes and Granny Smith apples, the per pound cost of bean coffee, the per pound cost of boneless, skinless chicken breast, and the cost of a thirty-two ounce jar of name-brand pasta sauce. Add up the cost of this "shopping list" to get a total cost in each city. Then add up the costs for all the cities, and divide by the number of cities to get an "average cost" of the shopping list among all the cities you are considering. Divide each city's cost by the average cost to get the "percent of the average" for each city. Multiply this "percent of the

251

average" by $2,600, a mentor-estimated annual food budget, to get an estimated food budget for each city, adjusted for cost-of-living differences. Subtract this amount from your after-tax salary.

Now estimate the cost of an average night out with friends in each city. Take the cost of a movie ticket, and add it to the cost of three premium draught beers at the local bar to get a hypothetical "cost of a night out" total for each city. If you aren't sure of the exact costs of these items, make some phone calls to get them. Add up these totals for all the cities you are considering, and divide by the total number of different cities you're comparing to get an "average cost of a night out" among the cities. Then divide each city's actual cost by this average cost to get a value called the "percent of the average." This figure gives you some indication about how much more or less expensive one city is compared to another. Still with me? Now multiply this percent of the average that you derived for each city by $2,500, your mentors' consensus about how much you will spend on entertainment in a given year. The result is your estimated entertainment budget for the year, adjusted for cost of living in the various cities you are considering. It's not perfect, but it's a surprisingly good estimate. Subtract this from your salary.

After doing these calculations, you have a rough estimate of how much money you'll be looking at after you've paid your taxes and essential costs of living. Now take your after-taxes and expenses salary totals, and as we did before, divide them by the billable hour goals for each firm you are considering.

Surprised?

I was. Doing these calculations revealed to me that I would actually be making a larger per-hour salary after taxes and expenses in New Hampshire than I would have made in Boston, even though the starting salary in Boston was about 90 percent higher, because the taxes, cost-of-living expenses, and billable hour goal in New Hampshire were much lower.

Fill out the chart on the next page for yourself. You may need to spend a couple of hours and make a few phone calls, but the time you spend will be well worth the insights you can gain.

THE SALARY COMPARISON CHART

FACTOR	Firm:__ City: __	Firm:__ City: __	Firm:__ City: __
1. Starting salary at firm	_____	_____	_____
2. Federal income tax percentage	_____	_____	_____
3. Federal income tax (row 1 x row 2)	_____	_____	_____
4. State income tax percentage	_____	_____	_____
5. State income tax (row 1 x row 4)	_____	_____	_____
6. City tax percentage	_____	_____	_____
7. City tax (row 1 x row 6)	_____	_____	_____
8. Total taxes (row 3 + 5 + 7)	_____	_____	_____
9. After tax income (row 1—row 8)	_____	_____	_____
10. Billable hour requirement	_____	_____	_____
11. Salary per hour after taxes (row 9 divided by row 10)	_____	_____	_____
12. After tax income (same as row 9)	_____	_____	_____
13. Annual rent	_____	_____	_____
14. Subtotal (row 12-row 13)	_____	_____	_____
15. Parking/registration/insurance	_____	_____	_____
16. Subtotal (row 14-row 15)	_____	_____	_____
17. Public tranporatation cost	_____	_____	_____
18. Subtotal (row 16-row 17)	_____	_____	_____
19. Annual food budget*	_____	_____	_____
20. Subtotal (row 18-row 19)	_____	_____	_____
21. Annual entertainment budget*	_____	_____	_____
22. Subtotal (row 20-row 21)	_____	_____	_____
23. Billable hour requirement	_____	_____	_____
24. Salary per hour after living expenses (row 22 divided by row 23)	_____	_____	_____

*see text above for suggested calculations

If you have taken the time to fill out the chart, consider the following thoughts. Are you working more hours for less money at one firm than you would be at another? Is there a compelling reason why you would want to do that? There might be—perhaps that firm offers more of the kind of work you want, has a better reputation, or is located in the city you most want to live in. Just make sure you know *why* you are choosing one firm over the other, because, as the above exercise shows, a higher starting salary does not always translate to more money in your pocket. Remember a couple of other things. Minor differences should not be overemphasized, since several of the calculations are rough estimations. Finally, keep in mind that the above exercise examines first year starting salaries only. You might want to look into how much, and by what method salaries typically increase from year to year at each of the firms you are considering. Are the annual raises merit-based (based on your performance), or lock-step (based on the number of years you've spent at the firm)? Once you have this information, you can begin to eyeball how the comparisons between the firms you are considering might play out over time.

Choosing a firm using the "relevance calculus"

Below, you will find the list of the thirty-three defined factors that comprise the "relevance calculus"—a non-scientific system to help you decide in what firm, and perhaps even in what city to practice. If you read the prior chapters on recruiting interviews, did your homework, and asked the right questions, you should already know where each firm you are considering stands with respect to each of these factors. After the list of these factors, you will find the "relevance calculus" chart, which will help you to really think about each of these factors and its importance to you and to your decision. You may want to photocopy this chart several times so you can fill one out for each firm you are considering.

Here's how it works.

First, read the descriptions of the various factors below, and assign each of these factors an "importance value" from zero to two in the space provided in the chart that follows. Give a factor a zero if it is of little or no importance to you, a one if it is somewhat important to you, and a two if it is very important to you. Be sure that once you assign a factor an "importance value," you use the same importance value for that factor across all the firms you are considering. Note that there are a couple of blank spaces intentionally provided in the chart in case you want to write in extra factors.

From there, assign each of the firms you are considering a score from one to five for each of the factors discussed. For example, on the factor "salary and bonuses," give a firm a factor score of one if the firm's salary and bonus structure is "lousy" compared to the other firms you are considering; a two if it is "below average;" a three if it is "average;" a four if it is "above average;" and a five if it is "outstanding."

After you have assigned each factor an "importance" score (zero to two), and a "factor score" (one to five), multiply the two scores together to get the "total factor score" for each factor. For example, if you assigned the factor "salary and bonuses" an importance score of two ("very important"), and gave a particular firm a factor score of three ("average") for salary and bonus, the "total factor score" for salary and bonuses for that firm would be six (two times three). Note that if you ruled a particular factor "not important," you will end up with a total factor score of zero for that factor because you are multiplying by zero.

Complete these calculations for each factor until you have filled the entire chart, and then add up the "total factor scores" of all the factors. The number you end up with is the "final firm score." Compare the final firm scores of each of the firms you are considering to help you decide among them.

DESCRIPTION OF FACTORS IN THE RELEVANCE CALCULUS

Salary and Bonus: Starting salary, including any bonuses (signing bonus, clerkship bonus), moving expenses, and the amount of bar expenses the firm will cover. Be sure to use "The Salary Comparison Chart" above to make a more accurate comparison between salaries.

Benefits/Vacation Package: The amount and quality of health, dental, and life insurance the firm will provide to you; whether your spouse and children are also eligible under the benefits package; number of weeks of paid vacation allowed per year; sabbatical program, if any.

Prestige of Firm: Overall rank of firm in city and nationwide among lawyers and law students. By the time recruiting season is over, you should have a good idea about this already, but for more information, consult your law school placement office and the annual firm rankings provided in *The American Lawyer* or *Law Weekly*.

Length of Partner Track: The number of years you must work before you can be considered for partnership. Ask whether there are different levels of partnership (junior partner, non-equity partner), and determine the number of years required to reach each level.

Potential to Become Equity Partner: Remember that only equity partners share in the firm's equity (and divide the lion's share of yearly profits), so if you're in it for money and control, find out what percent of first-year associates go on to become equity partners. If you receive an ambiguous answer, beware—the news is probably not favorable.

Billable Hour Requirement: 1800–2000 is average, but don't just accept the firm's "party line" on what the billable hour requirement is. Find out what the average associate billable hours were for the prior year, and then ask several of the associates you met during your callback interview what their previous year's billable hours were. Remember that the most efficient associates can still only bill about 80 percent of the time they spend in the office. Assuming that you take your three weeks of vacation and don't work weekends, you will need to work ten-and-a half or eleven hour workdays to meet a 2000 hour billable goal. Those are long workdays. If the requirement is higher than 2000 hours per year, well . . .

Ability to Do Type of Work Desired: First, does the firm have a thriving practice in the type of work you are interested in, or do they only do the occasional case or deal in that area? Will you be allowed to pick the department or the practice group you want to work with? Again, don't just accept the firm's "party line" answer to this question. Check with the associates you meet to find out whether the person that came to the firm to do First Amendment work is actually getting that kind of work, or has ended up getting stuck with routine contracts work instead.

Firm Training/Mentoring Program: Will you be assigned a mentor in the area of law you are interested in practicing? What kind of training does the firm provide you, in terms of learning how to use the computer systems, and offering writing and trial workshops?

Distribution of Assignments: Are assignments filtered to you through an advisor, mentor, or a central clearinghouse, or can partners and upper-level associates simply dump things on you willy-nilly? Is there anyone you will be able to turn to when your workload becomes unbearable, but the partners keep coming with more assignments? For incoming associates who have a difficult time refusing assignments from partners, this is a critical question to ask.

Firm Hierarchy: Simply put, what is the partner to associate ratio? Top-heavy firms can be very taxing on associates, since there are only so many people around to field assignments from partners. You might also want to find out how projects are typically staffed. Will it be just you and a partner, or will there also be a mid-level associate on the project who can help you over the rough spots?

Associate Satisfaction: How happy are the associates at the firm you are considering? Don't expect candid answers from the associates themselves. Instead, consult your law school placement office for the latest "Associate Satisfaction" poll anonymously collected from most of the country's largest law firms. If your firm ranks poorly, proceed with caution. There is no reason to expect that your experience will be any different.

Perception of the Other Attorneys at the Firm: Largely a "gut feeling" here, since you probably only met these people for part of a day, but how did they look? Were they smiling and cordial, or were they generally scowling, walking around with their heads down, and looking exhausted? Did they greet each other in the hallways, or just walk past each other like ships passing in the night? Did the people you meet seem to have interests outside the office, or was the office their life? Are these the kind of people that you'd want to hang out with socially?

Firm Culture/Environment: Is this a "white shoe" firm from yesteryear where your kind might be welcomed at the front door, but not really welcomed in the back hallways? Is there an obvious "old boys network" at play? Does the contingent of associates feel more like a college fraternity where boozing and partying after work is overemphasized? Is the place stiff and overly formal? Did it feel cold and austere, or warm and comfortable? More "gut feeling" stuff here, but first perceptions can be accurate ones.

How Do You Think You Would Fit in Here? Still more gut feeling stuff, but what do you think? Are the people at this firm enough like you that you'll have things to talk about? Would you be comfortable working in a place like this? Is this the kind of place you'd be excited to come to every morning, or do you already feel like you'd have nothing in common with a lot of the people you met? How does your personal style mesh with the firm culture discussed above?

Maternity/Paternity Policy: Want to have kids some day, but still keep your job? Better ask about this. While you're at it, inquire about whether the firm provides on-site day-care for its lawyers. Some do.

Percent of Minority Lawyers at Firm: Want to work in a diverse, or at least non-bigoted environment? Look around when you visit. What do you see? Does the place look ethnically diverse, or white as snow? Is there a mix of males and females in the partnership? If you have doubts, you'd better ask some questions. Better to find out now than after you start.

Firm's Attitude Toward Alternative Lifestyles: Are you gay, lesbian, or bisexual? Better investigate what the firm's reaction will be when they find out. Are there any gays or lesbians in the partnership? Check the NALP directory for this information. Is there a nondiscrimination policy in place that includes a clause on sexual orientation? Ask to see the firm's policy. If there isn't, you might want to look elsewhere.

Desirability of the Firm's Office Space: Where is the building located? What does the office space look like? Will you have your own office? How big will it be? Will you have your own legal assistant? Completely a matter of personal taste here.

"Perks": Does the firm have a luxury box at the arena or the ballpark? Does the firm provide discounted country club memberships or waived initiation fees? Health club memberships? Low interest home loans? Help getting a good mortgage? Meals if you are working late? A car to drive you home if you are working really late? Errand service? Ask!

Friends at the Firm or Going to the Firm: Don't underestimate the importance of having someone you can trust at the firm to commiserate with. Your job will have its moments, and having someone there to talk to who knows the personalities you are talking about and understands the firm culture can be very helpful.

Potential to Move Laterally: If your job at this firm ends up being less than spectacular, how easy will it be to go somewhere else from this firm? The general rule is that it is easier to move from a large, big-city firm to another large, big-city firm, or to a smaller market than it is to go from a smaller market to a large firm. Ask your law school placement office for more help here.

Desirability of City: Do you have a favorable o[...]
impression of the city where the firm is located?

Housing Options Near the Office: Are [...]
attractive places to live near the office? Ask th[...]
the firm where they live, and for any recomme[...]
options compare to the options in the other [...]
ing?

Length of Commute to Work: Pretty much speaks for itself, rig[...]
Also consider whether you will be traveling via public transportation
or driving. Do you prefer one over the other? Are both options available and convenient?

Proximity to Family: Can be good or bad, depending on your family. Whichever one it is, how do you feel about it? Are you close
enough to them or far enough away from them to feel comfortable?

Proximity to Close Friends: Sure, you'll be meeting lots of new
friends, but it helps to have an established network of friends in a new
place to get you started—or at least to have a friend or two nearby to
call on when times get tough. How far away are your best friends?

Proximity to Significant Other: Sure, some people try the long distance relationship thing, and a few of them even manage to make it
work for awhile. As a young associate at a law firm, you probably won't
be one of them.

Potential to Find a Significant Other in This City: Hoping to find
a nice Jewish boy in Boise? Ever heard of a cowboy named Goldberg?
Being single in rural anywhere probably isn't a good idea either.

Cultural Activities: How are the museums? Is there a live music
scene? Good movie theatres? Exhibitions?

Nightlife: How is the local bar and club scene? Is it the kind of scene
you'd enjoy? How close are the ballparks, stadiums, and arenas? Are
there generally seats available to the games, or is every game sold out
a year in advance?

Proximity to Favorite Outdoor Activities: When the snow starts to
fly, how far is the nearest good skiing? How far to the beach, the lake,
the mountains?

Sports Rooting Interest: Can you stomach working in the same city
as the Yankees? No, really. Can you?

you've read through and considered these factors, make
t you can give each firm an honest grade on each factor. If
eed more information, it's time to make some phone calls.
ce you have the information you need, fill out "The relevance
alculus" below to get scores for each of the firms you are considering. You may want to photocopy the chart to enable you to fill
one out for each of the firms under consideration.

THE RELEVANCE CALCULUS

Firm: _____

Factor	Importance to you 0 = not important 1 = somewhat important 2 = very important	× Score = 1 = worst 5 = best	Total
Salary and bonuses*			
Benefits/vacation package			
Prestige of firm			
Length of partner track			
Potential to become equity partner			
Billable hour requirement			
Ability to do type of work desired			
Firm training/mentoring program			
Distribution of assignments			
Firm structure (# of associates to # of partners)			
Associate satisfaction			
Your perception of other attorneys at firm			
Firm culture/environment			
Gut feeling about how you would "fit in" at firm			

Firm's maternity/paternity policy			
Number of minority lawyers at firm			
Firm's attitude toward "alternative lifestyles"			
Desirability of firm's office space			
Firm "perks"			
Friends at or going to this firm			
Potential to move laterally from this firm			
General "gut feeling" about this firm			
Desirability of city			
Housing options in city			
Length of commute			
Proximity to family			
Proximity to close friends			
Proximity to significant other			
Potential to find a significant other in this city			
Cultural activities			
Nightlife			
Proximity to favorite outdoor activities			
Sports rooting interest			
Other:			

*see the salary comparison chart above before scoring this factor

Surprised?

I was. I was having an extremely difficult time choosing between my favorite firm in Boston, and a great firm in the much smaller but rapidly growing city of Manchester, New Hampshire, where I grew up. After sketching out all the different factors that were relevant to my decision, I developed the "relevance calculus" to help determine which factors were more important to me, and to provide a way to objectively compare my options. After putting my two choices through the calculus, I determined that, given my interests, my career goals, and the factors that mattered most to me, my choice wasn't nearly as difficult as it first appeared.

Maybe the relevance calculus can do the same for you. At the very least, however, it should provide you with a way to think about and evaluate the factors that matter most to you in making this important decision. Remember, for most law students, a permanent offer of employment will come from the firm where you choose to spend your 2L summer, and accordingly, it is also likely to be the firm you'll end up staying with for at least your first few years after law school. It is a big decision, and should not be made cavalierly.

Here's what influenced your mentors in choosing their firms.

"I chose based on three factors: location, prestige, and variety of practice areas," Elizabeth explained. "I am close to my family, so I decided that I wanted to end up close to home. This turned out to be a good decision, because the life of an associate is so busy there isn't much time to be traveling. I also wanted to make sure I ended up with a prestigious firm because in today's legal market, no one knows how long they will be at their first job. My theory was that it's better to start off in a place that has a good reputation because from there you can go anywhere. Finally, I am interested in so many things that I wanted to get exposure to a bunch of different practice areas. I wanted to start my career with a wide variety of choices and then have the ability to specialize later."

"I paid particular attention to whether I liked the people I met, and whether I sensed that the attorneys were generally happy to be where they were," Carolyn adds.

"Try to find a place where you can learn to practice law. You need to find a place where there are people you can learn from, a place where you'll feel comfortable, and a place that is going to allow you to practice in the areas you're interested in," Pat counsels.

"I also looked for positive experiences from the 3Ls who had worked at the firm the previous summer," Joel mentions.

Keith adds a final word for those being drawn to a particular city, firm, or firm size by peer pressure.

"Avoid the lemming mentality. Don't go somewhere just because everyone else thinks it's the place to be. Decide what it is that *you* want, and then go after that. Forget what everyone else is doing. Most of them don't know what they're doing."

CHAPTER 20

Back on the Chain Gang:
Advice About Journal Membership

*We must all hang together, or assuredly,
we shall hang separately.*
—BENJAMIN FRANKLIN

MANY STUDENTS compete for membership on legal journals (in schools that offer writing competitions) or "walk on" to journals where membership is open to all without ever considering what the experience entails or what benefits are to be derived from membership. For them, it is just another blind decision for students climbing the ladder of ambition. If you read chapter 14, however, you should have already given enough thought to the reasons why you want to be on a journal that the sometimes monotonous nature of 2L journal membership should be easier to take.

But what distinguishes the law review from the other "law journals" that you've heard about, and what does being on one of these journals entail?

Essentially, the law review or any other legal journal is an academic publication, kind of like a magazine for scholars, lawyers, and judges. As discussed in chapter 14, among its contents, a law review typically contains several articles on current, controversial issues in the law (typically written by professors, practitioners, or judges); reviews of the most current cases coming out of the supreme court or the circuit in which your law school is located, called "Notes," (typically written by law review members); "Comments" illuminating confusing areas of uncertain law or criticizing current doctrines (written by law review members); and, perhaps, a book review or an essay. A law journal, on the other hand, typically focuses on a particular subject or area of law (constitutional law, law and economics, mental health law, etc.) and restricts its articles, notes, and comments to that one subject area.

Generally, a school's law review is the most prestigious, because it has the widest circulation, receives the most funding, gets the best articles, and is the most selective in choosing its student membership. It is not uncommon, for example, for a professor who has written an article on a topic in constitutional law to bypass a school's constitutional law journal to get his article in the law review. In the "publish or perish" world of academia, reputation means everything.

So how exactly does this work, and what will your job be as a 2L working on one of these journals?

When you "make" one of these journals, you will probably be given a key to the office, a desk and a mailbox in that office, and a library card which will enable you to check books out to the journal. You will no doubt also go through a period of orientation where you will learn how the journal operates and what you can expect your schedule on the journal to be like. You will also be introduced to the journal's officers (read: 3Ls)—the people who will really be running the show this year.

Who are they, you ask?

Every journal's board is slightly different, but generally, it will look something like this. There will be an editor-in-chief, generally the intellectual and motivational leader of the board, who is ultimately responsible for overseeing the other teams of officers, and making all final decisions about the content and style of the journal. The managing editor is the money person—the individual who handles the budget, advertising, distribution, accounts receivable, accounts deliverable, and anything else financially related to running the journal. The executive editors, generally a team of three to six people, are responsible for typesetting, generating, dividing up, and distributing the copy to the 2Ls, entering the editorial changes made by the 2Ls into the computer system, redistributing second, and then final edits of all articles, comments, and notes, and conducting a final check of all copy for errors. The articles editors, generally a team of three to six people, read every written submission and query made to the journal, check the author's background, and decide, usually with the editor-in-chief and the managing editor, which articles are selected for publication. They are also responsible for shepherding the author through the editorial process, and acting as chief negotiators between the author and the journal when any controversies arise with respect to content or style. Comments editors or notes editors, generally a team of three to six people, are the people responsible for guiding the 2Ls and 3Ls through the process of writing their note or comment (or both), developing topic, outline, and draft schedules for each student, making editorial suggestions about each note and comment written, and selecting the best ones for publication in the journal. Each journal also typically has a resource editor who is responsible for tracking down rare sources through inter-library loan, making sure that the journal stays current on all its library accounts within the university system, and returning all sources back to their proper library at the end of the editing process; and a symposium editor, who acts as the general overseer and manager of the journal's symposium issue (an issue devoted entirely to the treatment of one particular topic in the law).

As for you, well, you're just a plebean this year—the worker bee that makes the hive run. Your journal likely publishes between four and eight editions each year—each of which must be filled with the articles, notes, and comments mentioned previously. After the articles editors select which articles to publish in a particular issue, and the executive editors divide up the manuscript into manageable segments, it's your turn to shine.

At the beginning of every "edit cycle," you will receive a piece of manuscript to edit. Your first job is to search through the citations and footnotes, and retrieve all first-cited sources from the library system. Generally, these sources will be gathered on shelves and in binders devoted to the author in the journal office. Any sources you cannot find must be identified and handed off to the resource editor, who will then continue the search for you.

After you read the author's entire article to get a sense for what the article is about, and how his argument develops, it's time to edit the particular piece of manuscript to which you have been assigned. Almost inevitably, you'll discover that your author has no idea what the Blue Book is and has never heard of proper citation form, particularly pinpoint citation. This will probably be your largest source of frustration, as you find yourself stuck in the library late at night skimming through a four-hundred page tome looking for the two line quote your author has cited to the source without pinpointing the page for you.

Frustrating. But all part of the game.

After you've finished your first edit and turned it in to the executive editors' office, you'll receive a "second edit"—another section of the same article which has undergone its first edit in the hands of one of your fellow 2L editors. You are told to assume, however, that no one has seen the section before, and to check every source, quote, and citation again—and for good reason. Blue Booking is incredibly tedious and precise work, and even a momentary lapse of concentration can cause you to miss errors in a first edit. Of course, laziness, lack of effort, and the attitude that "someone else will catch it in a second edit" are more frequently the cause—which brings us to one of the most important pieces of advice about journal membership that you'll see in this chapter. It really should be very obvious, but every year, it seems that some people forget to heed this advice.

Do your share of the work, and do it well.

There is nothing that will destroy your reputation in law school faster than getting on the law review or another law journal, using the credential to secure a job and a clerkship, and then being a slacker, turning in sloppy edits, and dumping the burden to correct your work on your fellow editors. To police this problem, many journals post the names of the editors that worked on each section of a prior edit, but even if your journal doesn't do this, don't take advantage of the situation. In the law journal world, what goes around comes around, and generally the first thing to come around will be an angry fellow editor.

The cycle will continue with the circulation of "final edits"—which are generally already on galleys and typeset and formatted as they will appear in the journal when it is published. At this stage, your job is mainly to check for typographical errors, numbers in headings, and cross-references in citations. Upon completion of your final edit, the article will go to the executive editors for a final read-through, and then off to press.

But your job is never done.

Usually even before you see a final edit for an article, you are working on the first edit of something for the next volume.

It is impossible to generalize a weekly time commitment for 2L Law Review or journal membership, as the commitment fluctuates significantly between schools. An initial barometer is to check how many credit hours the registrar has assigned to membership on your journal—but don't stop there, because this number usually significantly underestimates your actual time commitment. Twenty or thirty hour weeks (on top of your classwork) are not uncommon, particularly in the weeks when you are writing. Check with current members of the journal for an idea of what will be expected of you.

Writing your note or comment

The case note

As I noted earlier, writing a case note usually entails dissecting a recent supreme court or circuit court opinion, reporting on its reasoning and conclusions, highlighting the controversial aspects of the opinion, discussing any dissents, and, depending on the style that your journal employs, perhaps editorializing a bit along the way. A case note is generally around ten pages in length.

Relax. You're basically writing a case brief on steroids. It's not as difficult as it sounds, and it can actually be an interesting and extremely educational exercise.

Unlike selecting a comment topic, choosing a note topic is fairly simple. The editorial board of your journal may pre-select a case for you, or provide a list of cases they want treated during the current year. If they don't, talk to the professors in the subjects of your greatest interest, and ask them about recent controversial cases that they feel would make good topics for a case note, or simply monitor the Westlaw and LEXIS legal news databases until you find something you like. Then follow your editors' instructions with respect to content and style.

The comment

Unlike the case note, the comment generally goes beyond the strict "reporting" of a recent case to a lengthier and more thorough evaluation of the controlling law in a particular area. Comments generally run between thirty and a hundred pages. The most fertile ground for comment development is in areas of the law where splits among the circuit courts of appeal have left the status of the law in doubt or disarray. Poorly reasoned supreme court decisions, or decisions based on untenable or recently disproved scientific or social-science research are also common sources for comments.

Although each journal has its own guidelines for comment writing, there are two general rules to follow when selecting a comment topic. First, if you are writing on a topic that involves a split of authority in the circuit courts of appeal, the supreme court must not have already granted *certiorari* to a case (indicating that they will hear the case in the next term). The practical reason for this is that, by the time your comment is finished, edited, and published, the supreme court may already have issued its opinion resolving the controversy—which will render your comment superfluous, and moot, and of little interest to readers. It is vital to monitor the appeals taken from circuit court cases in your area of interest, and the activities of the United States Supreme Court in granting those appeals during the early stages of your comment-writing process. There is nothing worse than completing a research outline having already committed dozens of hours to a topic, only to get preempted by a grant of *certiorari*.

Second, you must undertake a thorough review of all prior law review and journal articles written on your topic to assure yourself that you have not been preempted by another author. Note that this does *not* mean that if someone else has written on the same topic, you can't write on it. You are only preempted if that other article makes the same arguments and reaches the same conclusions that you do. As long as you approach the subject in a different way, make different or additional arguments, provide a more thorough review of the subject, or reach a different conclusion, you should be fine. When in doubt, however, consult your comment editor. The last thing you want is to write a great comment and then to have it ruled preempted and barred from any chance at publication.

So how do you find a compelling comment topic?

The best way is to talk to a professor in one of the subjects of your greatest interest and ask about the current controversies in the law. Inquire about circuit splits, vagueries in statutes, policy disagreements, or poorly reasoned United States Supreme Court opinions. Bring a pen and prepare to start writing. Professors usually have many of these areas on the tips of their tongues since they are also constantly searching for hot legal topics on which to write and publish. If the professor mentions anything that sounds interesting to you, always ask permission to use it as a topic for a journal comment and see if the professor has any books, case names, or other articles that might point you in the right direction. If the meeting goes well, you might consider asking the professor to mentor your work for you. Most professors are happy to assist students with journal articles.

Again, since every journal will have specific rules about the style and content of student comments, I won't go into further detail here. I will, however, offer a few pieces of advice that will be applicable to any comment written for any journal.

Choose a topic that fascinates you

Notice that I deliberately did not say "interests" you. I said *fascinates* you. Writing a comment, particularly a lengthy one, is a significant undertaking, and may consume six months or more of your law school career. If you pick a topic that fails to hold your interest over time, that can really be a miserable six months—and in the end, you final product will probably reflect your disinterest. Conversely, choosing a great topic can make working on your comment something you look forward to every day after class.

"Make sure your topic is not so general that you can't get it down to a clear thesis," Alison adds. "I picked what I thought was a 'sexy' topic—child sex tourism and how to prevent it under international law. It turned out to be a mess because it was too general. I think the most specific topics work the best."

Whenever possible, choose a topic in the area of your greatest legal interest. If you can combine that topic with an area of expertise from your undergraduate major (like history, political science, economics, or psychology), that's even better. The more layers of interest you have in your topic, the more likely that it will hold your interest, and the richer and more interesting it is likely to be. Take as much time as it takes to find a good topic, and be sure that you're not preempted before you begin.

"And make sure that if you're writing on an international or foreign topic, that enough of your source materials are in English or some other language you can understand!" Keith counsels from experience.

Find a mentor on the faculty

Trying to write a comment without advice from a faculty member is really inadvisable. In case you haven't figured it out yet—law is hard. Trying to keep intersecting doctrines straight and your argument on target in the midst of warring circuit court opinions discussing subjects you haven't studied yet can be difficult. Having a professor to guide you will help you to see the forest for the trees, keep you from veering off on unnecessary tangents, and help to pare down your topic to a sharp, solid thesis.

Stay organized, and stay on deadline

Writing a comment typically involves reading and citing to at least fifty, and sometimes as many as several hundred sources. If you're not careful, your apartment will quickly become littered with photocopies, and you'll end up spending more time looking for something that you previously read but now can't find, than you'll spend actually writing.

Stay organized!

Get yourself a couple of three-ring binders, some highlighters, some stick-on tabs, and a three-hole punch. When you begin reading source material, highlight any passages that you think are relevant, and when you finish reading a source, put it in a general section of your binder (cases, law review articles, legislative history, etc.) and tab it with an identifying moniker so you'll be able to find it again easily when you begin writing. Keep law review or other scientific or news articles alphabetized by author's last name. Tab all passages in books, and keep a sticky note on the front of the book denoting what you plan to use it for.

Staying organized can shave many hours off the comment writing process and will make the experience significantly less frustrating and more enjoyable for you. Finally, upon completion of your comment, you can also turn in your tabbed and organized source binders to your editor. Knowing that the comment is well-researched and well-documented and that the sources are readily accessible could give you a leg up on your competition for publication.

Writing a comment for a law journal can be the most challenging and academically exhilarating experience of your law school career. Make the most of it!

CHAPTER 21

Restoring Balance: Moot Court, Public Service, and How to Reclaim the Life You've Lost

I am not now that which I have been.
—LORD BYRON

BY THE TIME you hit the halfway point of your law school career, you'll have weathered the worst of what law school has to offer. With the dreaded first year, and all of its associated fears behind you, with journal membership decided, and with recruiting season over, it is time to step back from the day-to-day grind and take an accounting of where you are in the big picture.

Take a look at your life.

Wow. Scary, huh?

How bad is it? Have you completely lost touch with your non-law school friends? Have you put on fifteen pounds, fallen badly out of shape, or completely abandoned your hobbies and other interests?

When was the last time you took a whole weekend off without being worried or feeling guilty about it?

As much as I hate to admit it, I spent three years in Philadelphia without ever getting down to see the Liberty Bell, Independence Hall, or the Philadelphia museums of art or natural history. I never got out to Pennsylvania Dutch country, and only discovered the Reading Terminal Market, one of Philadelphia's most wonderful features, in the last months of my stay.

In short, I didn't do a great job achieving balance in my life until my third year.

And that's too late.

Your last three semesters of law school can provide a rich diversity of fulfilling experiences, and a much more relaxed pace, if you look up from your frenetic hustlings long enough to realize that the worst is over. It's time to restore some balance in your life.

Here's how.

First of all, you need to reclaim the life you've lost. In the first weekend after you get back from winter break (unless your school is on an odd schedule—in which case, you should just shift all of this to after your third set of semester finals), take the weekend off. No books, no reading, nothing. Go out of town and visit the best friend you've virtually ignored for the past eighteen months, or invite that friend to come visit you. Kick back and call friends and family. Reconnect with people. Give your spirit a lift.

Go out into the city (if there is one) and just wander around. See the sites. Go to a concert or an exhibit. Treat yourself to dinner at one of the city's renowned restaurants. Browse in the fiction section of the bookstore, or, if the thought of reading anything makes you want to wretch, find a music store instead. Bet there are a lot of new albums from your favorite musicians that you could catch up on.

Restore your gym membership if you've let it lapse, and recommit yourself to getting healthy again. Find a coffee shop somewhere where there are tables and a wait staff that isn't going to hustle you out as soon as you finish your coffee. Consider doing your class reading there as a change of pace.

When you're feeling relaxed and feel like you've regained some perspective, look back over the last eighteen months of law school. Recognize how far you've come and credit yourself for having survived such a grueling experience. Now look forward to the time you have left. Are you still clearly focused on why you came to law school? Have your goals or feelings changed? Are you narrowing your interests in terms of what kind of law you want to practice, or whether you even want to practice at all? Prod yourself a little bit to come up with some answers to these questions, and recommit to or establish a direction to follow as you move into the second half of your law school career.

As you move into the second half of your law school career, you can really start opening up to the myriad opportunities outside of classroom study that are available to you. In planning the spring semester of your second year—the first semester that you'll really have the time and flexibility to pursue some different interests—look to areas other than just garden-variety classes to fill part of your schedule.

"I would just say do something," Joel notes. "Employers like to see extracurricular activities of all kinds, and participating in something can round you out as a person. If you made a good decision going to law school in the first place, then there is surely at least one opportunity that interests you."

"Definitely do something," Alison agrees. "The competitive activities like law review and moot court may seem the most appealing, but other activities can be equally rewarding. The important thing is to do something other than just studying and watching TV, for your sanity as well as your resume."

Public service opportunities

Almost every law school offers some form of course credit (or has a mandatory requirement) for public service work. Commonly referred to as "internships," "externships," "clinics," or "practica," public service opportunities come in all shapes, sizes, colors, and political affiliations. Depending to some extent upon where you are, there may be internships or externships with the attorney general's office, the U.S. Attorney's office, or the public defender's office. There may be chances to earn credit in legal aid clinics, or small business clinics working on real cases with real clients which may ultimately require you to make appearances and arguments in a real court before a real judge. There are opportunities to battle discrimination, bigotry, and anti-Semitism by doing research and writing legal briefs through the mail for organizations like the Southern Poverty Law Center or the Anti-Defamation League. You can represent the poor in landlord-tenant battles against urban slumlords, or work with judges and lawyers in mediation clinics.

"I think participating in a public service activity is very worthwhile," Carolyn notes. "First, it gives you the opportunity to apply some of what you've learned in law school. Second, it gives you the opportunity to help someone who would otherwise have no one to turn to for help. Finally, participating in a public service activity is a great way to get your perspective back. It is very easy to get wrapped up in your own stressful little world as a law student, but taking part in one of these activities is a way to avoid having this happen.

"I participated in a civil practice clinic and had an externship with the Philadelphia D.A.'s office. The one thing I would strongly advise if you're going to do an externship is to research your placement thoroughly before you accept it. Don't bother going to work someplace where the program is unstructured, or where it is unclear both to them and to you what your duties will be, because you'll end up sitting around a lot and you won't learn anything."

The list of possibilities is so vast that you can almost certainly find something to satisfy even the most specific subject interest. Almost every law school has a public service office or a public service coordinator. Stop by, introduce yourself to that person, and get a sense for what the opportunities are. Public service placements provide great opportunities to work with clients, hone your research and writing skills, anchor your legal education in the practical world, and do some real good in the process. You'll be surprised at the life the law takes on when it is being applied to real situations involving real people, and the satisfaction you get from helping someone by using the law can help to cast law school in a whole different light.

Moot court

Whether run by your law school or an outside organization, moot court competitions provide an unparalleled opportunity to apply the research and writing skills you learned during your first year legal writing class to a specific set of facts, and then defend your work orally against an adversary and a panel of impartial judges. Generally, organizers of these competitions choose sexy topics that are the subject of widespread dispute in the legal community, especially issues that have produced a split of authority among the circuits or have just been granted *certiorari* by the United States Supreme Court.

Moot court is a must for anyone thinking about litigation.
—Keith

More than any other experience you will have in law school, moot court competitions prepare you for the realities of life as an appellate advocate and teach you to apply relevant law to the facts of a slightly different case. In a well-constructed competition, you will be forced to analogize and extend existing law to the facts of your case, and defend your arguments against vigorous questioning from the judges. If you are a timid student who was rattled by the Socratic interlocutories of your first-year professors, you would be well served by forcing yourself through one of these experiences to build up your confidence and to help learn to think on your feet.

My moot court experience is my fondest memory of law school. I would recommend it to everyone! There is just no substitute for free practice on how to think on your feet. The time to learn is now.
—Elizabeth

Inns of Court

The mission of the American Inns of Court is "to foster excellence in professionalism, civility, and legal skills for judges, lawyers, academicians, and students of law in order to perfect the quality, availability, and efficiency of justice in the United States."[1] An American Inn of Court is an organization composed of judges, lawyers, law professors, and law students which meets approximately once a month to discuss pertinent, cutting-edge issues facing the legal profession. Patterned after the traditional English model of legal apprenticeship, each Inn of Court is composed of masters of the bench (judges, elder lawyers, and law professors); Barristers (lawyers who don't meet the minimum requirements to be masters); associates (young lawyers); and pupils (law students), and is limited to a membership of eighty people. Inns concentrate

[1] From the Mission Statement of the American Inns of Court as expressed on their website at www.innsofcourt.org

on issues raised in civil and criminal litigation practice, although some Inns further specialize to address only specific areas of legal practice, like intellectual property, federal courts, or white-collar crime.

The membership of a particular Inn of Court is divided into "pupillage teams" consisting of a few members from each membership category. Each team is responsible for conducting one program for the Inn each year and also assembles outside of monthly meetings to discuss general matters of legal practice—an arrangement which allows the less-experienced lawyers in a pupillage team to learn from the experience of the masters and barristers. Finally, each younger member of the Inn is assigned a master who is to act as a mentor, and assist the younger member's development in the law.

There is a lot to be said for any opportunity to develop a mentoring relationship with more experienced people in the legal profession, since the law school atmosphere does not tend to foster these relationships between students and professors. Frankly, there is no better way to learn the practical realities of legal practice. Investigate whether there is a chapter of the American Inns of Court near you, and consider applying for membership if the concept interests you. You'll meet a lot of interesting people and learn a lot of things that are not taught in law school.

Law school committees

Finally, in your upper-years of law school, there are usually chances to get involved in your law school's administration through memberships on various student-faculty committees. Although selection processes vary at different schools, membership is typically decided either by an election or by simply volunteering for the positions.

Among the more interesting of the committees usually seating one or more student members are the admissions committee (which decides admissions criteria and often reads files of aspiring applicants); the hiring committee (which seeks out, evaluates, interviews, and hires new faculty members); the curriculum committee (which proposes courses and designs the law school's curriculum); and the disciplinary committee (which enforces the law school honor code and conducts suspension or expulsion hearings involving student offenders). Check with your law school's dean of student affairs to determine vacancies.

Obviously, membership on these committees can provide you with a great deal of influence in determining the philosophical direction of your law school. It also provides an excellent forum to cultivate close relationships with members of the faculty, and to learn a lot in the process.

CHAPTER 22

Demystifying Judicial Clerkships:
Heigh Thee to the Chambers

He that walketh with wise men shall be wise.
—PRV. 13:20

A<small>T THE TURN</small> of your third semester of law school, conversation will turn to the subject of "judicial clerkships," and you will find yourself in the midst of the newest law school feeding frenzy. But what exactly is a judicial clerkship, and why are all these people scrambling to get one?

A judicial clerkship is essentially a one or two-year paid internship with a state or federal judge which begins after your graduation from law school. A student accepting one of these clerkships must defer entering legal practice, but in exchange, will usually be given credit by her law firm for the number of years served. Thus, for example, a student deferring an offer with a firm in order to serve a two-year clerkship will typically enter the firm as a third-year associate. Although such policies vary from firm to firm (as do the bonuses offered by firms to students who clerk), they can be, and should always be negotiated.

The exact job description of a judicial clerk varies depending on the kind of judge you clerk for and the peculiar quirks of the individual judge; in most cases a judicial clerk functions as the judge's "research" person. The clerk's primary role is to read case files and the memoranda of law written by practicing attorneys, and then write "bench memos" summarizing her findings, or "draft orders" of the actual opinions to be delivered by the court. In the past, a clerk would also serve as the judge's "runner" during hearings or trials—retrieving cases or statutes needed by the judge during the proceeding. With the growth of in-court technology, however, most judges now have access to Westlaw and LEXIS from the bench—absolving the law clerk of this duty. Unfortunately, this advance in technology has consequently reduced the amount of in-court time the clerk gets to log during his clerkship—since his presence is no longer required during every in-court proceeding. Most clerks, however, are still welcome and are often expected to join their judges in the courtroom for major proceedings in the cases they are assigned to. In such cases, the clerk's primary functions are to serve as an extra set of eyes and ears in observing the proceedings, to evaluate arguments and testimony, to feed the judge important questions raised by the briefs, and to alert the judge to any discrepancies between the written record and the live testimony as those discrepancies occur at trial.

Clerkships are available at all levels of the federal and state court system. In the federal system, clerkships are offered by the United States Court of Claims, the United States bankruptcy courts in each jurisdiction, the United States district courts in each jurisdiction, each of the twelve circuit courts of appeal, and the United States Supreme Court. On the state level, clerkships are offered by every state's highest court (generally called the "supreme court"), and the majority of state appellate and state trial courts. Competition for these clerkships ranges from competitive (state trial and appellate courts), to intensely competitive (state supreme courts, U.S. bankruptcy courts, the U.S. Court of Claims, and the United States district courts), to extremely competitive (circuit courts of appeal), to damn near impossible (the United States Supreme Court). Experiences in these positions are widely disparate and are best summarized in turn.

STATE COURT CLERKSHIPS

State trial and intermediate appellate courts

When considering a lower state court clerkship, it is important to remember that the state court systems vary widely. In some states, the courts may be divided according to subject matter (domestic issues, criminal issues, corporate issues, etc.), while in others, the subject matter may be lumped together, but the courts' jurisdiction decided by the amount in controversy. In still others, the jurisdiction of state courts may be based on some combination of these factors.

Pay particular attention to whether the judges in a particular state court system are elected or appointed, as elected judges may have certain political agendas that you may be forced to adopt. Call the court and determine whether you will be in a central "pool" of clerks shared by all the judges in a particular court, or whether you will work one-on-one with a particular judge, bearing in mind that as a member of a clerk "pool," your opportunities to cultivate a mentor in the judiciary may be reduced. You should also keep in mind that many state trial courts carry exceptionally heavy case loads which may limit your opportunity to write extensive draft orders or bench memoranda, or delve deeply into the theory behind the law.

When considering a lower state court clerkship, the best advice is usually found by consulting lawyers who practice in the state court system. They will typically have more insight into the particular courts and judges than you could ever gather on your own.

State supreme courts (highest court)

If you know for certain which state you intend to practice in, doing a clerkship in that state's highest court can be an extremely valuable experience both for the law you'll learn, and contacts you'll make in the judiciary and among the practitioners. Some states' highest courts, like the supreme courts of California and New Jersey and the New York Court of Appeals produce exceptional opinions. Others harbor judges esteemed on a level equal to their federal counterparts. United States Supreme Court Associate Justice David Souter, for example, spent many years on the New Hampshire Supreme Court before being tapped for the First Circuit Court of Appeals and then the United States Supreme Court.

Some state supreme courts seem to attempt to decide every case on its facts and show little interest in developing a body of well-reasoned, precedential case law. Others still elect their supreme court justices, which, to put it kindly, opens the door for a more openly "political" experience.

Conventional wisdom says that the quality of legal scholarship is much higher in the federal courts than it is in the state courts, even at the highest level. There are, of course, numerous exceptions. To sum up, when pursuing a state court clerkship, you may want to employ some "quality assurance" tactics.

FEDERAL COURT CLERKSHIPS

Federal district courts

Federal district courts are the "trial courts" of the federal system. Although they are courts of limited jurisdiction, the combination of federal question and diversity jurisdiction, coupled with state law issues bootstrapped into a case via supplemental jurisdiction, provides a vast array of subject matter likely to keep even the most curious law student happy.

If you have eyes on a career in litigation, a tour of duty in a federal district court will provide you with invaluable experience and insight. You will read and evaluate dozens of legal memoranda prepared by some of the best lawyers in the region, which will radically improve your understanding of how to construct, organize, and support legal arguments. You will argue close legal points and proper case outcomes with your judge, which will give you insight into how judges think, and an understanding of what is needed to convince them. Finally, you will have the chance to observe and participate in federal court trials, which will give you the opportunity to watch trial strategy in action—and to get immediate feedback from the judge about what is effective and what isn't. If you're lucky, the judge may even allow you to observe while he questions the jury about the case in the jury room after a verdict is reached— which will give you a rare glimpse into the confounding world of jury deliberations.

Of course, the heart of any clerkship is research and writing, and you'll do plenty of that as a district court clerk. Motion practice is the bread-and-butter of the federal clerk's responsibility, and consequently, a large percentage of your time will be spent reading, researching, and writing draft orders deciding motions to dismiss, motions for summary judgment, and motions in *limine*. Although some district judges like to see their name in print, the majority of district court opinions are not published. Nevertheless, even in a quiet chambers, you'll still probably place two or three opinions per year in the F. Supp. (the compendium of published federal district court opinions).

Finally, on occasion, a federal district judge will be asked to "ride the circuit" for a few cases to substitute for an ailing or otherwise indisposed circuit court judge. When this occurs, the judge's clerks go with him to oral argument, and may even have an opportunity to draft a circuit court opinion.

A district court clerkship is perhaps best summed up as a one year tutorial in federal courts litigation where you will learn from the practitioners, from the judge, and from your own performance. It is a once in a lifetime opportunity, and is viewed with the requisite prestige by even the largest firms in the country.

Specialty courts

Frequently overlooked, federal clerkships are also available in a number of the federal specialty courts, including the bankruptcy courts (which hear all cases arising under the Bankruptcy Code), the U.S. Tax Court (which hears income, estate, and gift tax cases arising from decisions of the Commissioner of Internal Revenue), the U.S. Court of Claims (which has jurisdiction over cases involving claims against the United States government), the Court of International Trade (which hears cases concerning the valuation and classification of imported goods), and the Court of Appeals for the Federal Circuit (which hears appeals from the U.S. Court of Claims, the Court of International Trade, and the Patent and Trademark Office, among others).

Federal circuit courts of appeal

Appellate clerkships are viewed as the more "scholarly" of the two primary federal clerkships because there is a greater concentration on discrete issues and a frequent opportunity to "make new law." Since circuit courts have the "final word" on the law in a particular circuit (save the unlikely chance that a case will be granted *certiorari* by the United States Supreme Court), as a circuit court clerk, you won't spend as much time as a district court clerk worrying about the possibility of getting overruled. On the flip side, however, since most circuit court cases are decided by three judge panels, your judge will not always be the primary author of an opinion.

As a circuit court clerk, your primary duties are to read the appellate briefs submitted by the lawyers in a particular case, research the applicable law, and prepare your judge for oral argument by highlighting the uncertain areas of the applicable law in bench memos. Since nearly all circuit court opinions are published in the *Federal Reporter* and are frequently complex and lengthy, a clerkship in these courts will really help you to hone your writing skills, and guarantee that much of your work will be memorialized in print for posterity.

Finally, a circuit court clerkship is virtually a prerequisite for a clerkship in the United States Supreme Court.

The United States Supreme Court

Referred to as the "mother of all clerkships," these positions are so intensely competitive that perfect grades, membership on law review at a top ten school, a publication credit in your law review, and a distinguished circuit court clerkship may not even get you an interview. In a recent year, twenty-seven of thirty-eight Supreme Court clerks were drawn from Yale, Harvard, and the University of Chicago. Of course, that statistic also means that eleven clerks weren't drawn from those schools, and the fact is, you never really know what might draw the interest of a Supreme Court justice. What is certain, however, is that no Supreme Court justice regularly draws clerks directly out of law school, so you'll need to secure another clerkship first and apply during your third year. If you think you have what it takes to get this most elusive of all brass rings, speak to a professor at your law school for more information.

WHY PEOPLE CLERK

There are many reasons students give for pursuing judicial clerkships. Among them, students cite the "once in a lifetime" opportunity to observe and participate in the judicial process behind the scenes, to develop an understanding about how judges think and react to certain strategies, arguments, and approaches, and to gain a unique perspective on the litigation process by watching skilled practitioners in action and reading and evaluating their work product. Students also note the opportunity to cultivate a mentor in the judiciary—someone outside your law firm who can render advice and guidance during your critical early years of practice, the opportunity to explore a new city or region of the country without making a long-term commitment to being there, the chance to further develop research and writing skills, and the obvious credential that one of these prestigious positions provides.

> I applied only at the federal district court level because I was interested in litigation and felt that I'd learn more from the experience. I'd advise potential applicants to apply with judges and courts which would benefit them in a similar way. I also strongly suggest that you apply to judges who sit in the state you come from and to judges who went to your undergrad or law school since having these things in common may help put your application at the top.
>
> —Bess

Whatever your thoughts, consider these reasons carefully before dismissing the chance to pursue a judicial clerkship. While the salary paid to judicial clerks does not begin to compare to that paid by larger firms, many firms provide handsome bonuses and/or credit for years served during a clerkship. Your loans will wait, and you'll have forty years to practice law.

HOW TO APPLY FOR A JUDICIAL CLERKSHIP

Choosing your judges

By now, you probably understand that securing a judicial clerkship is not going to be an easy task. Competition is fierce, and reminiscent of first-year recruiting, you'll probably need to send out dozens and dozens of letters. As was the case in looking for first-year employment, however, you only need to strike gold once to end up a clerk!

To get started, go to your law school placement office and ask them for a current list of members of the state and federal judiciary. Chances are, your placement office keeps binders or computer programs with this information, and may even have an event scheduled to explain the clerkship application process, or to teach you how to run mail merge software from their database.

> I would caution you to ultimately apply only to places where you really want to go, and to judges that you really want to work for. I have several friends who were put in the awkward position of having to reject a clerkship offered by a federal judge, and several others who are instead clerking somewhere they wish they weren't because they haphazardly applied to forty or fifty judges without really thinking about whether these were all clerkships that they really wanted.
>
> —Joel

In trying to narrow your focus, ask yourself a couple of questions. Are you more interested in a federal clerkship or a state clerkship? Trial court or appellate court? It is okay to be interested in, and to apply for, both trial and appellate court clerkships, but it helps to have one as your primary focus. Here's how I did it.

When I began my clerkship search, I decided that, given my interest in litigation, I would be best served by pursuing a federal district court clerkship. I also knew that I wanted to settle in New England, and most likely in New Hampshire, the state where I grew up. Accordingly, I decided that my optimal clerkship would be in the United States District Court for the District of New Hampshire. The problem is, that court had only four judges, two of whom were not hiring for the term I was interested in (directly after law school). Accordingly, I expanded my horizons to include the districts of Maine, Vermont, Massachusetts, and Rhode Island (the other district courts in the first circuit), which brought me up to about twenty-five district judges. Since that number was still far too low to provide a good chance at success, I expanded my horizons further to include the United States District Court for the District of Connecticut, located in New Haven, where I did my undergraduate degree, and the United States District Court for the Eastern District of Pennsylvania, located in Philadelphia, which had a familiarity with, and a propensity to hire Penn students. That brought my number up to about forty district court judges. I then did a search for all district court judges who were alumni of either my undergraduate university or my law school, and applied to all of them, irrespective of their geographical location. This gave me about twenty more judges, bringing my total up to about sixty. I then consulted the list of newly appointed district court judges and added all of them to the list, figuring that they might not be on everyone's radar screen yet, which could increase my odds at getting an interview in those chambers.

I then decided that since I had a strong interest in research and writing, I should also pursue clerkships on the appellate level. Given the degree of competition for these clerkships, however, I thought it best to target certain judges with whom I had at least some connection. I chose the judges of the First Circuit Court of Appeals, the judges in the Second Circuit Court of Appeals who sat in New Haven, a judge in Little Rock who I knew lectured and wrote extensively on my law review comment topic, and all alumni of my undergraduate university and my law school, irrespective of their circuit. This brought my list to about eighty judges.

I then talked to the professors I was planning to use as recommenders, and asked them if they had any friends or colleagues in the judiciary. Most of them were able to give me at least a name or two, and I added these names to the list, figuring that my odds would increase with those judges because I had a recommendation from someone they knew. To top it off, I added the justices of the New Hampshire Supreme Court, figuring that since I knew I wanted to practice in New Hampshire, getting a clerkship in that particular appellate court would be a particularly relevant and worthwhile experience.

When I had my list, I went through each judge's biography looking for interests in common that I could highlight in a cover letter or on my resume. Whenever I found such commonalities, I noted them on the list next to the judge's name to assure myself that I would personalize his or her cover letter accordingly.

What to send

Whether you are seeking a state or federal clerkship, your application materials must contain (1) a brief, well-written cover letter; (2) a current copy of your resume, updated to contain membership on journals, forthcoming publications, and any other relevant law school honors or activities; (3) a copy of your law school transcript; (4) a copy of your undergraduate transcript (if it helps you); (5) a carefully edited, concise writing sample; and (6) two or three letters of recommendation from law school faculty members.

The cover letter

Your cover letter should be brief, certainly not more than one page, and laser printed on conservative, white bond paper. As before, avoid ostentatious monogrammed paper, and don't do anything funny with fonts.

In two or three paragraphs, describe your interest, as specifically as possible, in the type of clerkship that judge is offering. See my descriptions of the various clerkships above to help you highlight specific reasons for your interest. A cover letter expressing a well-reasoned and relevant desire to clerk for a particular court can go a long way in separating your application from the rest. It is also *critical* to highlight any geographic connection you have to the city, state, or region that houses the court you're applying to, and to put the name of your undergraduate school and/or your law school front and center if the judge is an alumnus. Although there is no "official" policy, many judges show a trend toward hiring former, present, or future residents of the city or state where their court is located, and graduates of their undergraduate and law schools.

Close by (1) mentioning what you've enclosed, (2) state that, if invited, you'd be willing to travel to the judge's chambers for an interview at your expense (since judges don't have interview budgets, there are no judicial "flybacks," and a judge might be disinclined to interview you if you will have to travel a long distance), and (3) provide a contact number and e-mail address.

Since you are personalizing these letters whenever possible, go over each one carefully to make sure that it is free of typos and other errors, as such mistakes show carelessness and are likely to be fatal to your chances.

Your resume

We've already discussed resumes a couple of times in this book, so I won't belabor the point here. Just make sure that the resume you send to judges is updated with your most current achievements, including journal membership and position, forthcoming publications (if any), moot court participation, externships, teaching assistantships, and first and second summer (forthcoming) employment. In addition, you should include a "personal interests" section on the resume you send to judges if you don't already have one. You will be spending a great deal of time in close quarters with your judge during your clerkship, and mutual interests can be influential in hiring decisions. Hobbies, recreational interests, and sports rooting interests can all be placed in this section.

Your writing sample

Whatever it is, make sure it is the tightest, best organized, and smoothest piece of legal writing that you've done to date. No matter how wonderful your grades are, to function successfully as a judicial clerk, you have to be able to research thoroughly and accurately, and write in a fluid, clear, and well organized fashion. Unlike law firms, which may or may not closely evaluate your writing sample, a judge considering whether or not to invite you to chambers for an interview will read your writing sample closely to determine whether it meets those qualifications. In many chambers, evaluation of the writing sample is the "final cut" before the interviews are granted.

Most judges will not want to read anything longer than ten pages, so unless you have a good reason to submit something longer (like a strong draft of a journal article you are authoring), keep your sample to ten pages or less.

In selecting your writing sample, be wary of submitting something you produced either for a judge or for a law firm during your 1L summer. Remember that strict confidentiality rules apply to the use of these works, and that you will need to obtain specific permission prior to submitting either to a judge. If you plan to submit work produced for a law firm, replace any identifying names or products with generic terms to maintain the flow of the written prose (in other words, do not simply "black out" identifying terms) and then obtain written permission from your employer to use the work product. When submitting the writing sample, be sure to include a cover sheet explaining to the judge that you obtained written permission for the use of the work product. This rule applies with even more force to draft orders prepared during a judicial internship. Don't even *think* of sending a photocopy of a judge's signed opinion as your writing sample without obtaining explicit permission from the authoring judge. If you plan to use a draft order as your writing sample, send a copy of the sample you intend to use to the authoring judge and request permission, in writing, to use the draft as a writing sample. Ask that in granting you written permission, the judge affirm, in writing, that the sample you are submitting is indeed your work product. If permission is granted to you, send a copy of your draft (not the signed, final order) with a copy of the authoring judge's permission letter to every judge you apply to. Note that failure to follow these instructions explicitly can be fatal to your candidacy for a clerkship.

How to choose your recommenders

Yeah, yeah . . . you don't know any professors well enough to ask them for a recommendation. Very few law students do. But you gotta ask anyway, so here's how to determine who you should ask.

Look at your transcript. Find the classes you did best in. If you have the luxury of choosing from among these classes, pick the professors who taught the classes most relevant to your clerkship. For example, if you are applying to a federal district court and you got A's in Constitutional Law, Federal Courts, and Real Estate, choose the Con Law and Fed Courts professors.

Make a photocopy of the most recent version of your resume, and then, in three or four double-spaced pages, type up a brief, autobiographical sketch of yourself, highlighting your major accomplishments in detail. Note that I said major accomplishments. You don't need to include the story of how you rescued your neighbor's cat from a tree in third grade and got your name in the town paper. We're talking major things here. Two or three major things you did in college, what your thesis was about, what you did if you took a year off between college and law school, how you chose to go to law school, what you did last summer. What you're trying to do is make your resume come to life, by putting some meat on the bones. Then write a brief note to the professor (one paragraph will suffice) alerting him that you'd like to solicit his recommendation and that you are enclosing your resume and a brief autobiography for his evaluation.

When you've finished your autobiographical sketch, go to each professor's secretary and set up an appointment. Leave your note, resume, and the autobiographical sketch with the secretary and ask that the professor review them in advance of your meeting. You should expect that it will take your professor six to eight weeks to prepare your letters of recommendation, so don't ask too late!

When the day of your meeting arrives, be on time for your appointment, and thank the professor for his time. Ask him if he has had the opportunity to review your materials, and if he has, whether he thinks he could forcefully recommend you as a clerkship candidate. In almost all cases, this method will produce the affirmative result you seek. Using this method will also provide the professor with a base of knowledge from which to ask you further questions. He can then use these materials to highlight the things in his recommendation that he feels will be most influential in the eyes of a judge. Take advantage of this opportunity to ask the professor whether there are any particular federal judges that he knows, or thinks would provide an excellent experience. This is your opportunity to add three or four names to your list where your chances for success may be highest.

Preparing your applications

Most federal judges adhere to the judicial conference's recommended March 1 commencement date for the extension of offers. Interviews are generally not scheduled to occur before March 1, but judges' secretaries may begin calling to schedule interview dates and times in early February. This means that your applications should be received in the judges' chambers no later than the first week of February.

In many cases, your law school will insist that professors' letters of recommendation be sent to your judges by the school. If this is the case, it is your responsibility to check to make sure that the letters were sent. We've heard horror stories about professors who have forgotten about deadlines, and stacks of letters being mislaid in the placement office. Take affirmative steps to make sure that these disasters do not happen to you.

Scheduling interviews

Anytime from early February on, your phone may start ringing with offers to schedule interviews. There is, however, an important piece of information that you need to have before you schedule anything.

You may get an offer at the end of an interview, and you may be asked for your answer right then and there. These are called "exploding" offers, meaning that the offer is rescinded if not immediately accepted.

Yeah, you read that right. You might have to make an on-the-spot decision about whether to accept or decline the offer. Right there, with the judge looking at you! No time to make phone calls, no time to mull it over, no time to wait for some other judge to make a decision. Yes or no. Simple as that.

Needless to say, this possibility puts you in a very precarious position, because you may be faced with the choice to (1) decline with the hope that your first choice judge will accept you, and run the risk that you will end up without a clerkship altogether if he rejects you; or (2) accept the offer and be happy that you have a clerkship, but have no chance to end up in the court or with the judge that you wanted most. While this scenario may play out despite your best efforts, there are a couple of things you can do to attempt to control this mayhem.

First, prioritize your list of judges. As multiple interview offers begin to arrive (and may you be so lucky), space them out during the first four days of March as best you can, scheduling your most favored judges during the first day, and other judges later in the week. That way, one of your top choice judges might make you an immediate offer, and even if that doesn't happen, the possibility of getting an exploding offer before you interview with your preferred judges is reduced.

Although this seems simple enough, it may not always work, because some judges may call and require that you interview on the first day of the process. You see, at the same time that you are angling for the most prestigious clerkship, the judges are also angling for the best candidates. They know that a delay of even a day or two can cost them their top choice applicants—so some judges rigorously pursue their top candidates by requiring them to interview on the first day of the process. If you are invited to interview with a judge and you are given a very early interview slot, ask yourself a single question before you accept the interview: Independent of my other options and considered in a vacuum, would I be happy clerking for this judge? If the answer is yes, take the interview. If not, decline.

One final thing about scheduling interviews. As soon as you are granted an interview with a judge in a particular court, it is appropriate to call the other judges in the area to let them know you will be there on a particular day. This may trigger one or more of these other judges to grant you an interview as well, significantly increasing your chances for success. Oh—and feel free to define the term "area" loosely!

The interview itself

You've been through many of these by now, so the standard rules for a legal interview apply. Arrive fifteen minutes early, dress conservatively, be prepared to be thoroughly searched by court security personnel, and try to relax.

When you arrive in the chambers, you will likely be greeted by the judge's secretary. Remember to treat this person respectfully, as, even more so than secretaries in law firms, a judge's secretary is likely to be very tight with the judge. Try to make some idle chatter while you wait.

When the judge arrives, it is proper to greet him either as "Your Honor" or as "Judge So-and-So." He will likely then take you into his chambers and close the doors. Don't let this rattle you.

From there, things can vary widely. The judge may open with some idle chatter, or jump right into things. Sit up straight, make good eye contact, and watch your body language. Remember that most judges are former trial lawyers and have been trained to read people. Crossed arms, leaning away, and downward glances show intimidation—which is not what most judges want in a law clerk. As a clerk, you'll need to have the confidence to argue legal points with the judge, and you can't do that effectively if you are intimidated. Of course, this doesn't mean to adopt a cocky attitude either. Deferential confidence is what you're looking for.

As far as content goes, know your resume cold, be sure you can talk specifically about why you want a clerkship in the particular kind of court you're in (see above for help on this), and be ready to discuss your connection to, or interest in the geographical area. If you submitted a draft of a journal article you are writing as your writing sample or listed one on your resume, be prepared to discuss it in depth. The judge I ultimately clerked for grilled me for almost forty-five minutes on my comment topic based only on the title I listed on my resume (as it turned out, the subject was one that interested him a great deal, and was one that he knew a lot about).

Know the judge's biography, and remembering that people like to talk about their families and their own accomplishments, try to get in a question or two about the judge's background at an appropriate time. Many times, these biographies also provide hints about the judge's hobbies and interests, and if you have anything in common in this area, find a way to get those common interests in play. Be sure to glance around the chambers and see if anything strikes your eye. For example, my judge had several pictures in the chambers showing him hiking with his family. Because I shared his passion for hiking, I acknowledged his interest, and we spent several minutes discussing the various mountains that we have climbed. Remember, a judge has to work in close proximity with his law clerks for a minimum of a year, so in addition to your academic qualifications, he's going to be looking for someone he likes and can work comfortably with. Common interests really help in this area.

Some people may tell you that you should brush up on the judge's recent written opinions, but none of the judges I interviewed with asked me about them or expected me to know about them. Nevertheless, to cover your bases, check the judge's five most recent opinions on Westlaw, find one that interests you, and read it for a basic understanding. That way, if you need to talk about an opinion for some reason, you'll have one. Anything more than that is probably overkill.

When the interview is over, shake hands and thank the judge for the opportunity to interview with him. Listen carefully to anything the judge might say. He might give you a timetable as to when you might expect an offer. He might ask you to call him before you accept an offer from another judge. He might say nothing, in which case, it is appropriate to ask him when you might expect a response. Finally, he might make you an exploding offer.

Of course, if you are faced with an exploding offer and the judge making the offer is one of your top choices, you can happily accept the offer on the spot and begin celebrating. If you are confronted with an exploding offer that is not one of your top choices, however, there is one tactic you may be able to use to buy yourself some time. Whenever a judge makes an offer to you, react enthusiastically, and humbly. Thank him sincerely for his faith in you, and express something about how fortunate you feel to have been granted such a rare and exciting opportunity. Then, when the judge asks you for an immediate decision, explain that you were not expecting this outcome, and that you'd like to have a few hours to discuss the ramifications of taking the position (e.g. the location of the position) with your spouse/fiancé/significant other and ask when the judge would like to have an answer. If you're lucky, your judge will give you twenty-four hours, though some will insist that you get back to them by the end of the day.

In either case, if you have an exploding offer and a brief window of time in which to accept it, as soon as you leave the chambers, call every other judge ranked higher on your list with whom you have already interviewed and explain the nature of your predicament. Make it clear on the phone that you would accept an offer if one were tendered, but that you'll need an immediate answer. These situations will generally work themselves out. Either the judges you've already interviewed with will make you an offer on the telephone, or they'll tell you that they cannot make a decision yet, which, in essence, is their way of telling you that you're not tops on their list and that you should probably accept the offer. No matter what the result, at least you'll have had one last chance to canvas your top choice judges. Whether you reach every judge or not, however, be sure to respond to the judge that made you the offer well within the time frame he gave you. A delay of even an hour beyond what he allowed could cost you your clerkship.

Finally, either before or after you meet the judge, you will likely spend some time talking to the judge's current law clerks. Use this time to ask the clerks questions about their experiences. Unless the judge has already made you an offer when you meet the clerks, **do not let down your guard** during this discussion. Many interviewees are under the false impression that their time with the law clerks is not part of the interview. Nothing could be further from the truth. Obviously, law clerks have the ear of their judge on a regular basis, and accordingly, in most chambers, law clerks play a vital role in the selection process. No matter how comfortable it might feel, the time you spend with the law clerks is a crucial part of the interview. Treat it accordingly.

Accepting an offer

Absent an exploding offer from one of the judges you interview with, you'll be playing a waiting game. Any offer you're going to get will come by telephone, so check your messages at least twice daily, especially if you are away on spring break, as you will need to make an immediate response to any offer you get. If you receive an offer from a judge other than your top choice judge, use the same stalling tactic I provided you in the section on exploding offers above. If you are granted a reprieve of any length, use the time to call your top choice judges and explain your situation. As before, the situation will likely resolve itself. Either you will get an offer on the phone from your top choice judges, or you won't, but at least you'll have given yourself one more chance.

When you do accept an offer, ask the judge whether he requires some form of formal acknowledgement. He may require a written acceptance letter from you, or he may send you a letter confirming your arrangement. If no formal acknowledgement is offered, call the judge's secretary and request a letter confirming the arrangement.

Finally, once you have accepted a clerkship, it is expected that you will call the other chambers where your candidacy is still active and withdraw. Don't even *think* about waiting to see if your first choice judge accepts you, and then calling the other judge back and rescinding your acceptance. The federal judiciary is a brotherhood, and exhibiting such unethical conduct will likely cost you both offers.

Finally, remember that the judicial clerkship process is a crapshoot, and every year, many qualified candidates fail to land clerkships. If you are unsuccessful, it is not necessarily a reflection on you or your abilities. Connections, alumni preferences, personalities, and timing all play roles in the process that you cannot control.

CHAPTER 23

Keys to Ascension:
Turning 2L Summer Employment
into a Permanent Offer

To the victors belong the spoils.
—ANDREW JACKSON

WHEN YOU ARRIVE at the firm on the first day of your summer program, you will, no doubt, be somewhat nervous. All of a sudden, there you are in the big city law firm, armed with two years of largely theoretical legal knowledge and some basic research skills that you're struggling to remember, thrown in with as many as sixty other 2Ls whom you've never met, with hundreds more nameless and faceless partners and associates going past you in a blur, and no idea what to make of it all.

Alternatively, you're at a smaller firm, or a public service organization, and once greeted by the recruiting coordinator or the hiring partner, you are shown the library and your office, given some brief instructions about how to use the computer system and the phones, introduced to your secretary, and handed your first case file and a due date.

How are you supposed to deal with these situations?

Relax. That's what this chapter is here for.

Although the summer experience is radically different at large urban firms than it is at smaller firms or public service organizations, there are basic performance concepts and "rules of the road" that are common to all summer experiences. I'll address each of them below, making specific references to any relevant differences in strategy between large firm, and smaller firm or public interest practice. So let's get started!

> The summer associateship is basically just an extended interview. Use the time to really get a good sense what it is like to work at the firm. Ask a lot of questions about the partners, the lifestyle, the culture, the projects that associates are given, the expectations of associates, associate turnover rates, and take some time to figure out who the movers and shakers at the firm are, who the respected partners and associates are, and why that is. Finally, be yourself. You are going to want to be at a place where you are comfortable, and this requires that during the summer that you are there, you be yourself.
>
> —Pat

When you arrive

At large firms, your first week will likely be consumed by mixers to help you get to know the other summer associates in your summer "class," and by telephone and computer training. Carry a legal pad and a pen with you to take down anything important that you might not be able to remember, like security codes, computer passwords, and names of people you meet and want to remember. You'll either get your own office, or share an office with another summer associate. If you're in a sharing situation, it will obviously be important for you to get along with your office mate, so spend some time early on cultivating that relationship. Whether you're on your own or have an office mate, strike up a friendship with your secretary. Chances are, your secretary has been around longer than you have, and therefore, can teach you things and provide good advice. Don't overlook this obvious resource.

There will be a number of social events scheduled for you during the first week. Make an appearance at all of them. As was the case in the first days of law school, bonds are established during the first few days of a summer program—bonds which can really enhance the experience. Having a good friend or a confidant in your summer program can go a long way to making the experience more enjoyable and less stressful.

Your first week at a large firm will be spent traveling from one orientation event to the next during the day, and one social event to the next in the evenings. Don't worry about it! You're being paid big money for doing nothing. Enjoy it while it lasts.

If you're at a smaller firm or a public interest position, your experience will be much different. You may be the lone summer person, or one of only a handful. There may not be any organized orientation program, and you may be put directly to work upon your arrival. If this is the case, you'll need to lean on the recruiting coordinator or the hiring partner to answer your questions and help you get settled. Don't hesitate to ask questions. They expect it, even if it doesn't seem that way.

In many ways, the early days of a summer associate at a smaller firm or organization are often much more stressful, chaotic, and isolating than in a large firm. Because there are fewer clueless people like you, you'll feel somewhat self-conscious and unsure of how you fit in. At first, you may find yourself going to lunch by yourself and leaving at the end of the day with nowhere to go but home. It's not that nobody wants to spend time with you or to make the effort to get to know you, that's just the way things work in a small firm. Once people start seeing you around and working with you, you'll begin to assimilate. It just takes longer at these smaller places, and consequently, your first days can feel pretty uncomfortable. That's normal, so don't worry about it.

Handling assignments

The way you handle assignments as a summer associate is almost as important as the work product you ultimately produce. Organization, punctuality, clarity about what is being asked of you, and improvement in performance from assignment to assignment are all critical factors in determining whether you will be extended a permanent offer at the end of the summer. The advice which follows is applicable whether you work in a large firm, a small firm, or in a service organization.

Do what you are told, and do it well. It's really as simple as that.
—Elizabeth

You may work on a dozen or more separate assignments during the course of your 2L summer, and each one will likely start off the same way. You'll either choose a project from a central pool of available assignments, or more likely, someone will wander into your office and hand you a piece of a project. This often happens in a hurry, and the person giving you the assignment is frequently unclear with her instructions, and, to be frank, is often unclear herself on the precise question she is looking to answer. You *must* force the person assigning you a project to sit down with you for five minutes, take a deep breath, and express to you in the king's English what it is she wants you to do. She may claim to be in too much of a hurry, or she may try and weasel away from you by getting defensive and abruptly stating "just find out so-and-so, okay?" and then walking away. If that happens, follow her. Ask for some context. Get clarification until you understand the issue and know exactly what it is you need to find out.

Yeah, it may feel awkward and uncomfortable to push someone on this, and yes, you may get a hostile reaction initially. But you know what? If you don't get absolutely clear on what it is you're looking for, the chances are great that you'll go up to that great summer associate wasteland known as the firm's law library and end up flailing around for days on a project that should have taken you hours and potentially coming back with an answer that is unresponsive to the question the assignor had in mind. And you know who ends up looking bad then? Not the person who gave you the ambiguous assignment. No doubt, she'll insist that the assignment was crystal clear in her mind. So you know who ends up holding the bag?

Yup. You.

This is one of the toughest lessons of the 2L summer, and many people end up learning it the hard way. So it's your choice. A little discomfort now, or the potential for embarrassment and humiliation later. Trust me, this really isn't much of a choice.

Managing your workload

The next monkey that many summer associates have on their backs is how to manage their workload. Here's the typical scenario.

It's 4 P.M. You've been asked to research a difficult issue for a motion for summary judgment that a partner is filing. It was given to you yesterday afternoon and is due tomorrow morning. You've been working on it steadily, but you still have more research to do and you haven't even started writing yet. Then, out of nowhere, a partner comes into your office and without introducing himself or inquiring about your workload, says, "I have an issue I need you to look into. The client wants an answer tomorrow morning, so read these cases, do some research, and have a memorandum explaining your position on my desk by 8 A.M. tomorrow."

The partner then starts to walk out.

Welcome to summer associate nightmare scenario number one. What do you do?

Many summer associates would say that there is only one correct answer, and that is to pull an all-nighter and try to get both assignments done by the deadline. Of course, the likelihood of veering off course in one of the assignments at 3 A.M. is pretty high, putting you at risk of looking incompetent when you turn in an average or below average work product, and potentially leaving one or both partners without the answers they need. Option two, of course, is to tell the partner that you're sorry, but you can't take the assignment because you have another complicated short-deadline project due tomorrow morning and that you won't have time to do a good job on both projects in the short time you have.

Believe it or not, most partners would prefer this answer to the former. Surely you're not so arrogant that you think that you're the only person in the office capable of handling this short-term research for the partner, are you? Remember that, at any one time, there are a number of other lawyers in the firm that aren't staring down a twenty-four hour deadline on another project. While it might be uncomfortable to have to turn work away, particularly from a partner, it is certainly better to turn the work away than to take it on without saying anything, and produce mediocre work for both people.

There is a third option, however, which is the best response of all. The partner who just arrived told you that his client needs an answer tomorrow morning. But what about the guy writing the motion for summary judgment? He told you that your deadline is tomorrow, but is the actual filing deadline for the motion tomorrow, or much later? You probably don't know the answer to that, but it is possible, if not probable, that the deadline he gave you is a "soft" deadline—meaning that it is a deadline for your part of the project to be completed, but is well in advance of the actual filing deadline. So here's what you do.

Explain to the partner with the client deadline that you'd be happy to help him, but that you've already been given another project which is due tomorrow morning. Give the partner the name of the attorney who assigned the other project to you, and let him know that if he talks to the other attorney and gets your first deadline pushed back by a couple of days, that you could take on the partner's last minute project.

This strategy does two things for you. First, it keeps you from having to say "no" to a partner, since many summer associates are (in most cases unnecessarily) afraid to do this. Second, it puts the responsibility for restructuring your schedule in the hands of the person making the demands on you. If he needs you badly enough, he'll talk the other lawyer into pushing off his deadline. If not, he'll tell you not to worry about it, but he'll be left with the impression that you were proactive and willing to try and help him out. Of course, there is always the possibility that the partner will be unreasonable and tell you to work your scheduling out yourself. If that happens, you need to explain to the partner that you cannot take his project until you talk to the other lawyer. You should then immediately call the other lawyer, explain the situation, and then let the two of them work it out.

Billing your time

There is one, and only one, thing to say on this subject. Bill all your time. That's it. No exceptions, no questions asked. Nothing to discuss. If you worked it, bill it. Period. End of story.

Yeah, but you got sidetracked on an issue that ended up being irrelevant, or you feel like it shouldn't have taken you twenty-five hours to write a memorandum, or you had no idea what you were doing because you never took Commercial Paper, or . . .

It doesn't matter. If you spent the time, bill the time.

The fact is, in most cases, the partner in charge of a particular client's account will look at your hours and bill the client according to what he thinks is a fair charge for the work you produced. Let the partner reduce your hours. Your job is to write everything down so you get credit for the actual amount of time you spent working, and to give the partner a fair idea of how long something actually took you to do. If over the course of a summer, you actually worked five hundred hours, but only billed three hundred of those hours because you were afraid you were inefficient, since the presumption is that people bill all the time they spend working on client matters, the firm is going to think you only worked three hundred hours, and conclude that you are lazy. The firm expects inefficiency from its summer associates and even from its young full-time associates. What the firm will not tolerate, however, is laziness. Thus, by reducing your own hours, you can end up shooting yourself in the foot.

If you worked the hours, bill the hours. 'Nuff said.

Using Westlaw and LEXIS at the firm

We've all heard the horror story of the hapless summer associate who, while working at a small law firm which had use-based online provider accounts, ran up a twenty-five thousand dollar bill doing online research for an internal memo to a partner. Needless to say, doing this could be disastrous to your future employment prospects, but how do you find out what the story is with online research?

Simple. Just ask.

At the beginning of the summer, ask your advisor, the recruiting coordinator, or an associate about how the firm handles billing for its online services. Most large firms now have monthly or annual "unlimited service" arrangements where the firm pays a flat fee for unlimited access to all databases. Some firms, however, still pass these costs through to their clients proportionally, so if you spend two hundred hours doing online research on one project, and only one thousand user-hours were logged by your firm that month, the client whose project you were working on is going to pay 20 percent of that month's bill. If you learn that the firm you are at uses proportional cost allocation for its online research services, you should ask every partner who assigns you a project whether you can use online research services, and if so, if he wants to cap their use at some level. This becomes even more important if you are working for a small firm or a service organization, where flat fee payments are less common, and the cost of online services may be passed directly through to the client.

Getting the work you want

Nobody likes a complainer, but, if after several weeks of work, you have not been given a project in any of the areas you are most interested in, it's time to talk to someone about it. If you have a mentor, bring your concerns to him, express what your interests are, and go from there. If you don't have a mentor or your mentor is on vacation or unresponsive to your concerns, then go to the recruiting coordinator and ask for advice. If that doesn't work, go through the firm directory yourself, find a couple of partners who practice in those areas, and seek out the work yourself.

Again, there is a difference between brown nosing, and expressing sincere interest in getting the work you want. Proactively soliciting work from partners, if the other channels fail you, constitutes the latter and should be done. While you will want to be a team player and should not expect that every assignment you will be given will be hand picked for you, the firm should make some efforts to find you projects in the practice areas you're interested in pursuing. If this isn't happening, you need to politely make it happen.

Getting feedback on your work

One of the most common complaints from both summer associates and full-time associates is that partners and upper-level associates don't provide any feedback to allow them to learn from their mistakes. As a summer associate, you will probably be scheduled for a "mid-summer review" about halfway through your tour of duty, but you should certainly not wait until then to get feedback on your assignments. When you first talk to your advisor at the firm, explain that getting feedback on your performance is extremely important to you so you can learn from your mistakes and make adjustments. This should be music to your advisor's ears, and consequently, you should ask him for advice on how to solicit feedback on a project if none is immediately forthcoming. My strategy was always to wait a few days after turning a project in, and then to stop by the partner's office to follow up, ask if he needed anything else, and then, at the same time, to ask him if he could provide any feedback for me.

Many times, the partner, impressed with my initiative, would sit me down right there and provide the feedback I asked for. Other times, if the partner was busy, he got back to me with feedback. The fact is, many summer associates feel that it is the firm's job to train them and to provide feedback on their performance. For the lawyers at the firm, however, life goes on, the work piles up, and deadlines come and go the same way they did before you arrived. For them, getting feedback to you is not a high priority task, unless you make it one. In the two summers I spent in law firms, I got feedback on every single project I worked on by simply stopping by the partner's office to follow up, and then asking for a suggestion or two for next time.

There's really no magic to this. You just have to make it a priority, and the partners will come to appreciate your openness to constructive criticism and willingness to learn and improve.

Escaping the clutches of a possessive partner

Although uncommon, if you do good quality work for a partner early in your tenure as a summer associate, you may find your time monopolized by more and more work from this one partner. Although this situation can frequently present a great opportunity to develop a mentor in the firm and a close working relationship with someone that could lead to a permanent position, it can also work against you by limiting your exposure to other partners in the firm.

If you find yourself trapped in the clutches of a partner who is monopolizing most of your time, talk to your mentor or the recruiting coordinator about it. If you are happy with the arrangement and like the partner and the work he is giving you, explain this, but express your concern about not being exposed to the rest of the firm. Listen carefully to what they tell you. If you hear that the partner is well-respected in the firm and that you are lucky to have the opportunity to work so much with him, then count your blessings. If they agree with your concern, ask them for help in soliciting work from other partners at the firm to increase your exposure.

Confront problems immediately

Now and again, you might find yourself in a sticky situation at work. You may have a personality clash with another summer associate, your secretary may resent you, a partner may treat you unprofessionally, or you may discover a huge mistake in your work product after you've handed it in. Personal problems between people are best handled directly after a discussion with your advisor or the recruiting coordinator, and after the situation has had a chance to cool down. Emotional responses are almost never productive, and drawing that kind of attention to yourself, justified or not, can jeopardize your chances of getting hired.

If you discover an error in your work product, bring it to the attention of the person who assigned you the work immediately, apologize, and take responsibility for your mistake. While the partner may be upset that the mistake was made, it is hard to remain angry with someone who accepted responsibility for the error without making excuses or trying to cover it up. Fortunately, most legal errors, especially in the projects you'll be given as a summer associate, are easily remedied. Handling the situation poorly, however, by getting defensive, trying to cover up the mistake, or trying to pass the blame off on someone else only makes the situation much worse.

Getting along with the other summer associates

The most important aspect in this department is diffusing any sense of "competition" for billable hours, attention of partners, or an offer at the end of the summer. The fact is, the majority of firms and organizations do their screening in the hiring process, and do not bring on many more associates than they feel they have the need to hire permanently. Accordingly, if you do a good job on the assignments you are given and get along with people, assuming that the market remains steady, you should get an offer.

Overt arrogance, brown-nosing, and gossiping or undermining others behind their backs is the way most summer associates get themselves into trouble. On the flip side, offering your assistance when another summer associate is in a crunch, asking questions, and being a good listener should put you in the good graces of your colleagues. Every once in a while, though, you'll meet someone who just seems to have it in for you. If one of those people just happens to be a summer associate with you, remember that you can never leave a battle with a skunk smelling like a rose. Steer clear, and involve your advisor if it gets really bad. Most of all, remember the bottom line—if you are productive, do good work, and get along with people, you will get an offer.

Proper etiquette at firm social events

In the two summers I spent as a summer associate in a law firm, I saw people make more clear blunders in this area than in any other area raised by this chapter. First of all, control your alcohol consumption at firm social events. Yeah there's an open bar at most of the events, and yeah, other summer associates and full-time associates get hammered and do really stupid things that people think are funny. Make certain that you're one of the people laughing, not the one that they're laughing at. These events are the occasions when people get to meet you on a personal level and learn more about you. If you are incapable of carrying on a conversation, or worse yet, end up embarrassing yourself, you may find yourself without an offer at the end of the summer.

> Don't be the person who is known to everyone merely as a big partier. In the end, remember that you want to be remembered for the quality of the work you did; not for the quantity of alcohol you drank.
>
> —Allan

If you have a spouse or significant other and the firm makes it clear that such people are welcome at certain events, then by all means, extend the invitation. Again, these events are organized to encourage people to socialize and get to know each other, and spouses and significant others are a part of that arrangement.

If the firm takes you out to expensive restaurants or to events where food and drink can be purchased and charged to the firm (like golf outings, concerts, etc.), show some discretion. It is not appropriate to order the most expensive thing on the menu unless everyone around you, including the partners and associates are doing so. Similarly, it is not acceptable to be a glutton just because you're not paying for things. At a summer concert outing for a large Boston firm where a full, lavish dinner, drinks, and dessert had just been provided, I watched a summer associate order a large shrimp cocktail, two more alcoholic beverages, and two desserts when nearly everyone else was ordering coffee or a beer. I was embarrassed merely to be sitting near her, and I noticed that several partners were talking about this indiscretion amongst themselves. Remember that just because you're on a firm's expense account doesn't give you license to lose your sense of decency. If you act like a boor, people will notice.

"Also, don't feel compelled to maintain a frenetic summer associate social life, or that if you don't go to every impromptu social event you're invited to, that you won't get an offer," Joel adds. "There will be a few relatively formal events or dinners with partners that should not be missed. Otherwise, if an event sounds like fun to you, go; and if it doesn't, don't. No one has ever lost an offer or failed to make partner because he failed to go on the brewery tour as a summer associate—although someone probably has lost an offer because he threw up on a partner's shoes at the brewery tour. . . ."

Finally, it should go without saying that as a summer associate, you need to be extremely careful about initiating romantic relationships within the firm. Dating secretaries, support staff, or other associates or summer associates can be a very risky proposition—and should either be avoided entirely or entertained with extreme discretion. Such relationships, when they sour, can be very devisive to the professional environment, and accordingly, many firms have policies to avoid the problem. Dating within the office is also frequently viewed as indiscrete by older partners, and can work against you when hiring decisions are made. The summer is short.

Use it to build a friendship, and if the relationship is still ready to bloom at the end of the summer, you can always entertain it then, and look to move down the street for permanent employment.

> To use a golf analogy, during your 2L summer, two-putt. Smile, be polite, show up on time, and do good work on the projects you are given, but, at least if you're at a large firm, don't think that you really have to distinguish yourself. Generally, the job is yours to lose.
>
> —Keith

Some closing thoughts

Your 2L summer experience will probably be unlike anything you have ever experienced before in your lifetime. If you go to a large, urban firm, you will be "wined and dined" from start to finish. The firm's box at the ballpark will be at your disposal. They'll take you to concerts, museums, and on tours of the city. You'll dine at the city's finest restaurants, go yachting at partners' beach houses, and drown yourself at weekly "open bar" happy hours. The excesses that you'll be exposed to can really take your breath away.

Of course, that's the point.

What you need to remember is that, once the summer is over, so is the fairy tale. With associate billable requirements of 2000 to 2250 hours per year (and many associates at these large firms who routinely bill over 2500 hours per year), most of the dining you'll be doing once you start as an associate will be at your desk. You'll be forced to work many late nights and weekends. Finally, because of the vast turnover at these firms, and their ability to routinely make students from the best law schools in the country swoon over them, if you aren't willing to produce at that level, you'll be expendable. Forget about doing quality work for fifty-hour weeks and then taking a stand to reclaim the rest of your life. Most associates at these firms do great work, so it's not just quality that counts. It's quality and quantity both. The associates who do the most great work, and concomitantly bring in the most income for the partners, will be the ones who survive the yearly bloodlettings.

A lot of my friends in law school went into these large firms with a naïve attitude and without really thinking about what the choice would mean. Now, after some of them billed 2500 to 3000 hours during their first year (do the math to figure out how much free time that leaves you for the "other things" in your life), bitterness, regret, and reconsideration abound.

"I laugh at people who go to these big firms," Steve notes. "They are fools. I guess some people just need to work hard all the time and have no social life to feel important. Some people get off on having a stressful life in an unpleasant work environment, and it's mostly those people that end up going to the sweatshops. I wish them the best of luck.

"The problem is that a lot of people go to law school right out of college and have never held a real job," Steve adds. "They have no idea what it's like to work every day, with no spring break and no summer vacation. These people go to a big firm during their 1L or 2L summer because they think it's prestigious, and they get wined and dined and spoiled rotten in that artificial environment of excess. These people never look around long enough to see what kind of life the associates who actually work there lead because these summer associates are too busy going to theatre nights and expensive lunches. Then they take a permanent offer there and get blindsided by the reality of what working at those places is really like, and they end up miserable! In choosing a firm, try to get a realistic view of what kind of lifestyle the lawyers lead there. Being a lawyer is hard enough if your job is 9 A.M. to 6 P.M. When you join one of these places and your work is 9 A.M. to 3 A.M. and there is a partner yelling at you and calling you a 'worthless sack of shit' every five minutes, and you are constantly being told that if you don't bill more hours you'll be let go, that job gets even harder."

Wow. Of course, it's not like that at every big firm, but I'm not making these quotes up, folks. I know several first and second year associates at some of the more notorious of these large firms who routinely pull at least one all-nighter a week, bill more than 3000 hours (figure THAT one out over fifty-two weeks), and have verbal abuse, and in one case, a stapler hurled at them by ornery and unhappy partners.

It's not my place to judge the choices you make. Just make them informed choices so you won't be surprised when the golden carriage you thought you were riding in turns into a pumpkin.

PART FOUR

. . . and the Third Year
They Bore You to Death . . .

CHAPTER 24

But It Doesn't Have to Be Boring . . . Designing a Plan to Avoid the Third-Year Doldrums

Plough deep while the sluggards sleep
—BENJAMIN FRANKLIN

IF EVERYTHING has worked out according to plan, you should be receiving a permanent offer from your 2L firm or public interest placement in early-to-mid-September. For many of you, when that day comes, your singular purpose for going to law school will have been fulfilled, and the future (or at least the immediate future) will be decided.

So what now? You still have another whole year of school to go, but the end result has already been revealed. It's kind of like watching a drama but already knowing the ending. So assuming that you have a job lined up and your immediate future plans are resolved, what can you do to make this year worthwhile?

Don't lose sight of the blueprint for your upper years of law school that you designed in Chapter 16. Many of your classmates will stop reading, and stop going to class. With a job offer in hand, many will trade in their books, laptops, and study aides for happy hours, road trips, and four-day weekends.

But should you?

"Oh, come on!" you say. "I've worked my ass off for two years following the advice in this book, and it has served me well . . . but if you're going to tell me I need to work as hard during third year as I did in my first two, you can go stick it in your ear."

Fair enough.

There's nothing wrong with allowing yourself a more leisurely pace than the frantic one you've been living during the past two years. But you know what? You're paying for your third year of law school whether you like it or not, and greens fees and bar tabs are not included. If you're like most of us, you'll be racking up another twenty-five thousand dollars in debt to pay for this year—debt which will take you more years than you'd care to count to pay off.

So yeah, third year of law school, and particularly your spring semester, is the "last hurrah" of your career as a student. It does provide the last clear chance for extended vacations, traveling, and camaraderie, and the last chance to "live like a student" with late nights and even later mornings. But you also need to make third year something more than just the year you lowered your handicap and raised your tolerance.

At the very least, don't forget the price you've paid for the ground you've covered. Many a student has blown his hard-earned top 10 percent class rank or an opportunity to graduate with honors by sliding through third year of law school, beer in hand. Others have gone on to get thrown off their journals for lack of effort, and even done poorly enough to fail to graduate and lose their employment offer.

With fading memories of the all-nighters you spent struggling over equal protection, personal jurisdiction, and choice of law rules, it's just too easy to turn your back on it all and let the marching lemmings pass you by. Never forget the price you've paid to get where you are, and exercise some moderation. Sure you can take more enjoyable classes, schedule yourself a three-day weekend, and opt out of taking seminars with serious writing requirements. But you still need a certain number of credits to graduate, and you might need to defend your position in the class against your still ambitious classmates eager to beat you to the finish line. While your rank in class, or graduating with honors might not matter to you now, do you know what the future will bring? What if there is a downturn in the economy and you suddenly find yourself out of a job? What if you later decide to change firms, move to a different city, or apply to business school? The four C's you could earn in that last semester could hang around your neck like an albatross.

Pep talk over.

So what are you supposed to do this year, you ask?

Go back to chapter 16 and refresh your memory about what your upper-year strategy was supposed to be. What were your goals and visions for the last two years of your law school career back then?

Were you following a bar review strategy in which you found out what subjects were fair game on your state's bar examination and decided to get a semester's worth of experience in each of those subjects? Were you majoring in a certain specialization by taking a carefully selected program of courses to flesh out your understanding of a particular area of law? Were you following an experiential strategy, trying to get as much clinical, pro bono, and trial advocacy experience as possible through internships, externships, and practica?

It's time for another self-assessment.

Whatever system you were following, is it still working for you? After an additional year of experience and a summer of work in the real world of legal practice, do you want to adhere to your strategy, deviate from it somewhat, or abandon it entirely in favor of a different approach?

Think about the experiences you had working this summer. What did you learn about yourself? Are you leaning toward corporate law or litigation? Firm practice or public interest work? Or are you just burned out on the law and thinking of alternative ways to use your law degree?

"One thing I did during my third year was take classes with professors that I had already had and enjoyed. It was easier getting myself to class knowing that I would find it worth my while to be there," Joel noted. "Further, if by the end of your 2L summer, you know where you'll likely be working after graduation, it might be worthwhile to ask the lawyers (or the judge if you're clerking) there which advanced law school classes they consider most relevant to their cases."

No matter what position you're in, you can design an approach to your third year to make it both worthwhile and interesting. If you're tired of taking classes, look for an interesting externship that can provide you with the skills and experience you'll use in the type of work you intend to practice after graduation, or an opportunity to do an independent study with a professor on a subject that interests you. More than one student has ended up co-authoring a law review article with a professor based on an idea conjured up in an independent study. If you have some interest in becoming a professor, you should also look for opportunities to teach legal writing to first year students, or to become a teaching assistant in first-year or undergraduate law classes. If you're trying to get away from law and your law school is part of a larger university campus, look for chances to cross-register in classes at the business school, or take graduate classes in relevant areas like history, political science, economics, or psychology. Many law schools will allow you to earn credits toward your law degree from courses taken in other departments. Does yours?

Go back and revisit our discussion of public service in Chapter 21. Have you done any pro bono or public service work since you've been in law school? Many students burned out on law find renewed interest in legal practice by interacting with real clients and actually using what they know to help real people with real problems. Check out the local offices of the U.S. and district attorneys. Go watch trials at the local courthouse. Intern for a federal judge. Just go *do* something!

"If you feel really burned out and don't want to take any more traditional law school classes, get involved in the clinical programs or do some public interest work where you can apply the things that you've learned," Carolyn suggests.

"Or just work part-time!" Elizabeth adds. "If you've arranged your schedule properly over your first two years, your course load will not be as demanding as it was during your first and second years. This should leave you enough time to work part-time and still have enough time for fun and the necessary studying. Working part-time while you're still in school will give you more experience outside of the traditional summer associate setting, and more personal contact with the people at your firm. The best thing is, when you finally start your real job after graduation, you won't have as many of those feelings of fear and cluelessness so typical of first-year associates."

Finally, many students, particularly those carrying a large debt burden, choose to work part-time for a law firm during their third year of law school. Aside from providing a significant source of income, part-time work can ease the transition between the worlds of academia and practice, and get you more practical training and exposure to different practice groups prior to your actually joining the firm. Some firms will even allow you to work through the mail if your law school is in a different city, by sending you research assignments and asking you to draft memoranda and send them back. Look into these possibilities.

The opportunities available to you during your third year of law school are vast, and extend well beyond the walls of your law school. Keep your grades up, but mix it up a bit. Pursue some experiences that you might not have the chance to pursue once you start your practice. Stretch your boundaries. Just don't sit idly by and let the year go to waste.

CHAPTER 25

Opportunity Knocks Again . . .
A Second Chance at Recruiting

The foolish and the dead
alone never change their opinion.
—ROBERT LOWELL

IN THE FALL of your third year, after you know whether or not you received an offer from the firm where you spent your 2L summer, recruiting season arrives anew. Although the primary focus will be on the 2Ls in the class behind you, almost every firm will be willing to talk to and hire 3Ls for permanent employment beginning in the fall after graduation without the need to summer at the firm.

Some 3Ls feel that there is a stigma attached to reentering the employment pool as a 3L, and thus, refuse to do so even though the firm they worked at during their 2L summer failed to live up to expectations. Nothing, however, could be further from the truth. Once you've been through a full summer of employment at a firm or a public interest placement, you will inevitably have a much better idea about what the real-life lawyering experience will entail. Did you like what you saw?

> I would suggest participating in 3L recruiting to anybody who is not one hundred percent certain about the place they have an offer from.
>
> —Pat

Think about the experience you had at the firm last summer. Did the people there treat each other with respect? Did they treat you fairly? Does the firm specialize in the kind of work that you are most interested in doing? Did you get to do any of it while you were there? Did you get good feedback from the partners you worked with? Can you see yourself working closely, on a longer-term basis, with the people you met at the firm last summer?

> I recruited third year because I wanted to do trusts and estates and I hadn't yet heard whether I would get a specific offer from the trusts and estates department at my firm. I went through five or six on-campus interviews with firms that had trusts and estates departments, got three or four callbacks, and then got an offer from the trusts and estates department at the firm I had worked at, which I immediately accepted.
> —Alison

Now step back and get a panoramic view of things. Did you like the city or geographic region that the firm was in? Have any factors in your academic or personal life changed since last fall that are prodding you to look in a different direction?

While few 3Ls are ever *really* secure about the employment choices they make, if any of the aforementioned concerns are nagging at you, there is no harm taking another lap or two in the recruiting pool before you make a final decision about the firm where you worked last summer. With an offer in hand, you are likely to be even more attractive to firms than you were last time around, since another firm has already staked its claim to you. This time, with a summer's worth of experience to draw upon, you can ask the tough, insightful questions that you may not have known to ask, or dared to ask last time, you can pursue the really selective firms, or your can barter for department-specific placements in a particular firm with more force and more credibility. With a much more clearly defined idea of what it is that you are looking for, it can't hurt to take another look around.

You'll typically have until November 1 to make a final decision about whether to accept the offer from your 2L summer firm, but you'll want to confirm this arrangement with your specific employer. There is nothing disingenuous or disloyal in exploring your options and seeking other offers until that date, nor is it improper to tell other employers, if you are asked, that you have an offer from the firm that you worked at last summer. People understand that interests change and that the choice of a first job is a large and important decision. Take your time, and make your decision the right one.

How to handle phone calls from people at your old firm

By the way, while you're shopping yourself around, don't think that the firm you got an offer from is going to sit idly by and let you get away. Although firms understand why you might want to take a second look around, they don't like it when people they wined, dined, and trained end up going elsewhere. There's nothing they can do to stop you, except one thing.

They'll start calling you.

It will start out as a casual call from the recruiting coordinator asking if you received the firm's offer letter. When you respond affirmatively, the coordinator might inquire if there is anything the firm can provide to help you in making your decision, or outright ask you if you've made a decision yet. It is perfectly fine to respond by saying that you are weighing your options and will give the firm an answer well ahead of the November 1 deadline.

That won't be the end of it, though.

By delaying your decision, you're opening the floodgates. You'll get more calls from people at the firm than you get from telemarketers. You'll hear from associates you socialized with, and partners you worked for. If the firm really wants you, you might even get a call from the hiring partner asking if your decision hinges on financial concerns.

How do you respond to all of these people?

Generally, I used my answering machine a lot during those days, and screened my calls to avoid having to tell the people at my firm for the third or fourth time that I was weighing my options and trying to come to a very difficult decision. If a firm subscribes to the NALP guidelines, there is nothing they can do to force your decision before the November 1 deadline. If you're dealing with a smaller firm that is only going to hire one or two people and is waiting on your decision, however, you should certainly understand their desire to fill their slots as quickly as possible with the most qualified candidates and get them a decision as soon as you can.

Until you've made a decision, however, there's not a lot you can say. If you have any questions or concerns, call the firm and get them cleared up. If you need advice, get it from people you trust. At the end of the day, though, like so many other things about law school, it's you alone that needs to step up and make the call. Make the decision, and then don't look back.

If you didn't get an offer from your 2L firm

There are two different species of "non-offers" that you can get from a law firm. A "soft offer" is an understanding that, although you are not welcome to return to the firm on a permanent basis, you are allowed to tell other employers that you were, in fact, extended an offer by the firm to avoid being stigmatized. These non-offers are typically extended by firms that would have hired you but for a downturn in their business or a strategic restructuring within the firm which has reduced the need for young associates. These offers can also be given to people with strong constituencies within the partnership favoring their being offered permanent employment, with a couple of strong detractors blocking the offer. In any case, a soft offer is a very effective tool, because it permits you to spin your non-offer any way you like.

The second, and much more difficult non-offer is the simple "thanks-but-no-thanks" non-offer. Fortunately it is rarely a surprise to its recipient, since most firms provide adequate warnings to summer associates at risk of failing to secure an offer. Typically, people who get non-offers either do something egregiously terrible during their summer associateships like making a pass at a partner's spouse (don't laugh, it has happened) or betraying client confidences. Others show no effort during the summer associateship, display intolerable arrogance, or reflect a repeated inability to handle the rigors of law practice. The first two of these examples would get you fired from your summer position, the last three would probably get you a warning at your mid-summer review first.

Occasionally, however, a non-offer will come from a particularly compassionless firm that has simply determined that it doesn't need you. This situation, although rare, can really leave you in the lurch. So what do you do if this happens to you?

If you get an unexpected non-offer from a firm, the first thing you need to do is swallow your pride and call the recruiting coordinator at the firm to make sure that your non-offer was not the result of an administrative error (which has happened). If your fears are confirmed and you really had no idea that your performance was lacking, it is appropriate to explain your surprise and ask the recruiting coordinator for an explanation. If you get some kind of equivocation that falls short of "you didn't get an offer because your work product was pathetically inept and so were you," you might ask the recruiting coordinator if the firm would consider making you a soft offer, or providing you with a blanket letter of recommendation to use in 3L recruiting. If the reason you didn't get an offer was due to a downturn in the firm's hiring needs, you are on solid ground making this request. If you don't get satisfaction from the recruiting coordinator, call your advisor at the firm and put the request to him. Do not simply roll over and play dead, because an unexplained non-offer from your 2L firm can be the kiss of death in 3L recruiting.

Almost every interviewer you'll see during 3L recruiting will ask you whether you received an offer from your 2L firm, and just in case you were wondering whether your unfortunate circumstances would justify a lie, the answer is no. Most employers will call your 2L firm to verify that you got an offer, and if you are discovered to be lying, you'll be finished anyway and potentially subject to disciplinary sanctions by your law school. Accordingly, if at all possible, try and get a "soft offer" or at the least, a letter of explanation from your firm explaining the circumstances that led to your not getting an offer. Without such a letter, you're in for some very tough sledding.

So what if you didn't get an offer because you really were arrogant or lazy or you rubbed somebody the wrong way? How do you spin that reality in 3L recruiting to make some other firm take a flyer on you? That's not easy, even in a good economy, but here's my advice.

First, be completely candid. Come clean about the mistakes you made, and what you learned from them. Don't try to explain why you behaved like you did, just make it clear that you understand what you did wrong, why it was wrong, and most importantly, that you are now clear about what the expectations are. Contrition goes a long way in a situation like this, and the fact is, you're now a gamble, so you need to sell the firms you interview with on the idea that you're a normal person who made a mistake but that you are now ready to take your place in the adult world.

A lot of firms will pass on you despite these efforts, because when another firm decides that you're not employable and not even worthy of a soft offer or a letter, that's pretty stigmatizing. You may need to call in reinforcements from your law school's placement office or get letters from faculty members to help you overcome the stigma—that is, if those people don't share the firm's opinion of you. If they do, and you don't have any family connections you can count on to bail you out, your last hope is volunteering to work at a firm for free to prove your worth.

CHAPTER 26

Last Semester Cross-checks

Caution is the eldest child of wisdom.
—Victor Hugo

Life in the real world is fast approaching. As you make the turn into your last semester, there are a number of cross-checks you need to make with various members of your law school administration—and with yourself—to ensure that no important details slip through the cracks as graduation nears.

Ensure that you have enough credits to graduate

Don't laugh—I've seen more than a few frantic "independent study" papers spring up after a call from the registrar around spring break. Your law school has a minimum number of credits or credit hours required for you to graduate. Do you know what that number is? Do you know how many credits or credit hours you've earned to date? Have you scheduled enough credits in your last semester to graduate?

Before the close of the registration period for your last semester, be sure you have a comfort zone here. Count the credits for the classes you've taken, making sure that you've assigned the proper number of credits for moot court, journals, and any externships you've completed. When registering for your final semester, don't put yourself in the position where failing a class would mean not having enough credits to graduate—motivation can be a significant problem in the final semester.

When you think you have an accurate count of your credits earned, stop by the registrar's office and check your count against the registrar's count—because it's the registrar's count that matters. Although this may all seem a bit paranoid, these cross-checks are for your own peace of mind. Clerical errors can, and do, happen.

Ensure that you've taken and passed all required courses

Most law schools have a certain number of "required" courses that you must take in order to graduate. Many schools require you to take the majority of these courses during the first year—but there may be a few other required courses, often Corporations, Federal Income Tax, or Professional Responsibility that can be reserved for the upper years. Do you know what courses your school requires? Before the registration period closes in your last semester, ensure that you've met each of your school's curricular requirements, or have registered for any that you've missed. Schools tend to be pretty unforgiving of mishaps and oversights in this area. A forgotten course could easily derail your graduation.

Co-curricular or extracurricular requirements

Many schools impose an upper-level writing requirement, an oral advocacy requirement, and a pro bono requirement. Does yours?

If your school allows a note or comment written for a legal journal to satisfy the upper-level writing requirement, have you checked to see if there is a length requirement or if your journal piece needs to be advised and approved by a faculty member? Check now so you won't be disappointed later.

What about public service? Some schools require you to have completed—and have the documentation to verify—a certain number of hours of public service work during your three years of law school. Have you met the requirement, and verified that your paperwork is in order? Don't make any assumptions here, because clerical errors can happen and paperwork can be lost or forgotten—especially if you're assuming that your externship sent the required documentation to your law school. Remember that in cases like this, the paperwork is important only to you—to someone else, it's just a nuisance that can easily be overlooked or pushed to the back burner. If your school requires public service to graduate, verify that you've made your hours, and be sure that the public service office concurs.

Verify that your tuition has been paid

Nothing can stop your graduation faster than an unpaid tuition bill, and remember that without a copy of your diploma, you will not be able to register for the bar exam in most states. As such, when you visit the registrar to cross-check your credits and required courses; verify that you've satisfied all financial obligations to your school. Don't wait until the last minute to do this, because if you discover any shortfalls, you might need time to secure additional funds to clear the lien against your diploma.

Once you're satisfied that your academic house is in order, it's time to start looking ahead to the future. There are a number of housekeeping items you'll need to take care of early in the semester before the approach of exams and the imminence of your graduation start to compete for your attention.

Register for the bar exam and get your firm to pay for it

I'm already on the record about this, but it bears repeating. I took the six-week BAR-BRI preparatory course for the New Hampshire Bar Exam and found it to be excellent preparation for both the MBE (the Multi-State Bar Examination—the two hundred question multiple choice part common to all bar exams in all states) and the state essay section. I make this point again because many students wonder whether these courses are really worth their hefty fees (the average bar review course costs between $1,400–$1,800), and whether they are not simply business ventures designed to prey on students' fears. While everyone is entitled to his own opinion, you bought this book because you wanted mine and those of the mentors, and we just can't imagine trying to study for a bar exam without taking one of these courses.

In addition to keeping you on a strict study schedule, showing you the common "tricks" used by the exam writers, and providing you with an endless supply of sample questions to work on—you will probably learn more black letter law during the six-week bar review class than you learned during your entire three years of law school. That's valuable! In fact, I've kept my bar review books and notes handy and have used them frequently as a "quick reference" and a starting point while researching issues during my clerkship. They're a great source of legal outlines for most of the common legal subjects you'll encounter in practice.

Once you've decided that you need to take one of these courses, how do you choose which course is right for you? Of course, you'll want to, and should, do your own research, but for my money, I wanted the best known, and most reputable company in my corner—and that came down to a choice between BAR-BRI and PMBR. I, and many of your mentors, chose to take both.

Now wait . . . before you throw the book across the room in disgust, hear me out. BAR-BRI offers the most widely reputed full-bar preparation—a six-week class that provides you with two- or three-day lectures on all of the MBE subjects, one-day state-specific lectures on all topics covered on your state essay section, and comprehensive outlines for all of these subjects. PMBR, on the other hand, offers (among its options) a fantastic three-day MBE-only review course designed to be taken in conjunction with BAR-BRI, after you have completed your study of the multistate subjects. This course assumes that you've already studied the substantive law, and simply want to practice applying your knowledge.

On the first day, you take an entire MBE in real-time test conditions—a very difficult "harder-than-the-real-thing" exam which provides a great exposure to what the "real thing" will be like. On days two and three, an instructor (live or on videotape) will walk you through the entire exam question-by-question, discussing all the tricks used in each subject, and going over each wrong answer choice and explaining why it is wrong, and how they tricked you into picking it. I found this "dry run" and review extremely helpful, and would highly recommend it as a supplement to BAR-BRI.

Way back in the beginning of the book, I told you not to sign up for a bar review class during your first year of law school despite the discounts that the various companies might be offering. There were two reasons for my giving you this advice. First, you probably didn't have as clear an idea then about which courses you'd want to take, and second, now that you have a job offer, if you've decided to work for a firm, the firm should be willing to cover some, if not all of your bar-related expenses—including the review course.

How do you approach asking them to pay?

If you have signed on with a large firm, they may have already offered to pay your expenses, or cover up to a certain amount. If so, simply call the recruiting coordinator to request the necessary paperwork, and send it in. If your firm has not broached the subject with you, contact BAR-BRI and PMBR, or whichever company you choose to use, and obtain the course registration paperwork from them. Among the materials you receive will be a sign-up form, which includes a space for your firm's billing address and contact person. Once you have this form, call the recruiting coordinator at your firm and ask him what the firm's policy is on bar fees and expenses. Explain that you have the necessary paperwork, and ask if you may send it directly to the firm for payment. Most firms (even small ones) will either cover some or all of your bar expenses, or, at a minimum, will advance you the money to cover these expenses. You should certainly negotiate with any firm that does not immediately offer to do so, as covering these expenses is virtually standard practice these days.

Register for and take the MPRE exam

Officially, the MPRE, or "Multistate Professional Responsibility Exam," is the first part of your bar exam, and is required by almost every state's board of bar examiners. Requirements change from year-to-year, so check with the state where you intend to practice to confirm that you must take it. The MPRE is a somewhat tricky, fifty question, one hundred and twenty minute multiple-choice exam administered three times each year (in March, August, and November), with a curve so generous that the exam is more of a nuisance than a threat for those students that take it seriously. Note that I did not say that you can blow off the exam and still pass it. I said it is relatively easy to pass if you study for it.

The exam measures your knowledge and understanding of the rules of professional conduct as established by the American Bar Association's (ABA) Model Rules of Professional Conduct, the ABA Model Rules of Judicial Conduct, controlling court decisions, and generally accepted principles established in federal procedural and evidentiary rules. There are three major points to make about the MPRE. The first concerns when to take the exam. Many law schools offer the required course in Professional Responsibility as an elective during the first or second year, and consequently, students wonder whether they should take the exam during or shortly after completing this course. Take the exam early if you can, but check with the jurisdiction in which you intend to practice, because some states require you to pass the MPRE before you take the bar exam, while others will not allow you to take the MPRE until you've graduated from law school.

This leads us to point number two—what to study to prepare for the MPRE. When you register for the exam, the National Conference of Bar Examiners (NCBE) will send you a nifty little package of preparatory materials, including a study guide and a series of sample questions. You can order more sample questions from the NCBE website (and you should, if you're having trouble with the questions provided). I, and most students I know, carefully read through the materials provided by the NCBE, worked all of the sample questions provided, and never consulted the materials from our law school ethics classes. For the average student, a solid week or ten days of preparation involving a few hours a night should be sufficient to pass the exam, but leave enough time to work additional practice problems and to conduct additional review if you're not getting 75 percent of the practice problems correct. In an informal canvas of my classmates, 70–80 percent correct on the practice problems was about average, and assuming that the NCBE's grading scale doesn't change, getting 70–80 percent of the real MPRE questions correct should get you a passing score in every jurisdiction.

One other thing about the MPRE. Don't worry if you feel like you failed it when you leave the test center after taking the real exam. Most of us felt that way. Remember that the scale is friendly. The general consensus is that if you take the exam seriously and study diligently for it, you'll have little trouble passing it. Those who fail the MPRE typically (1) didn't study seriously for it and tried to take the exam "cold," (2) misbubbled on their answer sheet, or (3) had problems with time by getting hung up on a particular question. These things are all preventable and should not happen to you. If you have further questions about the MPRE, consult the NCBE's comprehensive website at www.ncbex.org.

Arrange a start date with your firm, judge, or placement

The bar exam is typically given in the last week of July. Judicial clerkships usually begin right after Labor Day. Everything else can be negotiated.

Smaller firms may be counting on your presence in the office soon after the bar exam—while big-city firms may grant you a start date as late as November. Whatever your individual situation is, make your arrangements early so you know what the expectations are and can plan accordingly.

Two bits of advice here. First, if you have any other option, don't work while you are studying for the bar exam. The schedule you'll get from your bar review course will be demanding enough—and any free time you have should be spent doing sample problems or relaxing. If money is tight, ask your firm for an advance on your salary to cover summer living expenses, and if they won't give you that, then ask them for a low-interest loan. Most firms have an interest in your passing the bar the first time around and will do whatever they can to help make sure that happens. If all else fails, get a loan from a relative or a bank. It's only two months we're talking about here—and during those two months, your time is best spent studying and resting. There will be plenty of time to pay back your loans later. First things first.

Once the bar is over, plan to take a vacation if you can afford it. You'll be wiped out—and many students report feeling a kind of post-partum depression when all of a sudden, every moment of your day isn't scheduled. Remember that the days between the bar exam and the beginning of your employment may represent the largest chunk of free time you'll experience between now, and, well . . . retirement.

Make the most of it.

Make advance accommodations in your new place of employment

Most bar review courses begin around June 1, which may not leave you a lot of time between graduation and the beginning of the course to find living arrangements in your new city and to get settled there. Remember the importance of this choice—you're choosing the place where you'll be studying for the bar, and probably living for the foreseeable future, and, if you're going to work for a large firm, they may pay for your relocation expenses, including moving costs. They'll only pay this once, however, so you'll need to get it right the first time. For this, and many other reasons, many students like to stay in their law school accommodations through the bar exam because the surroundings are familiar and their living arrangements are already established.

Whatever your choice, let it be guided by two primary considerations. First, choose a place with minimal distractions, where you'll be comfortable and able to concentrate. This is not the time to risk failure for the fleeting pleasures of studying on a crowded beach. An isolated carrel in an air-conditioned, quiet library, away from phone calls, e-mail, and the Internet is a good choice. As unappetizing as this seems, the sacrifice must be made, as the alternative—possibly failing the exam—is definitely worse. The goal is to take the bar exam once, and to never have to think about it again. For most law students, this means giving up most of June and July to study, and taking (at least) the month of August off to play and recover. Second, try and find accommodations reasonably close to the location of your bar review course. Typically, the daily classes begin at 9 A.M. sharp—and these are not classes you'll want to miss, or walk into late. Every missed class or late start translates directly into lost opportunities to score points on the bar—and if you're like most people—you can't afford to give any points away. Tacking a long commute onto your day won't make things any more pleasant.

Make arrangements for your move well in advance

If you live in a high-rise or a large apartment complex, don't assume that you can just move out whenever it suits your schedule. I had already rented a U-Haul and signed a lease to move into my new apartment before I discovered that my apartment building in Philadelphia had strictly enforced moving times—and the date I needed was completely booked weeks in advance. Only a fortunate "arrangement" struck with the keeper of the freight elevator key and loading dock schedule saved me from disaster.

Don't get yourself into this situation. To be safe, make your moving arrangements at least sixty days in advance, and remember that you'll need to make compatible arrangements on both ends of your move. Oh—and you might as well assume that the day of your move will be the hottest and most humid day of the year to date. Somehow, it always seems to work out that way.

"And don't miss the deadline for picking up your family's commencement tickets!" Joel urges. "This is the voice of experience speaking."

CHAPTER 27

The Final Hurdle— Strategies for the Bar Examination

"... but you're not a Jedi yet ..."
—DARTH VADER TO LUKE SKYWALKER

SO YOU'RE A LAWYER.

Congratulations! You now have an impressive looking piece of parchment that you can hang on your wall to commemorate the struggle you've just endured. There's just one problem. If your intention is to practice law, that diploma isn't worth the paper it's written on until you slay the dragon.

Your law school diploma is merely your ticket into the final and grandest battle of them all—the bar exam.

It's time for a real reality check here. Although this is the penultimate chapter of the book, and the bar exam is your final antagonist—this is not Hollywood, and you are not guaranteed a happy ending.

Do not underestimate the difficulty of the bar exam. It is a worthy adversary.

In many states, the failure rate for the bar exam lies around 50 percent, and no one stands invincible against it. Every year, the bar exam claims unsuspecting victims from top law schools around the country—primarily individuals who failed to give the exam the respect it deserves.

Don't be one of them.

Around June 1, bar review classes begin in cities and towns around the country. If you read the last chapter, you should have registered for one of the six-week preparatory classes, and if you took our advice, you'll be supplementing that with the three-day PMBR mock exam and review.

Yes, I've known a couple of people who wrote away for a couple of sample bar exams, never took a review class, and passed the bar exam. I also know someone who won the lottery. You bought this book because it provides the best advice available to you as a current law student—in this case, advice from eleven people who just took bar exams in six different jurisdictions without a single failure—and we're telling you that it's worth every penny for you to take these bar review courses. Disregard this advice at your own peril.

On the morning of your first bar review class, bring a duffel bag to class—as you'll be on the receiving end of about sixty pounds of books and binders, and you'll need a way to transport these items home with you. You'll also be given a class schedule, and a lot of advice about how to pace yourself through the summer as you prepare for the exam.

For every student that takes the bar exam, there is a slightly different war story and a slightly different idea about what is the best way to prepare. This includes all of us as well, and as such, several of your mentors' bar exam study suggestions are abstracted for you throughout this chapter. In general, however, the consensus is that, if you're taking the July exam, you should follow the class schedule given you as closely as possible during the month of June. Treat each day as if it were a day at the office. Clock in at 8:45 A.M. to prepare for your 9 A.M. lecture. Drink as much coffee as it takes to remain rigidly attentive—because unlike your lectures in law school, these lectures are crammed full of black-letter law and explanation, and you really can't afford to miss a minute. In BAR-BRI, the lectures closely track the large outline. Follow the lecture in your large course outline and highlight the material covered in the lecture. Take written notes only where necessary to supplement or clarify the outline already prepared for you. Don't waste time writing what is already written for you. Listen carefully and actively and try to process the information.

When the lecture ends, take a quick break for lunch, and follow that with whatever preparation the course schedule recommends. Generally, among the tasks assigned to you that day will be to go over your outline and notes. Take that time to consolidate your lecture highlights and anything additional you wrote onto the large outline onto the small, concise outline also provided to you. Once you've performed this consolidation, study *only* the concise outline, and do not refer to the large outline for that subject again. There's only so much information you can retain for each subject. Concentrate only on what's most important—and in BAR-BRI, that's what's covered in the lectures.

"I think I had an effective strategy in preparing for the bar exam," Carolyn recalls, "which was passed down to me by my brother Keith who took the exam the year before. I took BAR-BRI and the three-day PMBR strategy course and never missed a moment of the classes. During the first month, I treated studying for the bar exam like a job: I went to class at 9 A.M. did my assignments, quit by 6 P.M., and didn't do a whole lot on the weekends. Starting July 1, though, I pretty much worked from 9 A.M. to 11 P.M. with breaks for meals and exercise, and spent lots of time doing and going over problems."

"Slow and steady wins the race," Keith insists. "It's a marathon, not a sprint, and you want to peak at the right time. Start preparing early so you can leave a little bit of time each day for some fun."

"Go to the bar classes, do the work they assign you, but don't overdo it too early or you'll burn out before the critical days," Bess agrees. "Heavy-duty studying should begin around July 1. Eat well, exercise, and try to stay healthy."

"I studied like hell for two months," Pat notes. "I took BAR-BRI and studied with a friend. Studying with someone else helped me because it provided me with an additional source of motivation. Knowing that another person was relying on me helped me to stay committed to my study schedule."

"I'd rather study ten times harder than I need to and pass, than underestimate the exam and fail," Allan noted. "Having said that, try to remember that the bar exam is designed to be a minimum-proficiency exam. If you do the recommended studying, you should pass."

"Try to relax. Lots of people who are not that smart pass this exam," another mentor adds. "Don't be too rattled by the low pass rates. You have an advantage simply by being a native speaker of English because a number of people who take the bar, particularly in New York, are international students."

Steve agrees. "Think about this: For every person sitting in your bar review class, there is a hapless person who decided that he could review old outlines from classes to prepare for the bar exam; or an even more hapless person who decided that the summer after third year of law school was the last bit of free time he would have, and chose to spend that time traveling around and cramming for the bar exam in the last week instead of studying for two months like you will. Then there are the people that speak English as a second or third language who will be at an immediate disadvantage to those of you who will be taking the exam in your native tongue. Essentially, it comes down to this: The people who work diligently and put forward a legitimate effort usually pass."

The real key to your success on the bar exam lies in those practice problems. Remember that simply doing the problems and correcting them is not enough. You must not leave a problem you got wrong until you understand *why* you got it wrong, and *how* the problem tripped you up. If the problem contained a legal point not in your concise outline, go back and write it in so you won't forget it. It is the little distinctions that you'll make by getting hundreds of practice problems wrong in each subject, and learning from your mistakes over the next six to eight weeks, that will earn you points when it counts. Keep a "cheat sheet" for each subject, noting the things you got wrong and the tricks that keep tripping you up, and consult it and add to it every time you work problems. Avoid the temptation to be lazy. Repetition is the mother of skill.

Many students wonder how to strike a proper balance between the MBE and the state essay topics. In BAR-BRI, sometime near the end of June there will be a transition from the six multistate topics (constitutional law, torts, property, contracts, criminal law and procedure, and evidence) into the essay subjects listed as "in play" by your state's board of bar examiners. Again, the best advice we can give is to follow the schedule provided to you. Prepare for each state subject on the day it is to be introduced—particularly if it is a subject that you did not study in law school, but do not go overboard trying to master the intricacies of these subjects. Read the subject outline provided by BAR-BRI and try to master the material it provides. Do not even consider going to outside sources to supplement your understanding. Your degree of understanding will be stronger in some subjects than in others. Accept that and move on.

Once you have a working knowledge of a state essay topic, take the outline provided to you by your bar review course and boil it down to a one- or two-page bullet point outline. Going through this process accomplishes two things. First, it forces you to really engage the material, select what is most important, and organize it in a way that makes sense to you—all of which will help you to understand the material and commit much of it to memory, and second, with every bullet outline you complete, you progressively reduce the amount of material you need to cover. Remember, you can't possibly memorize everything the bar review course will give you. You need to make choices.

Every state's essay day is different. Some states put ten subjects in play, and put six, one-hour essays on the state portion of the bar exam. Other states put as many as sixteen subjects in play, and ask twelve thirty-minute essay questions. Still other states fall somewhere in the middle. Obviously, your strategies for these state essay sections would be quite different. On the former, there are fewer subjects to master, but the level of mastery required to write a one-hour response can be expected to be fairly sophisticated. On the latter, there are more subjects to master, but with only thirty minutes to craft a response, a rudimentary, working knowledge of each subject will probably suffice to get you over the hurdle. Listen carefully to the advice your bar review instructor provides and don't be afraid to ask him questions about allocation of study time if it is not clear to you from the outset.

The general consensus is that, for the state essays, there are three possible levels of knowledge you might attain. The first level is superficial competence—an understanding of what's in the outline, and no knowledge of the subject outside of that. The second level is angry confusion—understanding what is in the outline, thinking that things in the outline contradict what you learned in your law school classes, and spending lots of time needlessly and frustratingly attempting to reconcile the two. Finally, the third level is mastery—which can only be the product of long hours working on the intricacies of a subject in law school.

It should be obvious what level of knowledge you're looking for on the state essay section of the bar exam. Sure, there will be subjects that you have mastered that are fair game for the state bar exam—and be thrilled for each one of those you can count. For the rest—you're looking for superficial competence—enough to comprehend the rudiments of the subject, but nothing beyond what's in the bar review outline. Forcing yourself to settle for superficial competence is one of the keys to staying on pace in your preparation, and however uncomfortable it might feel, you *must* do it.

Once you have a working knowledge of the state essay subjects and determine the depth of knowledge required, work up a bullet point outline for each subject, work at least one sample essay in each topic "in play," and figure out the timing for your particular state's exam. Most students feel that the majority of their time is best spent drilling on MBE questions. This strategy actually serves a dual purpose—as nearly every state essay exam will feature at least one torts question, and at least one contracts question—so the time you spend working with those subjects on the MBE section actually helps you with the essay section as well. Don't obsess about the essays. By the time you graduate from law school, you've probably written dozens of them. Conventional wisdom has it that very few people who do well on the multistate day fail the bar exam because of their performance on the state essay day. As long as you have a rudimentary understanding of the subjects in play, you'll survive the second day. Spend your time on the MBE.

The magic number is 75 percent. If you can routinely get 75 percent of the questions in an MBE subject correct, you're ready for the big day.

When exam day nears

The two or three days that you spend taking the bar exam will be among the most stressful and grueling days of your life. The worst thing you can possibly do after six to eight weeks of intense preparation is deprive yourself of sleep or relaxation on the eve of the exam. Your bar review course will work hard to drum this into you, and for good reason. You should approach the bar exam like an athlete approaches the most important athletic event of his training year. A day or two before the exam, you should begin to taper your studying to a few hours a day, coupled with lots of rest and relaxation. If you've stayed on schedule and worked hard for the entirety of the six to eight week preparatory period, this should pose no problem for you.

The day before the exam, shut down no later than mid-afternoon, and make peace with yourself. You've done everything you possibly could to prepare, and you must now try to relax and get ready to show the examiners how much you know. There is nothing to be gained by studying up to the closing bell. Go to a movie, go out to dinner, and do whatever it is that you do to regain your center and your perspective. Remember that, in spite of the stress and anxiety you feel, you are not suffering from a fatal disease—and your life will go on no matter what happens. Think of the thousands of people who have gone before you and passed this exam.

Rest easy—you can do it.

Final thoughts

You'll get all the strategy you need from your bar review course, but given that we've been looking over your shoulder since you started law school three long years ago, permit us to make three final suggestions. First, on the MBE, watch your time, and stay on pace. Break the morning section up into workable segments with time checkpoints, and make sure that you hit every one. The only sure way to fail the bar exam is to fail to finish the exam. Be disciplined! Remember, you don't need to get every question correct!

Second, no matter *how* you feel about the morning session of the MBE, go back for the afternoon. Almost every year, either the morning or the afternoon session of the MBE is noticeably harder than the other. Don't get rattled.

Finally, on the state essay section, watch your time and stay on pace. Take the time to read the question carefully and sketch out a response before you start writing. Don't worry if you don't have time to cover everything. Write a well-crafted response that hits the major points and you'll be fine. Never spend more than the allotted time on an essay response. Better to get three eights in the morning session and complete every essay, than to get two tens and a three because you took too much time on the first two essays. Rudimentary understanding wins the day.

CHAPTER 28

Parting Thoughts

There is a certain relief in change even though it be from bad to worse; as I have found in traveling in a stagecoach that it is often a comfort to shift one's position and be bruised in a new place.
—WASHINGTON IRVING

So THERE YOU HAVE IT. The secrets to law school success neatly packaged between the covers of a book. Suggestions gathered from students of different backgrounds and interests from law schools across the country, and advice gleaned from more mistakes, gaffes, and errors than any of us thought we would ever admit to publicly.

But you know what? We survived and we've gone on to chase a hundred different dreams all over this great country, and so will you.

In the end, I think law school is less about the degree you get, or the first job you take, than it is about the things you'll learn along the way. Yes, to some degree, especially in the first year, law school is about survival. It's about reading more than you ever have, forcing yourself to be more disciplined than you ever thought you could be, and replacing confusion and fear with confidence and mental acuity. It's about learning to write clearly and concisely, to question the way you think about things, and to look at everything in the world through a more critical, analytical prism.

"The main lesson I learned in law school was to be myself and make my own decisions," Joel counsels. "I think the peer pressure in law school, especially during the first year, is greater than it is at any time since junior high. It is crucial that you not blindly do whatever it is that the majority of your peers are doing. Make informed decisions. I truly believe that most unhappy law students and most unhappy lawyers are the people who did not know what they were getting themselves into. Reading this book is a good start."

"It's really all about being committed to law school before you start," Carolyn concluded. "I'm not sure I was when I started, and I paid a price for that first semester."

"A lot of people end up unhappy as lawyers," Steve concludes. "Maybe they just weren't cut out to be lawyers. More likely, though, is that they didn't think about the choice they were making before they made it. The people I graduated with who enjoy being lawyers each put a lot of thought into the kind of lawyer they wanted to be, and the kind of lifestyle they wanted to live, and made their choices accordingly. You do the same."

Law school is exhausting and exciting, annoying and awe-inspiring, frustrating, all-consuming, and exhilarating. It will, at times, drive you to tears, drive you to drink, and drive you to the edge. It will tear you apart like you've never dreamed, but, just when you feel that you've been irreparably reduced to an emotionally wrecked, mentally ravaged, vacant bundle of exposed nerves, it will rebuild you into a more thoughtful, more intellectually critical, and more mentally astute, thinking human being. You see, at its core, law school is really about teaching you a different way to think—and once you've experienced it, it's really impossible to ever go back to the way you were before.

Like most people, I had a love-hate relationship with law school. In the end, however, the experience, as miserable as it sometimes was, was definitely worth the benefits it imparted. There is an awful lot you can do with a law degree, and despite the rather sorry state of the profession in the minds of the public these days, people still have a lot of respect for the degree and the set of skills it stands for. For all the jokes and punch lines, people still look at you with a certain respect when you tell them you're a lawyer.

So get clear on whether or not you want any of the things a law degree can provide. If you decide you do, you've thought carefully about it, and you've committed completely to the experience, then there's only one thing left to do.

Go for it.

ABOUT THE AUTHOR

R OBERT H. MILLER, 28, is an associate with the law firm of Sheehan, Phinney, Bass & Green in Manchester, New Hampshire, specializing in federal courts, intellectual property, and constitutional law issues. Prior to joining the firm, he served as law clerk to the Honorable Chief Judge Paul J. Barbadoro in the United States District Court for the District of New Hampshire.  Mr. Miller graduated from the University of Pennsylvania Law School in May 1998, where he was a Senior Editor of the *University of Pennsylvania Law Review,* an H. Clayton Louderback Legal Writing Instructor, and the Chairman of the Executive Committee on Student Ethics and Academic Standing. His article *Six of One is Not a Dozen of the Other: A Reexamination of Williams v. Florida and the Size of State Criminal Juries* was published in the January 1998 issue of the *University of Pennsylvania Law Review.*

Mr. Miller graduated with distinction from Yale University in 1993. He lives in the village of Hopkinton, New Hampshire, with his wife Carolyn, who is also a lawyer.

This is his first book.